PHILOSOPHY
AND
RELIGION

RELATED TITLES PUBLISHED BY ONEWORLD

The Fifth Dimension, John Hick, ISBN 1–85168–191–4
Global Philosophy of Religion: A Short Introduction, Joseph Runzo,
    ISBN 1–85168–235–X
God: A Guide for the Perplexed, Keith Ward, ISBN 1–85168–284–8
The Phenomenon of Religion, Moojan Momen, ISBN 1–85168–161–2
The Meaning of Life in the World Religions, Edited by Joseph Runzo and
    Nancy M. Martin, ISBN 1–85168–200–7
Love, Sex and Gender in the World Religions, Edited by Joseph Runzo and
    Nancy M. Martin, ISBN 1–85168–223–6
Ethics in the World Religions, Edited by Joseph Runzo and Nancy M. Martin,
    ISBN 1–85168–247–3
God, Faith and the New Millennium, Keith Ward, ISBN 1–85168–155–8

PHILOSOPHY AND RELIGION

FROM PLATO TO POSTMODERNISM

MAX CHARLESWORTH

ONEWORLD
OXFORD

PHILOSOPHY AND RELIGION: FROM PLATO TO POSTMODERNISM

Oneworld Publications
(Sales and Editorial)
185 Banbury Road
Oxford OX2 7AR
England
www.oneworld-publications.com

ISBN 1–85168–307–0

Cover design by Design Deluxe
Typeset by Saxon Graphics Ltd, Derby
Printed and bound by Bell & Bain Ltd, Glasgow

CONTENTS

INTRODUCTION

THE REVOLUTION IN PHILOSOPHY OF RELIGION

The present work is a substantial revision of a book first published in 1972.[1] Coincidentally, in the thirty years between 1972 and 2002, an extraordinary revolution has taken place in the field of philosophy of religion both with respect to its content, or scope, and its method. First, the scope of the philosophy of religion has been vastly enlarged mainly as a result of the long overdue recognition of the radical diversity of religions. As a result, we can no longer speak of 'religion' as though it were a specific and unified field of human life; rather, we must speak of 'religions' in their irreducible plurality.

These religions range from the great 'world religions', such as Judaism, Christianity, Islam, Hinduism and the several kinds of Buddhism, to the minority or 'local' religious systems of indigenous peoples such as the Australian Aborigines and Amerindian groups. They also include the quasi-religious 'ways of life' of classical antiquity in the West – Stoicism, Epicureanism, Plotinian neo-Platonism – and the many forms of Gnosticism[2] as well as those of small and obscure sects such as the seventeenth-century Muggletonians in England and the multifarious 'Californian' syncretistic sects of our time.[3] And, of course, there is a profusion of hybrid and unorthodox forms of all these religious systems, and we must also note the powerful, and enormously influential, forms of religious dualism: Zoroastrianism, Manichaeism, and medieval Catharism.[4] In short, religions

1

are as various and diverse as human languages. One might say, indeed, that there is a religious Tower of Babel.

That diversity of religions has always been there, so to speak, but Western philosophers of religion have not recognised it and taken it seriously until very recently.[5] For the most part they assumed that all religions were basically the same, despite their outward forms of expression, and could be eventually reconciled with each other by a kind of special providence. However, whether we like it or not, the diversity of religions, great and small, is a real and irreducible 'brute fact' which cannot be glossed over or explained away.

Confronted with that diversity we can no longer simplistically define 'religion' as being about 'the Holy', or 'the numinous' (Rudolf Otto), or 'the Sacred' (Emile Durkheim), or the object of 'unconditional concern' (Paul Tillich), as though it were possible to discern a common denominator among all the religions, and as though Western Christianity were a kind of gold standard or benchmark for 'real' or authentic religions. Nor can we complacently assume that at bottom all religions say very much the same thing.

Jacques Dupuis, the noted scholar of world religions, writes that we must 'repudiate a universal theology of religions that would transcend the various religious faiths... There is no such thing as a universal theology of religions; there is only a plurality of theologies'.[6] This recognition of the radical plurality and diversity of religions has presented a direct challenge to the philosophy of religion in that the claims to universal and exclusive validity of the major monotheistic religions, especially Christianity and Islam, raise *prima facie* insoluble questions about how their respective assumptions that they are the sole legitimate vehicle of God's revelation to the whole of mankind, can be reconciled with each other. Again, they raise difficult questions about how religions may be measured against, and compared with, each other. We are, then, now acutely aware that the comparison of religious systems and their evaluation as more or less 'evolved', or 'developed', or more 'primitive' (as in a great deal of nineteenth-century philosophy of religion), is at best a very delicate, and perhaps dubious, business.

The second reason for the enlargement of the scope of philosophy of religion is to be found in the invasion of the social sciences – anthropology, sociology, psychology, history – into the study of religious systems. Most contemporary anthropologists and sociologists, as against late-nineteenth-century positivistically inclined social scientists, now see religion as an essential part of any human culture. Thus Geertz and other anthropologists see religious myths and rituals and practices as supporting the networks of meanings that make cultures possible and give them a particular shape.[7] It is, then, no longer possible to study religions and religious phenomena apart from their cultural contexts and for philosophers of religion to disregard anthropologists and sociologists. Our awareness of the diversity of religions, for example, has been powerfully aided by the anthropologists' and sociologists' emphasis on the plurality of quasi-incommensurable cultures.[8]

It remains true, however, that the social scientist's concern with religion and religious phenomena differs essentially from the interest and focus of the philosopher of religion. Philosophy of religion is concerned to adumbrate what might be called, in Kantian terms, the 'conditions of possibility' of the religious sphere, as distinct, for example, from the ethico-political sphere, or the aesthetic sphere, or the sphere of scientific enquiry. The inquiries of the social sciences into religious phenomena, on the other hand, presuppose that there is such a sphere, however loosely it may be defined, and they cannot themselves investigate whether or not there is actually a domain which transcends the world of our ordinary experience and which is not accessible to empirical enquiry.

Third, the emergence of new ways of doing philosophy, as in the various tendencies misleadingly called 'Postmodernism', have emphasised how much religions are 'constructs' or 'inventions' (akin to great artistic movements like Classicism and Romanticism), and how the appropriate method of inquiring into religion and religious phenomena is a 'deconstructive' one, that is, an attempt to reveal the historical and cultural and other ways in which a discourse, or discipline, or sphere of human thought, is built up.[9]

Thus, from Nietzsche to Heidegger and Derrida there has been a sustained critique of the philosophical (metaphysical) presuppositions of Western religious belief. Modern Western philosophy, so Derrida claims, has been obsessed by 'foundationalism', that is seeing the task of philosophy as the uncovering of the ultimate foundations or fundamental principles of knowledge and of reality. This has traditionally chimed in with Western and Middle Eastern religious views which see God as the foundation or ground (*arche*) of being and the question is whether Western religions such as Judaism, Christianity, and Islam, can be conceptualised without the older, and what is taken to be the discredited, philosophical or metaphysical view. In this context the 'death of God' which Nietzsche proclaimed is in effect the death of a metaphysical God, and the task of the philosopher of religion is to see what meaning can be given to religious discourse once the traditional (and untenable) metaphysical God has been exorcised. Martin Heidegger and Jacques Derrida have been the two main contemporary figures concerned with this central issue upon which the possibility of a philosophy of religion depends.

VARIETIES OF PHILOSOPHY OF RELIGION

The intention of this book is not to provide an encyclopedic survey of the vast number of attempts over some two thousand years to understand the relationship of philosophy, relying on what the medieval thinkers called 'natural reason', and religious faith in all its dimensions from its 'conditions of possibility' to revealed truths believed by 'faith'. Rather, what this study attempts is to display the various basic ways in which philosophy, in its diverse incarnations in Western thought from Platonism and neo-Platonism, through medieval (Jewish, Christian and Islamic) Aristotelianism, the Kantian revolution in the eighteenth century and beyond, to the contemporary movements of Wittgensteinian analysis and Postmodernism, has come to terms with the religious domain as that is defined within the great monotheistic systems in the West and the Middle East.

It is the contention of this book that there is a limited number of possible approaches to the way in which philosophical reason can relate to religious faith and some five of these approaches are considered in detail. Paradigmatic instances of each approach are discussed, for example Platonism is seen as a 'type' of one approach, the medieval Aristotelianism of Aquinas of another, Kant's philosophy of another, and Wittgensteinian analysis and Postmodernism, though in very different ways, of another. These last two propose a minimalist approach to the philosophy of religion and it may be argued that neither really provides a space for the religious domain. But both Wittgenstein and Derrida clearly wish to go beyond any kind of Kantian agnosticism.

This study, then, claims that these five approaches constitute a 'grid' on which most varieties of the philosophy of religion may be located. As a result, many philosophers of religion – for example, Spinoza, Hegel, Feuerbach, Whitehead and others – receive only incidental consideration. This is especially the case with contemporary philosophers of religion even though, as already noted, philosophy of religion has undergone a vast transformation in the twentieth century. Despite Nietzsche's prophecy of the impending 'death of God', and the confident predictions by Max Weber and other sociologists of the increasing secularisation of Western societies, philosophy of religion is now a flourishing industry. However, many contemporary philosophies of religion are of a quasi-Kantian kind (as with the various forms of 'religious agnosticism'), while still others are of a Platonic kind which identify religion with philosophy (as with 'Process theology'), and still other philosophers of religion (such as the American thinker Alvin Plantinga) have constructed a neo-Thomist position based on Aquinas's natural theology. The two contemporary examples of philosophy of religion discussed in chapters 4 and 5 have been chosen because they seem, at least *prima facie*, to represent a new minimalist and distinct variety.

It is necessary here to make two final disclaimers: first, as already noted, this book is focused on the relationship of philosophical reason with the religious domain and, in effect, for the purposes of this book the latter is identified with the great monotheistic religions, Judaism, Christianity and Islam. No mention is made of the ancient and enormously important religions of India, Japan and China, such as Hinduism in its many forms, or of Buddhism in its multiple manifestations, or Jainism, Sikhism, Shintoism, or Taoism. To enquire whether or not there is a discernible philosophy of religion in these religious systems, and whether a typology of the kind proposed here would 'work' with these venerable religions, would require another, and very different, book. In a sense, the philosophy of religion is very much a creation of the Western philosophical and theological tradition, and although there are analogous developments in Hinduism and Buddhism (Tibetan Buddhism, for example, uses Madhyamika 'philosophical' ideas to elaborate its 'theology')[10] philosophy has never had for them the autonomous status it has enjoyed in the West.

In passing, it is worth remarking that the two thousand-year-long debate between philosophy and religion has been an astonishingly creative tradition in the history of Western thought comparable to the emergence of the natural sciences in the sixteenth and seventeenth centuries in Europe, and to the development of the idea of democratic society from the eighteenth century onwards. It may be that most other civilisations have got along quite happily without a debate of that kind, none the less this does not detract from the achievement that it represents.

The second disclaimer concerns the omission of any detailed reference to feminist views on philosophy and religion. French, English and American thinkers such as Luce Irigaray, Ursula King, Sara Coakley, Sandra Harding and others have argued that there can be a distinctive feminist view on philosophy, religion and theology, and even natural science.[11] However, while there is no doubt that there may be a valuable feminist *perspective* on philosophy and theology and an indispensable contribution of women's experience to these disciplines, it is difficult to maintain that there can be a feminist (or masculinist) form of rationality and mode of doing both philosophy and theology. In order to show to both women and men that there is such a *sui generis* feminist mode of philosophical rationality, feminists would have to explain themselves in terms of commonly acknowledged canons of philosophical rationality which transcend gender differences.

There is an analogy here with the ideas of certain feminist philosophers of science who have questioned the gender neutrality of 'objectivity' and other central criteria of scientific discourse. Thus, some have concluded that science is irretrievably a masculine project and that the only alternatives for feminists are either to reject science altogether or to envisage a radically new form of science with different criteria of what is and is not 'scientific'. With regard to the first alternative, Evelyn Fox Keller, an American philosopher of science, has argued that it is 'suicidal'. So she says: 'By rejecting objectivity as a masculine ideal it simultaneously lends its voice to an enemy chorus and dooms women to residing outside the Realpolitik male modern culture: it exacerbates the very problem it wishes to solve.' Again, with respect to the second alternative Fox Keller has this to say: 'The assumption that science can be replaced *de novo* reflects a view of science as pure social product, owing obedience to moral and political pressure from without. In this extreme relativism, science dissolves into ideology; any emancipatory function of modern science is negated, and the arbitration of truth recedes into the political domain'.[12]

One must conclude, then, that despite the fact that there can be a feminist *perspective* on philosophy of religion, there cannot really be a distinctively feminist *philosophy* of religion any more than there can be a distinctively male philosophy of religion.

FIVE APPROACHES TO THE PHILOSOPHY OF RELIGION

This book contends that there are five main conceptions of the nature and scope of philosophy of religion, ranging from a virtual identification of philosophy and religion, to a position where philosophy has a minimal role with respect to the religious sphere. The logical structure of each of these conceptions or approaches is analysed so as to show their respective presuppositions and consequences, as well as their strengths and weaknesses.

The first approach argues that it is the business of philosophy to lead us to a quasi-religious view of reality and even to a quasi-religious way of life. As has been mentioned already, philosophical positions such as Stoicism and Epicureanism were seen in classical antiquity as 'ways of life' involving quasi-religious 'exercises'. In this view philosophy is in a very real sense identical with religion. One might say, indeed, that this position makes a religion out of philosophy. Though there are intimations of this conception of the philosophy of religion in the pre-Socratic philosophers, it is above all with Plato and his heirs that it is made fully explicit. However, it is not only the Platonists, and Plotinus and the neo-Platonists of the third century after Christ, who adopt this view, for it also emerges in modern philosophy with Spinoza and, in quite a different context, with Hegel, as well as in certain contemporary forms of Gnosticism.

The second conception of the philosophy of religion is associated with the name of the great medieval thinker St Thomas Aquinas, who sums up a long tradition of thought that begins with the Jewish sage Philo of Alexandria in the first years of the Christian era and passes through thinkers as various as Origen, St Augustine and the eminent Jewish thinker Moses Maimonides. It also includes Islamic philosopher-theologians in the early Middle Ages such as Ibn Rushd (Averroës) and Ibn Sina (Avicenna). One must also mention the neo-Platonic Christian thinker known as Denys the Pseudo-Areopagite (possibly a Syrian monk of the sixth century) who had a profound influence on Aquinas and the whole of medieval philosophy and theology.

For Aquinas and his predecessors the task of philosophy of religion is above all a defensive or apologetical one, justifying the 'preambles' of faith (the existence of God and his attributes or 'names') and defending the 'articles of faith' derived from Christian revelation, by showing that they are not, *prima facie*, self-contradictory or incoherent. Aquinas insists that philosophy does not enable us to know what God is in his essence, but that our minimal knowledge of God only can be attained by the 'way of negation'. In other words, we know what God is by knowing what he is *not*. Again, with regard to the articles of faith contained in revelation, we cannot know what they mean in any positive way.[13] Compared with the Platonic conception of the philosophy of religion, Aquinas's conception of the philosophy of religion is a much more restricted and 'negative' one. On the other hand, compared with Kant's agnostic position, for Aquinas the role of philosophy *vis-à-vis* religion is much more positive.

The third approach to the philosophy of religion is that of the great German philosopher of the late seventeenth and early eighteenth century, Immanuel Kant. According to Kant, philosophy has no justificatory role with regard to religion. Rather its function is to establish the conditions of possibility of the religious domain by showing that we know neither that God exists nor that he does not exist. Kant's monumental work *The Critique of Pure Reason* attempts to show that, as far as speculative reason is concerned, we must remain agnostic about the existence of God because the traditional metaphysical arguments of Aquinas and others involve going beyond the bounds of our experience. In this way, philosophical reason 'makes room' for the realm of religious faith by showing its own inadequacies. However, the space left by speculative reason can be filled, Kant argues, by reflecting on the implications of 'practical reason', which is concerned with our reasoning in the realm of morality and obligation. When we reflect upon morality we see that a supreme legislator is required to justify the principle of moral obligation. It is not clear whether this amounts to a strict proof of the existence of a supreme legislator, or whether it is through an experience of a sense of morality and duty that we intuit the existence of a God. Later thinkers in the nineteenth century, John Henry Newman for example, use the experience of having a moral 'conscience' in the latter way. This approach to the philosophy of religion has had, as we shall see, a very long and influential career in post-Kantian thought down to the contemporary movement of Postmodernism.

The fourth approach to the philosophy of religion sees the role of philosophy as being a purely analytical or meta-logical enterprise. It is not the business of philosophy to engage in metaphysical speculation about any realm that purports to transcend the world of our immediate experience, but rather to analyse the conditions of meaningfulness of the various languages (scientific language, moral language, aesthetic language etc.) or areas of discourse.

For some, like the English philosopher A. J. Ayer, the 'verification principle' specifies the conditions that any assertion must meet in order to have meaning, and we can show that all metaphysical and religious assertions are simply meaningless because they flout this principle in that they cannot possibly be verified. For others, like Wittgenstein, the verification principle is surreptitiously positivist in character in that it assumes that *scientific* language is the only one that meets the principle's criterion. For the analysts who follow Wittgenstein the business of philosophy is not to provide explanations about the world but rather to remind us of the way we use language in the various 'language games' we engage in. Thus philosophy of religion becomes the analysis of the ways we use language in religious contexts.

The fifth approach to the philosophy of religion is that advanced by the Postmodernist thinkers Martin Heidegger and Jacques Derrida. The main task of philosophy, for the Postmodernists, is to purge itself of the 'metaphysics' which has distorted traditional modes of philosophy by assuming that we must seek ultimate and absolute foundations for reality and for human thought. This disease of 'foundationalism' is linked with the idea that it is possible to transcend all 'contexts' in our interpretations of the world and of human thought, and to occupy a totally transcendent, or 'context-free', point of view. However, this is impossible. This means that traditional conceptions of God as being the absolute ground, or foundation, of all beings have to be rejected. However, this does not necessarily lead to atheism since classical atheism has also been guilty of foundationalism and of seeking to adopt a vantage point above or outside all contexts.

Heidegger and Derrida then leave us with a philosophical situation where we can say neither that God exists nor that God does not exist. Both, however, suggest that while we cannot conceptualise God and the religious domain, we can none the less gain an 'understanding' of it through classical mysticism (Meister Eckhart and others) and 'negative theology'. It is clear that for the Postmodernists philosophy has the most attenuated view of the role of philosophical reason *vis-à-vis* the religious domain and that we are here at the furthest extreme from the Platonic approach.

The danger of typologies of the kind proposed here is that they tend to lead to extreme schematism and abstraction and leave out of account the rich detail of what the Postmodernists call the 'local' situation. It is hoped, however, that in this book violence has not been done to the thought of the philosophers of religion referred to, and that there has not been too much Procrustean lopping of limbs to fit them into our five beds.

1

PHILOSOPHY AS RELIGION

*If our hearts have been fixed on the love of learning and true wisdom and we have
exercised that part of ourselves above all, we are surely bound to have immortal or
divine thoughts if we should grasp the truth; nor can we fail to possess immortality to
the highest degree that human nature admits.*

PLATO, *Timaeus*

INTRODUCTION

In this work we will be mainly occupied with the philosophy of religion in
the Western tradition and only incidentally with Eastern thought. This is,
first, for the sake of convenience, for the study of Eastern religions would
take us too far afield; and, second, because the philosophy of religion is a
peculiar creation of Western thought and occurs, in a pure form at least, only
within that tradition. There are, no doubt, some Eastern thinkers – Sankara
and Ramanuja, for example – who are concerned to speculate about religious
themes in a quasi-philosophical fashion; but it remains true that in Eastern
thought generally philosophy is never really disengaged from religion in the
explicit way in which it has been separated out within the Western tradition.
Some may see this lack of differentiation as an advantage and as a mercy to
be grateful for, while at the same time judging the distinction between

philosophy and religion that began with the Greeks, and that has persisted in Western thought ever since, as some kind of unfortunate original sin or 'fall'. However, unless philosophy or 'pure reason' is accorded some kind of autonomy or independence, then there cannot be a philosophy *of* religion. All that we will have, as in Eastern thought, is religious speculation, with a more or less philosophical colouring, where the final arbiter is religious revelation and faith and not pure reason.

However, if it is the Greeks who are the first to separate off philosophy from the popular mythical religious speculations of their time, they are also the first to attempt the invention of what one might call a philosophical religion – the construction of a religion out of philosophy which is intended to take the place of 'mythical' religion. Thus, for Plato and his later followers it is the task of philosophy to lead the sage to a supra-mundane vision and illumination; indeed, religion in this sense is the culmination of philosophy in that the end of philosophical wisdom is coterminous with the end of religion. In contrast with Eastern thought where philosophy is absorbed into religion, with the Greeks religion tends to be absorbed into philosophy, though philosophy itself suffers a change in the process. Here the task of philosophy is not to analyse religion as something already given, but rather to invent and constitute religion and, as it were, to serve the purpose of religion.

Since the Protestant Reformation, with its rejection of natural theology and its suspicion of the pretensions of philosophy with regard to religion, the very idea of a philosophical religion has come to be seen as almost self-contradictory, for if religion is the invention of our unaided and 'natural' reason, it cannot by definition be religion. In Christianity there has always been a sharp distinction made between what we may discover by natural reason and what by supernatural religious faith – the latter going beyond and transcending philosophical reason. God's revelation is precisely a disclosure or revealing, on God's own initiative, of what cannot be known by pure reason alone. And with the Protestant tradition this disjunction between faith and reason, the natural and the supernatural, what we can know by our own efforts and what we are given to know by God's gratuitous revelation or disclosure, is so understood that it comes to be taken as self-evident that there cannot be any commerce between philosophy and religion, let alone any identification of the two. So Karl Barth, for example, attacks the idea of natural theology because of its very nature it involves reducing religion to philosophy and so denaturing it. Again, it has been argued that commitment to a religious revelation involves that one cannot accept the possibility of any human judgement on this revelation, otherwise it would not be a religious revelation. We cannot expect a religious revelation to fit in with our ordinary canons of knowledge, for 'everything that did fit in with these canons could be known ipso facto not to be revelation'.[1] In much the same vein Rudolf Bultmann argues that if we admit that we can have a 'natural' knowledge of God in the light of which we may judge the Christian view of God, then 'we have given up our Christian belief from the start; for it would be given up by the admission that its authenticity could be decided from a standpoint outside itself'.[2]

Within this context, the mere idea of a philosophical religion is rejected out of hand in that it is alleged to involve a gross confusion between philosophy and religion. In such a conception of philosophical religion there can be no room for the dimension of the supernatural, or for revelation, or faith, or grace, and a religion which has no place for these concepts can scarcely be thought to be a religion at all.

Quite apart from these objections made from within the Christian or 'supernaturalist' conception of religion (and to that extent limited in their force and scope), there are other more general objections that seem to make the identification of philosophy and religion an impossible undertaking. For instance, the late-nineteenth-century French philosopher Édouard Le Roy criticises all philosophical or 'intellectualistic' forms of religion in that they make religion into a matter of speculative or theoretical assent and belief rather than of practical commitment. Le Roy, along with a good many other thinkers both ancient and modern, claims that it is of the essence of religion that it should provide a 'way' of life. Religion is of its very nature practical, and whatever theoretical content a religion may have is strictly subordinate to this practical purpose – the 'conversion' of our lives. This is, in fact, the great difference between religion and philosophy, for while the latter is concerned with speculation for speculation's sake (philosophy is useless, as Aristotle remarked), religion is pre-eminently concerned with action and practice. For Le Roy, then, any religion that merely exacted speculative assent to a number of doctrinal propositions, or that consisted solely in philosophical contemplation, would precisely not be a religion, save in the most attenuated sense.[3]

There is another consequence of this philosophical or intellectualistic conception of religion, namely, that it leads to a kind of religious élitism or esotericism. For, as only the few intelligent or philosophically wise can assent to the truth of a philosophical system, if religion depends upon philosophy only a choice few will be able to be religious in the full sense, just as in Plato's *Republic* only the philosophical élite can know what 'the Good' is and so be moral in the full sense, and just as for Aristotle only the fortunate few can be fully happy.[4] In this view, ordinary non-philosophical people have to rest content with a lower-level morality and a lower-level religion. But, Le Roy claims, this once again demonstrates the impossibility of a philosophical religion, for if philosophy is incurably élitist or esoteric, religion cannot be so and still remain religion in the full sense. Religion is essentially popular or universalist, that is to say it must be within the reach of everyone, lettered and unlettered. It is not 'relative to the variable degrees of intelligence and knowledge; it remains exactly the same for the scholar and the unlettered man, for the clever and the lowly, for the ages of high-civilisation and for races that are still barbarous'.[5] There have, of course, been ventures in religious esotericism – Gnosticism in Christianity, Ibn Rushd's 'Two Truths' doctrine in Islam, élitist forms of Buddhism – but it may be argued that these are very much exceptions that prove the rule, for these experiments have usually been rejected by the mainstream of religion and regarded as aberrations. To demonstrate that any form of religion implies, or leads to, this kind of philosopher's religion is therefore in effect to question its validity as authentic religion.

There is a good deal of force in these objections against the idea of a philosophical religion and they are objections that weigh very much with us at the present time (heirs of the Reformation that we are) and that prevent us from viewing sympathetically the strain of philosophical theology we are about to consider. However, whatever the objections, it is a brute historical fact that there is a substantial and important tradition in Western thought which identifies philosophy with religion and which sees religion as the culmination or highest realisation of philosophy. We can, of course, simply deny that this represents genuine religion by insisting upon the sharp and irreducible distinction between the natural and supernatural, and by defining religion in terms of supernatural revelation, faith and grace – the gratuitous, unmerited intervention of God. Or again, we can define religion as practical in mode so that the notion of a philosophical or speculative religion becomes self-contradictory. But the 'intellectualistic' tradition is too large and central to be dismissed in this way,[6] for it includes Plato and Aristotle, Plotinus and the neo-Platonic school, including the sixth-century Christian Pseudo-Dionysius (who had such a large effect upon the thought of the Middle Ages). Again, it is manifested in the philosophical theology of certain of the great Moslem thinkers such as Ibn Rushd in the twelfth century and, in quite a different context, in the thought of Spinoza and the deists of the Enlightenment in the seventeenth and eighteenth centuries, and of Hegel in the nineteenth century. Even within the Christian tradition, at least up until the Reformation, there is a persistent inclination towards 'intellectualism', despite the theological condemnations of it as being destructive of the distinction between nature and the supernatural, faith and reason. This tendency can be traced in the early thought of St Augustine (354–430) for example, and certainly in Boëthius's (480–524) *De Consolatione Philosophiae*. The *De Consolatione* had enormous influence upon subsequent Christian thought, and yet it is a work in which philosophy is seen as a way of life that culminates, without any kind of break, in religious enlightenment. Again, in the so-called 'dialectical' movement in the eleventh and twelfth centuries in the Christian West, there is this same tendency (though often ambiguously expressed) to identify 'true philosophy' with faith. It is indeed against this movement that in the early Middle Ages St Peter Damian and St Bernard of Clairvaux, for example, protest so violently, and the violence of their attacks on the religion of the philosophers or dialecticians bears witness to its reality and importance. Even such orthodox Christian thinkers as St Anselm of Bec have a strong dose of intellectualism in their theology, though in practice they make the necessary reservations and qualifications about supernatural faith being discontinuous with philosophical reason.[7] Finally, contemporary with Aquinas in the thirteenth century there is the movement of 'Latin Averroism', which holds the philosophical life to be the highest state available to humans, and which is important enough to earn ecclesiastical condemnation.[8] Aquinas's mentor, St Albert the Great, had been deeply influenced by the eleventh-century Islamic thinker Ibn Sina (Avicenna) who had identified Aristotle's conception of the life of philosophical contemplation with the prophetic life. It is interesting to note that Eckhart, in the thirteenth century, reformulated this idea in his doctrine of 'radical detachment', which leads to the mystical indwelling of God in the soul. As de Libera notes, Aristotle's ideas were transformed into a doctrine about the mystical life.[9]

It is, therefore, very difficult to define away this conception of the philosophy of religion simply by claiming that, within the Judaeo-Christian context, it represents a kind of contradiction in terms. For this way of viewing the philosophy of religion has in reality been of very great moment in the history of Western thought. We shall, therefore, look critically at some typical essays that have been made in this kind of philosophy of religion. Once again, we shall not be concerned to present a complete history of this tendency in Western thought, but rather to understand its motivation, its logical structure, and its implications for both philosophy and religion.

PLATO'S PHILOSOPHICAL RELIGION

Plato's philosophy of religion is elaborated by way of reaction against the mythological and superstitious character of the popular religion given credence by poets such as Homer and Hesiod, and supported by the priests and religious 'professionals'. Plato argues that this kind of mythical religion lacks any rational basis in that no proofs or reasons are offered by its devotees for what they believe. Nor, again, does it give a true and adequate account of 'the divine', for the infantile stories of popular religion show the gods engaging in all kinds of morally dubious behaviour and as being subject to change and multiplicity.[10] This view of the divine is childishly anthropomorphic and the first task of the philosopher is to demythologise the traditional theology and to replace it by a true, rationally based, theology. So Plato forbids the poets to speak of Zeus giving portions of good and evil to men, because he wants to make it clear that since God is good, he cannot be the cause of evil.[11] Again, he forbids the poets from talking about the various metamorphoses of the gods, for God is immaterial and cannot change; likewise he is truthful and cannot deceive us. Thus, as it has been put, 'Plato's religion ... is above all based upon rational convictions, on intellectual beliefs, on truths'. Again, it has been said, 'For Plato a life aimed at salvation takes the form of a rational inquiry, a philosophical life'.[12]

Apart from demythologising the popular anthropomorphic and irrational religion and substituting a purified rational religion in its place, the philosopher also must combat the atheism of those, like Empedocles, for whom God is an unnecessary hypothesis since the workings of nature are explicable in purely materialistic and mechanistic terms. In these atheistic views everything in nature comes about by chance, and religion, together with human morality and social institutions, are claimed to be mere products of convention.[13] For Plato, both the atheistic philosophers and the exponents of mythological religion have this in common – neither see that the world is the effect of an intelligent cause or principle. So in the celebrated passage in the *Phaedo* Socrates recounts his disenchantment with Anaxagoras's philosophical system which allowed no place for teleology and thus for a designing Intelligence. In fact, Socrates argues, we cannot explain the workings of nature in mechanistic terms, for the order and design of things and the adaptation of part to part in organic wholes implies purposiveness, and this in turn implies a purposing Intelligence.

As has often been remarked, Plato is here exploiting ideas that were in the air long before his time. Diogenes of Appolonia, for example, had put forward a finalistic proof of a supreme Intelligence in very much the same terms as the proof in Plato's *Phaedo*: 'No,' Diogenes argues, 'this would never have been possible without an Intelligence – this distribution that regulates the measures of all things, summer and winter, night and day, the rains, winds and sunshine. So also for everything else: anyone who wishes to consider things will find in them the most complete order'.[14] Equally, as Jaeger shows, Plato's philosophical religion is foreshadowed in certain of the pre-Socratics. Thus, for example, he says: 'Anaximander's explanation of nature is something more than mere explanation of nature: it is the first philosophical theodicy'.[15] Jaeger gives Xenophanes a major role in the demythologising of popular religion and its replacement by a philosophical religion,[16] and he sums up this new approach to religion with the profound remark: 'Though philosophy means death to the old gods, it is itself religion'.[17]

With Plato, however, the transcendence of the divine order becomes clearly marked for the first time. The earlier philosophers had spoken of the basic stuff out of which the world was made as being 'divine'. But Anaximander's 'Air' and Herakleitos's 'Fire' belonged to the world of 'becoming' and so could not really be 'divine'. For Plato it is rather the immutable, eternal, universal objects of pure intelligence – the Forms – that are divine in the strict sense. The totality of the intelligible Forms (together with the supreme Intelligence that contemplates the Forms) makes up 'the divine, the immortal, the intelligible, the indissoluble, the eternally identical' of which the *Phaedo* speaks.[18] Plato calls this totality the universal Being, Being without limitation, Being that is totally being, the Whole, and for him it is this alone that is divine in the strict sense, and not the physical world of the pre-Socratic philosophers.[19]

If the intelligible world is coterminous with the order of the divine, then the Form of the Good, upon which all the other intelligible realities depend, will be the quintessence of divinity. So Plato says in the *Republic*[20] that the Form of the Good is Goodness itself, Being itself, Justice itself; it is not a member of the class of good things, or of the class of beings – rather it is that by which things are good, existent, just and so on. (This is an idea that the medieval philosophers will take up and powerfully exploit later on.) We can say indeed that the Form of the Good transcends existence and goodness, for that which is the principle of existence and goodness cannot itself be called existent or good, any more than, to use a modern analogy, the standard metre in Paris (that by approximation to which any length is called a 'metre') can itself be called a 'metre'. (Once again, this is an idea that will be taken up and developed by the neo-Platonists.) Again, for Plato, the Form of the Good is mysterious not through any obscurity or unintelligibility attaching to it, but rather through its own excess of intelligibility. Just as we cannot look directly at the sun, which is the source of the light by which we see other things, so also we cannot look directly at the source of intelligibility by which we understand everything else. This pregnant idea, that the mysteriousness of God springs from his super-intelligibility, will also subsequently have a very deep influence upon both the neo-Platonists and the medieval philosophers of religion. If Plato's God is a hidden God he is that only in the paradoxical sense that he is so obvious and luminously clear that we find it difficult to see him. The obscurity is not in him but is due to the limitations of our intelligence.

This is a truly extraordinary conception and it represents a revolutionary development in human thinking about God and the religious order in general. It is, of course, intellectualism of the boldest and most uncompromising kind, for the divine is seen not as being discontinuous with the rational order (the sphere of philosophy) but rather as being completely continuous with it. In fact, the divine represents an intensification or deepening of the intelligible realm accessible to philosophical reason. And, as we have seen, its mysteriousness derives from an excess of intelligibility rather than from a limitation of it or from a break with the intelligible order, as is the case with primitive religion where the divine is held to be mysterious precisely because it is not accessible to reason. If it is possible to speak of Plato's 'mysticism'[21] then it is very much a mysticism that is the fruit of philosophical contemplation and vision, for the supra-rational is attained only through the intensification of the rational.[22]

For Plato, therefore, the sphere of the divine is not discontinuous with the rational order. Rather it is by carrying through the activity of intelligence to its ultimate limit or highest point that we reach the divine. As has often been remarked, for Plato the 'divine' is a kind of continuum covering the intelligible world as a whole,[23] the degree of divinity being proportionate to the degree of reality and the degree of intelligibility. Thus the philosophical ascent of the mind from the sense world to the intelligible world is also at the same time a religious ascent. For Plato, it has been said, 'Reason – as well as Soul, is found in the Universe and is due to the action of God, who is himself identified with Reason. In other words, the universe is rational and good in so far as God's rational nature and goodness are imparted to it; it is irrational and bad in so far as God's rational nature and goodness are not wholly imparted to it'.[24]

Plato is quite willing to accept the élitist consequences of this severely intellectualistic view of religion, and it is clear that for him the truly moral life and the truly religious life are only for a few choice souls and not for the many 'lovers of sights and sounds' who remain imprisoned in the world of *doxa*. Just as the philosophers are the only ones capable of true wisdom and of morality in the full sense, and so of political guardianship, so also they are the only ones capable of attaining to true religion. The Guardians are then both philosopher rulers and religious leaders. As Plato says in the 'Laws': 'The care of the State cannot be entrusted to those destined for this task unless they take steps to acquire all the knowledge that can be had of the Gods'.[25]

Again, as we have seen, Plato's view of the religious state is a purely speculative or visionary or contemplative one; religion for him is very much a concern of the intellect and not of the will or the desires. As he expresses it in the magnificent passage in the *Timaeus*:[26]

> If the heart of man has been set on the love of learning and true wisdom and he has exercised that part of himself above all, he is surely bound to have thoughts immortal and divine, if he shall lay hold upon truth, nor can he fail to possess immortality in the fullest meaning that human nature admits; and because he is always devoutly cherishing the divine part and maintaining the guardian genius that dwells with him in good estate, he must needs be happy above all.[27]

With Plato we have the first systematic attempt to construct a philosophical religion that will take the place of popular or 'mythical' religion. The great merit of such a philosophical religion for Plato is precisely that it is rational and intelligible and thus worthy of human beings at their best and most human. Mythical religion, on the other hand, is irrational and unintelligible and unreal, and so is suitable only to children or to the ignorant multitude who cannot rise above the world of dreams and illusions. The price we pay, however, for this is, first, that religion is wholly dependent upon philosophy and is only as valid as the philosophy on which it depends; second, that such a philosophical religion is inevitably élitist in that it is only the fortunate few sophisticated intellectuals capable of philosophical speculation who will be able to be religious in the full sense; and, third, this kind of intellectualistic religion is predominantly speculative or contemplative in character.

However, Plato is quite prepared to pay this price and we cannot plausibly claim that because his conception of religion is based upon (indeed, issues from) philosophy, and thus is subject to philosophical verification, as well as being élitist and intellectualistic, it is therefore not a religion at all.

We may conclude with the words of one of the most perceptive Platonic scholars: 'There is certainly such a thing as Plato's religion. It derives from his philosophy, it obeys the same principles and expresses the same aspirations, and it is, so to speak, the culmination and the flower of that philosophy'.[28]

ARISTOTLE: THE CONTEMPLATIVE IDEAL

At first sight Aristotle's philosophy seems notably to lack the religious orientation that is so marked in Plato. Certainly the gods and the general realm of the 'divine' occur as a constant feature of Aristotle's thought right from his early 'Platonic' treatise *On Philosophy* up to his later and more mature works. But, as Pascal complained of Descartes's God, the Aristotelian divinities appear to be dragged in to fill philosophical gaps, or to put the finishing touch upon a purely philosophical construction. Aristotle's theology, it has been said, seems to be a 'sort of appendix to physics, and to his particular physical theory'.[29] Thus, it has often been claimed that both the Prime Mover of the *Physics* and the ever-active Mind of the *Metaphysics* are wholly unconcerned with the affairs of humans or with the world in general, and the impression one gets is that the Aristotelian God is a cold and bloodless being, the 'self-absorbed object of unreciprocated love'.[30] Aristotle's God is one to whom we assent speculatively, the supreme object of philosophical contemplation; but he (if we can even call Aristotle's divine entity 'he') is not one whom one could love and trust and pray to. Commenting on Aristotle's observation in the *Poetics*, that the tragic denouement should spring from the hero's character and not be factitiously engineered by the gods, a recent commentator has this to say: 'Nothing could show more vividly how things have changed. The Gods are gone, except as a curtain raiser, and there is nothing to replace them except an Aristotelian Prime Mover sitting forever beyond the heavens'.[31]

Jaeger's view of Aristotle's religious ideas goes even further than this, for according to him Aristotle's philosophical development or evolution was away from a preoccupation with the supra-sensible world and the sphere of divinity (characteristic of his early Platonising phase) to a growing interest in the physical sciences. So in this view Aristotle's early metaphysics and theology, of a quasi-Platonic kind, give way to a philosophy of a strongly empiricist bent that is wholly unconcerned with theology.[32]

Nevertheless, despite these unpromising first appearances, there is in reality a definite and strong religious or theological orientation to Aristotle's philosophical system as a whole, and it is not too much to say that we find in Aristotle very much the same attempt to make religion the conclusion of philosophy as we have already noticed in Plato. In fact the notion of God is intimately involved in Aristotle's metaphysics, his psychology, his ethics, and his philosophical astronomy.

In Book VIII of the *Physics* Aristotle sets out an elaborate argument to show that the change or mutability that is of the essence of the material world cannot be explained without reference to an extra-physical cause of change which is not itself subject to change or mutability. Given that, for Aristotle, change or mutability is explained in terms of potentiality and actuality, this means that the unchanging cause of change is not itself subject to potentiality of any kind but is rather a purely actual thing. It *is*, and it cannot be otherwise than it is; and it is purely and ceaselessly active or dynamic without any kind of passivity or receptivity.[33] Aristotle's God, then, is full of life and energy to the highest degree – 'boiling with life', as Plotinus was to say later. Again, Aristotle's Prime Mover is not any kind of absentee landlord, or – to vary the analogy – a deistic God who winds the world up like a clock and then leaves it to run itself, for the influence of the Prime Mover upon the material world is direct, instantaneous and constant.

In Book X of the *Metaphysics* the nature of God's operation on the world is described in some detail. It is as a final cause that God acts on the world of mutability, and all the various changes in the universe, from the rotations of the heavens to the changes of material sublunary things, are seen as attempts by matter to approximate as far as possible to the perfection of God's eternal and immutable activity or dynamism. For Aristotle the circular movements of the planets are the most impressive manifestation of this approximation to the divine – so much so that he holds the contemplation of the movement of the stars to be one of the main sources (together with the prophetic power of the soul in dreams) of the religious impulse in man.[34]

Indeed this is for Aristotle the one tenet of popular religion that the philosopher can retain in his account of the divine. As he puts it at the end of Book X, chapter 8, of the *Metaphysics*:

> It has been handed down from the dim ages and left to posterity in the form of myth, that these principles [the stars] are gods, and all Nature is set round with the divine. The rest is mythical accretion designed to cajole the popular mind and to be used in the interests of law and utility... But if we strip this off and take the central fact alone, that they called the primary substances gods, it may well be thought god-inspired... So far, and so far only, are the beliefs of our society and those handed down to us by our ancestors, plain and true for us.[35]

Aristotle's low-keyed and modest prose in the *Physics* and *Metaphysics* conceals the very radical conception that he has of the relationship between God and the world – a world maintained in a state of dynamic process out of theocentric desire to imitate or approximate to the eternal energy or activity of God. The same idea is implied by his remark that God brings about order and goodness in the world just as the leader brings about order in the army.[36] 'The image of the leader', says a commentator on this passage, 'shows that the principle of order not only transcends the world as a model of perfection but also pervades the world as a force exercised by the supreme power'.[37]

This theocentric character of Aristotle's metaphysics is also evidenced in his account of the relationship between 'first philosophy' or metaphysics and 'theology'. Thus Aristotle certainly suggests on occasion that the object of 'first philosophy' – 'being *qua* being' – is identical with the divine in that it is only God that exists or has being in the fullest sense. As Merlan has put it:

> When Aristotle speaks of being *qua* being, ancient readers up to the time of Plotinus seem to mean: only of God can it be said that He is, whereas everything else is not only being but also becoming. Right or wrong, they seem to take the phrase 'being as being' as a kind of definition of the divinity. Therefore they do not see any essential difference between Plato and Aristotle in this respect.[38]

The theocentric character of Aristotle's psychology is certainly much less clear than that of his metaphysics but, in his enigmatic observations on *Nous* in the *De Anima*,[39] there is the hint that human thinking depends upon the Supreme Mind or *Nous*. Alexander of Aphrodisias, at any rate, interprets the passage in the *De Anima* as meaning that the human mind cannot engage in the activity of thinking without in some way participating in the ever-active divine *Nous*. In fact, he suggests that in so far as it is active (and not just receptive or passive) it is assimilated to the divine Mind and is 'divinised'.[40]

At first sight, Aristotle's ethics does not seem to have any explicitly religious dimension, for the portrait of the good man that emerges from the *Nicomachean Ethics* is hardly that of a religious mystic, but rather that of a 'well-rounded personality' who knows how to pursue his enlightened self-interest. Again, Aristotle does not see God as the origin of moral values nor as the sanction of them. Nevertheless, he clearly acknowledges that the culmination of the good life is the life of contemplation, and that this also represents the closest imitation of, or approximation to, the life of God of which men are capable. Thus in the famous passage in the *Nicomachean Ethics*,[41] Aristotle says that the highest form of happiness lies in the activity of *theoria* or pure contemplation, and he goes on to claim that the activity which brings the greatest happiness to man must be that which imitates the activity of God.[42] Now God's activity cannot be either of a practical or productive kind, for it would be absurd to think that God needed to be courageous or temperate or that he needed to make artefacts. But 'if you take away from a living being action, and still more production, what is left but contemplation? Therefore the activity of God which surpasses all others in blessedness, must be contemplation; and of human activities, therefore, that which is most akin to this must be happiness'.[43] If, then, this contemplation, which is the highest point of the moral life, is not strictly speaking *religious* contemplation,[44] nevertheless through this *theoria* man imitates the divine life in the closest way possible to him. Reason (*Nous*), as Aristotle says, is 'the best thing in us' and the most divine element in our nature;[45] and in its most intense form of activity (contemplation) we approach closest to the divine. Thus Aristotle argues:

> If the Gods have any care for human affairs, as they are thought to have, it would be reasonable both that they should delight in that which was best and most akin to them [i.e. reason] and that they should reward those who love and honour this most, as caring for the things that are dear

to them and acting both rightly and nobly. And that all these attributes belong most of all to the philosopher is manifest. He therefore is dearest to the gods. And he who is so will presumably be also the happiest, so that in his way the philosopher will more than any other be happy.[46]

This theistic orientation of Aristotle's ethics is even more marked in the *Eudemian Ethics* where good and bad are defined in terms of that which leads to the contemplation of God and that which hinders the contemplation of God respectively.[47]

Despite these religious implications of Aristotle's metaphysics, his psychology and his ethics, there are, however, two great lacunae in Aristotle's conception of religion, at least from a Christian point of view. The first is that Aristotle has no doctrine of personal immortality, and the second is that Aristotle's conception of God seemingly excludes any kind of providential interest and concern for the world and for human beings. With regard to the first, it seems that for Aristotle the contemplation of God (or the human contemplation that imitates God's contemplation) does not continue after death since the individual intellective *psyche* or soul is not capable of existing independently of the body of which it is the 'form'; although *Nous*, which is not bound up with a bodily organ and which enters the human *psyche* 'from without', is eternal and immortal.[48] However one may interpret the relation between *psyche* and *Nous*, it is clear enough that Aristotle did not envisage that the individual psyche could survive the death of the body and that Ibn Rushd's later interpretation of Aristotle's mysterious dicta in the *De Anima*, as implying a kind of soul of the human species which is immortal, is the most plausible one.[49]

Though it is, no doubt, possible to believe in God without believing in the immortality of the soul, this denial of personal immortality obviously limits Aristotle's view of religion in that for him religion becomes purely a 'this-worldly' business, even though God remains eternal and 'other-worldly'.

It is, however, Aristotle's apparent denial of divine providence that has given greatest scandal and caused many commentators to deny that Aristotle has any real conception of religion at all. In Book X of the *Metaphysics* Aristotle gives his celebrated definition of God as intelligence (*Nous*) intellecting itself: 'It must be of itself that this divine thought thinks (since it is the most excellent of things, and its thinking is a thinking on thinking)'.[50] This has commonly and naively been interpreted as meaning that God is self-centredly concerned and preoccupied with himself, and that he cannot in any way think of particular and changeable material objects outside himself, without, as it were, demeaning himself and violating his own unchangeable nature. However, it is not at all clear that this is Aristotle's meaning. Certainly he says precious little about God's providence, though he does suggest in the *Eudemian Ethics* that some kind of *philia* or friendship is possible between God and man.[51] But it cannot be Aristotle's view that God is not able to think of things outside himself, for his whole theory of the Prime Mover rests upon the assumption that God can act (albeit as a final cause) upon things outside himself without demeaning himself. And if God can *act* upon the material world and the world of men, it would seem to follow that he can equally *think* about them. The passage about *Nous* thinking on *Nous* cannot, then, mean that the possibility of divine providence is excluded. More probably it means that God's thinking must be wholly active without any of the passivity or receptivity that characterises human knowledge, in that this latter is dependent upon (and so passive with respect to) the object of knowledge. Perhaps Aristotle is wanting to say here that, whereas in human knowledge there is always a subject–object distinction, there cannot be any such distinction in divine knowledge, otherwise it would be object-dependent or 'passive'.[52] There is still a problem in explaining how God can think of material things without them being objects of his knowledge and without his thinking being passive or receptive with respect to them, but at least Aristotle himself does not see it as an impossibility.

It remains true, however, that for Aristotle religion is primarily a matter of vision and contemplation of God without there being any expectation of reciprocal interest or concern from God. For Aristotle, we contemplate God, but we do not love God or enjoy God's love in return. Our attitude to God is a quasi-aesthetic one, for just as we contemplate objects of beauty without the expectation of any return, so also we contemplate God. If this seems to be an austere kind of religious view we ought to remember that this is also the way religion is seen in certain forms of Buddhism and Hinduism. Again, as we shall see for St Thomas Aquinas, our final happiness consists primarily in the beatific vision or pure intellectual contemplation of God, and only secondarily in the love of God, and in being loved by God.

Ross complains that Aristotle's analysis of the religious consciousness is finally inadequate because, as he puts it, 'God is required not only by the intellect, to round off our knowledge of the world, but by the heart, to give us strength and courage to live'.[53] And he goes on to say: 'In a general sense

Kant was probably right in holding that the practical reason has more to tell us about God than the pure reason'.[54] Certainly, we may admit that Aristotle's conception of religion is not a post-Reformation or post-Kantian one and that it is very different from the 'religious consciousness' that is typical of much contemporary Christianity. But this gives us no warrant for claiming that Aristotle's view of religion is therefore in some way inadequate or defective, unless, of course, we gratuitously assume that Ross's own Kantian view of religion is normative or paradigmatic.[55]

In conclusion, then, even if we cannot claim Aristotle to be a 'God-intoxicated' man, nevertheless it is clear that for him, as for Plato, philosophy is itself a religious way of life in that through philosophy we approximate to the highest degree possible to the life of God. Aristotle is certainly not a cold rationalist suspicious of religion; rather he is, in line with Plato, concerned to show that the culmination of philosophy is religion. As his medieval commentators sometimes put it: true philosophy is religion, and true religion is philosophy.

THE NEO-PLATONISTS: PHILOSOPHY AND MYSTICISM

Whatever reservations one might have about the interpretation of Plato and Aristotle just offered, and of their effort to construct a religious philosophy or, what comes to the same thing, a radically intellectualistic form of religion, there is very little doubt that this was the way in which their thought was seen by their later followers. One can trace out the chequered career of this conception of the philosophy of religion, according to which religion is seen as the highest point of philosophical wisdom, in the complex movement of neo-Platonism that emanates from Plotinus in the third century CE as well as in the movement of Christian Platonism in the early centuries of the Christian Church, and the tradition of Arabic or Islamic philosophico-religious speculation from the ninth century onwards. Echoes of this view also sound, as we shall see later, in medieval Christian thought. It is worth while saying a brief word about each of these movements in order to emphasise how important and far-reaching the Platonic–Aristotelian conception of the philosophy of religion has been. It has been said that 'it would be difficult to name a later theological system that is not in some way or other, directly or indirectly, indebted to Plato';[56] and if, with the ancient commentators, we see Plato's theology as complemented by that of Aristotle, this observation is profoundly true.

With Plotinus (204–70 CE) and his followers Porphyry (232–305) and Proclus (410–85) the central themes of this Platonic–Aristotelian philosophy of religion are elaborated in the most dramatic way. Plotinus's 'One' plays the same role as Plato's Form of the Good and is at once the supreme meta-physical and ethical principle – that on which everything depends for its being and value, and that which is the final end of man. The One, again like the Form of the Good and Aristotle's God, is mysterious to us precisely because of its super-intelligibility and not in any way because the knowledge of the One breaks with rational knowledge. Again, Plotinus's 'mysticism' is of a radically rationalistic kind, for if we must transcend philosophy to achieve the ultimate vision of the One, this transcending of philosophy is done through philosophy and is itself a philosophical act. Plotinus certainly does not imply that there is some kind of supernatural realm discontinuous with the realm of pure philosophical reason. For him, it has been said, 'the mind has to be purged of its philosophy to find the Good. The supreme achievement of the intellect is to leave itself behind. But for Plotinus there is no way of passing beyond intellect than through intellect. We cannot leave our philosophical minds till we have used them to the full. There is, in his way of thinking, no alternative route to God for non-philosophers'.[57] It is then, Plotinus makes clear, not by prayers or rites that the soul returns to its source in the Good and so finds its true happiness, but rather by philosophy which raises the soul to the highest level of contemplation through which it finds union with the One. This contemplative vision is described in the *Enneads* in ecstatic terms (the intellect 'goes out of its mind'),[58] but, as we have said, it is an ecstasy that comes about *through* the intellect and not by negating it.[59]

For Plotinus then, and for the neo-Platonists generally, the whole purpose of philosophy is a religious one, so that the metaphysical effort to understand reality and man's own quest for ultimate enlightenment and happiness are one and the same. Anyone who thinks that this form of intel-lectualistic religion, with its emphasis on the pure intellectual contem-plation and vision of God, and with no – or at least a very impoverished – conception of God's reciprocal love and providence with regard to human beings, must inevitably be a cold and heartless kind of religion, has only to read Plotinus's *Enneads* in order to realise their mistake. For the *Enneads* shows once and for all that a philosophical religion is not, as has so often been alleged, some kind of unviable monstrosity. In its own way, indeed, the One of Plotinus and his followers perfectly fits the definition of the central religious reality which Rudolf Otto calls 'the Numinous', and which he defines as 'mysterium, tremendum et fascinans'. Again, the example of the great neo-Platonists' lives is significant in this respect. For the life of Plotinus, as his disciple Porphyry recounts it, shows a seriousness and devotion and sense of vocation that is very similar to that of the Eastern religious sages. And the same is true of Porphyry himself and of Proclus. Thus it has been said that 'philosophy produced some of the most striking ideal types, the saints of antiquity. Around all the prominent figures who founded or developed schools there grew not only anecdotes but also haloes'.[60]

This merging of philosophy and religion, entailing as it does a denial of any distinct supernatural order, is of course very difficult to reconcile with Christianity. But it is surprising how much this intellectualistic view of religion persists even within the Christian tradition. Thus, although the early Christian thinkers in practice make the necessary reservations in order to safeguard the distinction between what is supernaturally revealed and accessible to faith and what is accessible to philosophical reason, there is a tendency in Christian neo-Platonists such as Origen (185–254), St Gregory Nazianzen (330–90) and St Gregory of Nyssa (330–95) to see the end of Christian wisdom and of 'true philosophy' as identical. Speaking of St Augustine, a recent commentator says that 'he does not appear to have felt any sharp need, at the time of his conversion, to disentangle the teaching of Christianity from that of the "Platonists". It was easy to pass from the atmosphere of Plotinus and Porphyry to that of St Paul and the Fourth Gospel, and Augustine had no sense of any radical transition'.[61] The same writer goes on to say that 'in the works written at the time of his conversion to Christianity and immediately following it, Augustine interpreted his conversion as the result of his quest for wisdom, and often speaks of having arrived in the "haven of philosophy". "Christianity" and "true philosophy" are practically synonymous terms'.[62] So, in the famous passage in the *Confessions*, Augustine describes his conversion from rhetoric to philosophy in wholly religious language:

> Among these people, being not yet in manhood's strength, I was learning books of eloquence, in which I wished to shine with a purpose flighty and to be condemned, in the joy of human vanity. In the usual order of studies I had come to a book of a certain Cicero, whose speech is admired by almost all though his heart is not. But that book contains his exhortation unto philosophy and is called *Hortensius*. Now that book changed my affections and turned my prayers to Thee thyself, O Lord, and made my

wishes and desires quite other. Suddenly all vain hopes grew cheap in my eyes and I yearned for the immortality of wisdom with a burning zeal which passes belief and I began to rise that I might return unto Thee.[63]

It is, however, in the work of the Christian thinker Pseudo-Dionysius that this neo-Platonic religious intellectualism is given its most extravagant expression. Pseudo-Dionysius was a Christian thinker (possibly a Syrian Christian monk) of the sixth century who put forward a Christianised version of Proclus's thought under the name of Dionysius the convert of St Paul.[64] With Pseudo-Dionysius indeed it is difficult to know whether he is putting forward a neo-Platonic view of reality illustrated by Christian themes, or whether he is proposing a Christian world-view in neo-Platonic categories. Pseudo-Dionysius himself would probably not have seen the difference between the two, for seeing philosophy as religion, or religion as philosophy, would for him have come to one and the same thing.[65] Pseudo-Dionysius had enormous influence upon medieval thinkers – Erigena, Simon of Tournai, Bonaventure, Aquinas – and there is no doubt that his religious intellectualism rubbed off on them to some extent.

The same tendency to identify Christianity and 'true philosophy' occurs in a different context in the influential work, the *De Consolatione Philosophiae*, of the sixth-century Christian thinker Boëthius. The aim of the *De Consolatione* is precisely to show that philosophy leads the soul to God, and though the teaching of the work harmonises generally with Christian teaching about God, human beings and human freedom, there is no explicit reference to Christianity in it. Indeed, it has been claimed that Boëthius wrote the *De Consolatione* at the end of his life when he had abandoned Christianity and returned to philosophy as a secular way to salvation.[66]

Despite this infiltration of Platonic religious intellectualism into early Christian thinking, it remains true that in the last resort, Christianity sees the sphere of natural reason and of philosophy as distinct from the supernatural sphere of religious faith. In other words, one can never attain to religious faith simply by intensifying the exercise of pure reason. It is this realisation that forces the medieval Christian thinkers to formulate a completely new conception of the philosophy of religion.

MEDIEVAL ISLAMIC THOUGHT AND THE 'TWO TRUTHS' THEORY

The philosophical religion whose career we have been tracing among the Christian neo-Platonists also has interesting echoes in the tradition of thought that springs from the meeting of neo-Platonic philosophy and the religion of Islam. Apart from the orthodox Moslem apologists – the *mutakallimun* – who use philosophical instruments to defend and explicate the Islamic faith proposed in Mohammed's revelations in the Qur'an, there is a line of philosophers who seek to construct a purely philosophical theology of much the same kind as they find in their Greek masters, Plato, Aristotle and the neo-Platonists.[67]

Thus, for example, a Persian Platonist of the ninth century, Al Razi (Rhazes, 865–925), puts forward a purely rationalistic view of religion in the following words: 'Philosophy', he says, 'is the imitation of Almighty God so far as lies within man's power'.[68] The revealed religion of the prophets, Moses, Jesus and Mohammed, is superstition, and philosophy is the only true and universal way to salvation. 'God, glorious is his name, has given us reason in order to obtain through it from the present and future the utmost benefits that we can obtain; it is God's best gift to us... By reason ... we succeed to the knowledge of God, which is the highest knowledge we can obtain'.[69]

Similarly, the great Al Farabi (870–950) attempts to reconcile the Islamic religion and Platonic–Aristotelian philosophy by arguing that religion simply presents in a symbolic and limited form what philosophy presents more adequately and universally. As he puts it, the philosopher alone knows the truth in the full sense, and it is made known to others 'through symbols which reproduce it analogically'.[70] This idea is of course a very old one; it is found, for instance, in Plutarch of Chaeronia in the second century in his *De Iside et Osiride*. 'There is one divine mind', he says, 'which keeps the universe in order and one providence which governs it. The names given to this supreme God differ; he is worshipped in different ways in different religions; the religious symbols used in them vary, and their qualities are different; sometimes they are rather vague and sometimes distinct'.[71] The same equation of the religious with the symbolic will also, as we shall see, have a long history in subsequent speculation right up to the present times.[72]

According to Al Farabi, philosophical theology is the outcome of human reason alone and is, as such, universally valid. The symbolic expression of religious truths in the various 'revelations', however, are valid only for those who accept them and who understand the particular set of symbols they employ. It is worth while citing Al Farabi on this at length since he provides the first expression in Islamic thought of what has been misleadingly called the 'Two Truths' theory – in other words, the theory that philosophy and religion express the same truth in two different ways and at two different levels. Thus Al Farabi writes:

> According to the ancients, religion is an imitation of philosophy. Both comprise the same subject and both give an account of the ultimate end for the sake of which man is made – that is, supreme happiness – and the ultimate end of every one of the other beings. In everything of which philosophy gives an account based on intellectual perception or conception, religion gives an account based on imagination. In everything demonstrated by philosophy, religion employs persuasion. Philosophy gives an account of the ultimate principles ... as they are perceived by the intellect. Religion sets forth the images by means of similitudes of them taken from corporeal principles.[73]

It may seem that Al Farabi's position is one of religious scepticism, but this would be to misunderstand him, for he clearly thinks that he is giving an account of true religion superior to that of the *mutakallimun*, and that it is only through philosophy that one can achieve salvation and eternal bliss in the next life.

Ibn Sina (Avicenna, 980–1033), perhaps the central figure in Islamic philosophy, also maintains very much the same view of religion and philosophy though he is, perhaps, less severely 'reductionist' in his account than Al Farabi. In other words, he does not reduce the teaching of the Qur'an to a set of philosophical truths, without remainder, but rather attempts to harmonise the basic tenets of Islamic religious faith with Aristotelian and neo-Platonic philosophy. There is no doubt, however, that for him philosophy has the final say with regard to any conflict between faith and reason. Again, for him mystical contemplation is identified with philosophical insight. Thus a recent commentator writes: 'The highest form of the ritual prayer of the mystic is for Avicenna identical with the silent contemplation of the neo-Platonic philosopher which is the outcome and the culmination of intense and protracted philosophical studies'.[74]

A more nuanced version of the 'Two Truths' theory is put forward by the great twelfth-century Spanish Muslim Ibn Rushd (Averroës, 1126–96), who had considerable influence upon the Christian thinkers of the Middle Ages, especially Aquinas. The Qur'an, according to Ibn Rushd, is not opposed to philosophy. In fact, since it is the function of philosophy to lead men to the knowledge of God, the Qur'an implicitly commends philosophy. Again, we can only know the inner meaning of the Qur'an through philosophy, so the Qur'an cannot be opposed to philosophy as the religious fundamentalists pretend. There are three different levels of interpretation and understanding of the religious revelation contained in the Qur'an. First, there are those capable of understanding the latter through strict philosophical demonstration, and there is no doubt that for Ibn Rushd this is the highest and noblest form of religious understanding. Second, there are those who assume the truth of the Qur'an and argue for it dialectically. These are the theologians, and their understanding is inferior to that of the philosophers since it rests upon undemonstrated assumptions. Third, there are the 'people of rhetoric', or ordinary unsophisticated believers, who understand revelation through poetic analogies and metaphors. Thus, it has been said, for Ibn Rushd, 'there is absolute and esoteric rationalism for the philosophers; absolute and exoteric fideism for the ordinary people; and semi-rationalism and semi-fideism for the theologicans, who form a hybrid class'.[75] And the same commentator concludes that for Ibn Rushd 'religion does not teach any truth that the reason of the philosopher is not able to discover for itself. It is strictly only a system of symbols for the use of the masses who alone have to take them literally'.[76]

Though the 'Two Truths' theory had indirect antecedents in early Christian thought with the distinction between the theologians who have 'knowledge' (*gnosis*) of the true meaning of the gospels and the 'simpler' Christians (*simpliciores*) who are capable merely of 'belief' (*pistis*),[77] there is nothing in medieval Christian thought to compare with the radical kind of religious intellectualism to be found in this line of Islamic thinkers. Though they were attacked by orthodox theologians and other philosophers, such as the remarkable Al Ghazzali (1058–1111), who opposed their reduction of Islamic revelation to Platonic–Aristotelian philosophy, they themselves do not see their work in this light or as being sceptical in intent. In fact, it is clear that they thought that, by showing the concordance between the essentials of Islamic religion and the philosophico-theological conclusions of Greek philosophy, they were saving religion and making it respectable in that it could now be seen to be intrinsically rational. For them, as for their Greek masters, to rationalise religion was not to destroy it but rather to enhance and ennoble it and make it more fully worthy of our attention. For if religion were not the expression of philosophical reason, it would be irrational and unintelligible – a tissue of imaginative myths with no more truth-value than poetry. The 'Two Truths' theory enables us to see what is of universal value in the Qur'an and other religious revelations, and at the same time makes it possible for the philosopher to be a religious person in the fullest sense.

THE ENLIGHTENMENT: PURE REASON AND RELIGION

Though, as we have already remarked, the kind of religious intellectualism we have been examining has some repercussions in the philosophico-theological thought of the medieval Christian West, medieval thinkers such as Aquinas formulated a distinct position of their own according to which philosophy plays a defensive or apologetical role with respect to religious faith, the latter being seen as transcending philosophy or 'natural reason'. We will examine the structure of this position in the next chapter.

With the break-up of the medieval synthesis, however, and the emergence in the seventeenth century of a new rationalistic style of philosophy, there was a curious reversion to, or reinvention of, the older conception of the philosophy of religion. Thus, though Leibniz (1646–1716) and Spinoza (1632–77), for example, operate within a philosophical and religious context profoundly different from the Platonic/neo-Platonic tradition, they nevertheless, in their own way, also see religion as the culmination of pure reason. Or, to put the matter more exactly, philosophy for them expresses in a rational mode, accessible to the intellectually sophisticated few, the substance of what religion expresses in a symbolic or mythical mode accessible to the simple-minded many. And later on, Hegel (1770–1831) – although his philosophical perspectives are different again from those of Leibniz and Spinoza – adopts very much the same point of view. As Hegel puts it: 'The substance of the Christian religion, the highest developmental stage of any and all religion, coincides completely with the substance of true philosophy'.[78]

There is of course a large difference between the philosophy of religion of these thinkers and the philosophy of religion of the Greeks and their direct descendants. The distinction between turning philosophy into religion and turning religion into philosophy is a very fine one, but it could perhaps be said that, whereas for the Platonic/neo-Platonic tradition philosophy comes to have a religious dimension, for Spinoza and Hegel, on the other hand, religion tends to become a branch of philosophy. It is this, no doubt, that led Croce to remark of Hegel that he is at once the most religious and the most irreligious of philosophers, and that caused some of Spinoza's contemporaries to condemn him as an atheist, even though his philosophy culminates in the 'intellectual love of God'.

It is difficult, however, to make this point without aiding and abetting the usual misleading criticisms that are made of the rationalist philosophers (and, in another way, of Hegel), namely, that they were deists who arbitrarily introduced God into their philosophical systems in order to extricate themselves from difficulties and paradoxes or, even more damagingly, that they gave their philosophy religious trappings to escape sanctions from the ecclesiastical and civil powers. Pascal has expressed the first kind of criticism in his famous remark apropos Descartes: 'I cannot forgive Descartes. He would have liked, in the course of his philosophy, to by-pass God. But he could not help making Him give a shove to set the world in motion; after that he has nothing further to do with God'.[79]

But Descartes's God is not really a *deus ex machina*, and neither are the Gods (all very different) of Leibniz, Spinoza and Hegel, for in all these philosophical systems God is a necessary and indispensable element. Of course Spinoza's God – the object of 'intellectual love' – and Hegel's God – the Absolute Self-Conscious Spirit – are very far removed from the God of Judaeo-Christianity, and their conception of popular religion as giving mythical or symbolic expression to truths known in their fullness by philosophy is equally at odds with traditional Christianity. But unless we arbitrarily define 'God' and 'religion' exclusively in traditional Judaeo-Christian terms, we cannot protest that Spinoza and Hegel are not 'really' talking about God or religion at all.[80]

Again, there is no reason to doubt these thinkers' personal religious concern. Leibniz was deeply interested in religion and religious affairs all through his life; Spinoza was described by Novalis as a 'God-intoxicated man'; and it has been said of Hegel that he is 'in a sense the most Christian of thinkers, for while the official defenders of Christianity have usually borrowed their logic and the cast of their thought from Aristotle or from other sources, Hegel alone among thinkers has borrowed the whole cast of his thought from Christianity'.[81]

It is of considerable interest to see in the strain of thought represented by Leibniz, Spinoza and Hegel very much the same moves being made as in the older Platonic/neo-Platonic tradition. There is, for instance, the same denial of any distinction between the 'natural' order of reason and the 'supernatural' order of religious faith. Leibniz does indeed give lip-service to this distinction, but in practice he constructs a philosophical religion quite independently of revelation. As it has been put:

> Leibniz writes with perfect seriousness and decency about the Christian scheme of redemption, but it hardly looks like being for him a crucial

deliverance from perdition. It is not the intervention of Mercy by which alone he possesses himself of us: it is one of the ways in which supreme Benevolence carries out a cosmic policy; and God's benevolence is known by pure reason, and apart from Christian revelation.[82]

The same denial of the supernatural dimension of faith is also made even more firmly and explicitly by Spinoza and Hegel.

Again, these philosophers of religion betray the same religious élitism or esotericism already noticed in the older religious intellectualists. In other words, for them it is only the few intellectual experts who can grasp the true substance of religion in its rational mode. As Hegel expresses it in the celebrated conclusion to his *Lectures on the Philosophy of Religion*:

> For us philosophical knowledge has harmonised this discord [about religious belief], and the aim of these lectures has just been to reconcile reason and religion, to show how we know this latter to be in all its manifold forms necessary, and to rediscover in revealed religion the truth and the Idea. But this reconciliation is itself merely a partial one without outward universality. Philosophy forms in this connexion a sanctuary apart, and those who serve in it constitute an isolated order of priests, who must not mix with the world and whose work is to protect the possession of Truth.[83]

Spinoza also makes a sharp distinction between the philosopher's knowledge of God and the belief of the ordinary *croyant*. The philosopher attains to the 'greatest good of the mind' which is the knowledge of God,[84] and he enjoys the satisfaction and spiritual pleasure that goes with this knowledge.[85] This 'intellectual love of God', which Spinoza describes in terms analogous to those appropriate to religious mysticism, is 'the very love of God with which God loves himself, not in so far as he is infinite but in so far as he can be expressed through the essence of the human mind, considered under the species of eternity'.[86] On the other hand, the ordinary man's approach to religion is a completely non-speculative one. Faith at this level is a matter of 'obedience' to God's moral commands and a man is to be accounted religious in so far as he does good works. As Spinoza puts it: 'It follows that we can only judge a man faithful or unfaithful by his works. If his works be good, he is faithful, however much his doctrines may differ from the rest of the faithful: if his works be evil, though he may verbally conform, he is unfaithful'.[87] The imaginative utterances of the religious prophets, so Spinoza implies, are neither true nor false; they are simply more or less rhetorically effective in that they lead us to that love of our neighbour that is the heart and soul of religion. So he says, 'the sphere of reason is truth and wisdom ... the sphere of theology is piety and obedience'.[88] 'It is not true doctrines', he goes on, 'which are expressly required by the Bible, so much as doctrines necessary for obedience, and to confirm in our hearts the love of our neighbour, wherein (to adapt the words of John) we are in God and God in us'.[89] This practically oriented religion is 'adapted to the understanding and established opinion of the multitude',[90] and although Spinoza is sympathetic to the value of this popular religion, there is no doubt that for him it is inferior to the philosophical religion that culminates in the intellectual love of God.[91] Later on, Schopenhauer (1788–1860) mocks this distinction between the philosophical religion of the few and the allegorical or mythical religion of the vulgar. Thus in his dialogue *On Religion*, his *alter ego* Demopheles speaks of 'philosophers for the few, the emancipated; founders of religions for the many, for mankind as a whole'.

> Religion [he goes on] is the metaphysics of the people, which they absolutely must be allowed to keep: and that means you have to show an outward respect for it, since to discredit it is to take it away from them. Just as there is folk-poetry and, in the proverbs, folk-wisdom, so there has to be folk-metaphysics: for men have an absolute need for an *interpretation of life*, and it has to be one they are capable of understanding. That is why it is always clothed in allegory; and, as far as its practical effect as a guide to behaviour and its effect on morale as a means of consolation and comfort in suffering and death are concerned, it does as much perhaps as truth itself would do if we possessed it... The people have no direct access to truth; the various religions are simply schemata by which they grasp it and picture it, but with which it is inseparably linked. Therefore, my dear chap, I hope you'll forgive me for saying that to ridicule them is to be both narrow-minded and unjust.[92]

In his own way, Hegel makes much the same kind of distinction between philosophical religion and popular religion. The philosopher knows that God is not an independent objective entity, but is rather identical with the self-conscious Spirit which is becoming manifest in mankind as a whole. This does not mean for Hegel that God is identified with man, so that religion becomes a kind of humanism, but it does mean that the traditional 'theistic' God has to be done away with and that in this sense we may say that 'God is dead'.[93]

Popular religion, on the other hand, involves 'representational thought'. 'Representation' (*Vorstellung*) for Hegel does not simply mean thinking by means of images or mental pictures conjured up in the imagination. An image is always particular and so has no rational content, since rationality and universality are synonymous. A 'representation', however, is involved in a pictorial way of thinking which presents some universal, and so rational, truth. Thus, for example, the popular idea of God creating the world is a 'representation', for it represents, in an image taken from human making, the origin of the world as an event taking place in time (though for philosophical understanding, of course, the creation of the world is not an event, nor does it take place in time) and so gives us some dim idea of the philosophical truth that the Idea externalises itself by an eternal and timeless process.[94] This kind of representational thought is typical of popular religion and is of course accessible to the majority of non-philosophical people; but the inner meaning of what is represented by religious representations is available only to the 'isolated priesthood' of philosophers.

We may remark as well that for both Spinoza and Hegel philosophical religion is essentially speculative or visionary, as contrasted with popular religion which is above all concerned with moral practice. Thus, Spinoza expressly rejects any reciprocity in our intellectual love of God. We love God, in so far as we intellectually contemplate him, but God certainly does not love us in return. 'He who loves God', Spinoza says, 'cannot endeavour to bring it about that God should love him in return';[95] indeed, for a man to want God's love would be tantamount to desiring that 'God whom he loves should not be God'.[96]

Hegel also proposes the same severely intellectualistic view. 'The aim of philosophy', he says, 'is to know the truth, to know God, for he is the absolute truth, inasmuch as nothing else is worth troubling about save God and the unfolding of God's nature'.[97] Thus, for Hegel, all the doctrines of Christianity, despite any 'practical' appearance they may have, are translatable into speculative or theoretical terms. His account of the meaning of the death of Christ (the doing away of the human side of Christ's nature) is typical in this regard. 'The real point of importance', he says, 'is an infinite relation to God, to God as actually present, the certainty of the Kingdom of God, a sense of satisfaction not in morality, nor even in anything ethical, nor in the conscience, but a sense of satisfaction beyond which there can be nothing higher, an absolute relation to God himself'.[98]

In addition to these characteristics which Leibniz, Spinoza and Hegel share with the older religious intellectualists, they bring out very vividly another aspect of the 'logic' of this position. For Leibniz, Spinoza, and Hegel it is what is necessary and universal and essential and eternal that is of primary value in true religion, so that the contingent, particular, accidental and temporal or historical features of religion are disregarded as being of no real significance. There are elements of this 'necessitarianism' in the neo-Platonists and, as we have seen, in certain of the Islamic thinkers who contrast the particular and limited character of the various historical revealed religions with the universal and eternal character of philosophical religion. But with Spinoza and Hegel this tendency is strongly emphasised. For them the historical facts of Christianity – that, for example, Christ was born at a certain time and place; that he lived, suffered and died and rose again from the dead – are, as historical facts, of no relevance to religion at all. Thus Spinoza writes that 'it is not entirely necessary to know Christ according to the flesh, but we must think far otherwise of the eternal son of God, that is the eternal wisdom of God which has manifested itself in all things, more especially in the human mind, and most of all in Christ Jesus. For without this wisdom no one can attain to a state of blessedness'.[99] Again, Hegel says that we must distinguish between the 'outward history' of Christ, and the universal and necessary meaning of the events of His life, this latter being the concern of true religion.[100]

This radically a-historical conception of religion, which derives from Hegel's whole conception of philosophy,[101] is brought out very dramatically in a remarkable essay by the English neo-Hegelian F. H. Bradley, and it is worth while citing him at some length:

> Suppose (let us say) a man convinced of the truth of Christianity, and rightly or wrongly to understand Christianity as the unity of God with finite souls, a reality at once consummated and eternal and yet temporal and progressive. Christianity is to such a man a main aspect of the Universe, conscious of itself above time, and yet revealing itself in the historical growth of spiritual experience. And imagine the same man asked to compare with this principle the truth about some happening in time. I will not instance such events as the virgin birth and bodily ascension of Jesus of Nazareth, but I will take the historical assertion that Jesus actually at a certain time lived and taught in Galilee and actually died at Jerusalem on the cross. And by 'actually' I mean so that, if *we* had been there, we should have seen these things happen.
>
> 'All such events', our supposed man might reply, 'are if you view them as occurrences, of little importance. Inquire by all means whether and how far there is good evidence for their happening. But do not imagine that

Christianity is vitally concerned with the result of your inquiry. Christianity, as I conceive it, covers so much ground, fills such a space in the Universe, and makes such a difference to the world, that, without it, the world would be not so much changed as destroyed. And it counts for much that this eternal truth should have appeared on our planet (as presumably elsewhere), and should here (we hope) be developing itself more and more fully. But the rest, if you will take it as mere event and occurrence, is an affair so small – a matter grounded by the very nature of its world on so little – that between the two things there can be hardly a comparison'.[102]

SUMMARY AND EVALUATION

So far we have attempted to expose the anatomy of this view of the philosophy of religion which sees philosophy as leading to and issuing in religion. There is, it will now be clear, a kind of logic operating in this position in the sense that, given the identification of philosophy with religion, the other aspects of this position follow with a kind of necessity, and are also interconnected. Thus, for example, this kind of philosophy of religion results in an austerely contemplative or speculative approach to religion; it involves the denial, or at least the blurring, of the distinction between the sphere of natural reason and that of supernatural faith; it results in religious esotericism; and, finally, it leads to a radically a-historical approach to religion. Let us look at each of these aspects in more detail.

First, according to this position, religion is defined as consisting essentially in the intellectual vision or contemplation of 'God'. The latter, as we have seen, has been variously understood as the Form of the Good (Plato); the purely and eternally actual and dynamic source of change and mutability, and the ever-active *Nous* or Mind (Aristotle); the one transcending all our finite categories (Plotinus and the neo-Platonists); the creative and providential God of Islam; Spinoza's infinite substance (*Deus sive Natura*) of which finite beings are 'modes'; and Hegel's Self-Conscious Spirit working itself out in the world. And the intellectual apprehension and contemplation and enjoyment of God, in these several senses, is held to be of the essence of 'religion'.

In each case, no doubt, the philosophical knowledge and contemplation of God is accompanied by practical or ethical effects, so that, for example, through our contemplation of God we will be led to live virtuously and to be morally happy. But it remains true that the speculative aspect is primary, and the ethical aspect merely secondary. Spinoza expresses this order of precedence between the speculative and practical very nicely in one of his letters:

'I know (and this knowledge gives me the highest contentment and peace of mind) that all things come to pass by the power and unchangeable decree of a Being supremely perfect'.[103] Here it is the vision of the supremely perfect God on whom all else depends that is central, the resulting contentment and peace of mind being seen as an incidental concomitant.

It has been said, apropos of Spinoza's 'intellectual love of God' (and it could be said also of the other forms of speculative religion), that 'the love in question is more akin to the pleasure or mental satisfaction accompanying a scientist's vision of a complete explanation of Nature, rather than to love in the sense of love between persons'.[104] But perhaps it would be more enlightening to see the speculative vision of God as analogous to aesthetic appreciation. Aesthetic appreciation is primarily non-discursive or contemplative, though it may have concomitant emotional and even moral repercussions; it is disinterested or impracticable or 'useless', and it is non-reciprocal in that it does not expect any response from the object contemplated; and, finally, it is 'ecstatic' in that through intellection we are, as it were, led beyond intellection. It is, at all events, these aspects of philosophical knowledge – its non-discursive or contemplative character, its disinterestedness, and its ecstatic dimension – that the philosophers we have been considering wish to stress.

If then it should be objected that the identification of religion with philosophy makes religion too abstract and coldly intellectual an affair, we ought to remember that it is philosophy in the above sense that is in view. Aesthetic appreciation, it could be argued, is not cold and abstract, even though it is a form of intellectual contemplation, and if our analogy holds any water, the same could be argued of the intellectual contemplation of God. The prejudice (deriving from the Romantic movement) that the intellect is 'cold', as against the heart and passions which are 'warm', is really no more than a prejudice, for the intellect can be warm just as the heart can be cold.

Again, aesthetic appreciation does not have any direct practical or ethical implications, but it is not therefore without human value of its own. And in the same way, it might be urged, religious contemplation may very well have its own value even though it does not have any direct practical effect.

Objections against this kind of intellectualistic religion, on the ground that it must inevitably be abstract, and of no immediate practical concern to us, do not then seem to be fatal. In other words, there is nothing bizarre, as has often been alleged, about the notion of a philosophical religion which, to use Hume's words, 'affords no inference that affects human life, or can be the source of any action or forbearance'.[105]

In the same way, we may agree that this concept of philosophical religion involves a denial of the distinction between the natural and supernatural, and so renders otiose the whole notion of 'revelation' as the gratuitous disclosure by God (through prophets and 'inspired' agents) of truths inaccessible to natural reason. And in this way it would seem that philosophical religion cannot be squared with any form of religion, such as traditional Judaeo-Christianity or Islam, in which the notion of a supernatural revelation has a central role.[106] But it does not follow that philosophical religion is incompatible with forms of religion other than traditional Christianity, or even with forms of 'liberal' Christianity which do not hold a strictly supernaturalist view of revelation. It seems to be quite possible to have a religion without the notion of a supernatural revelation, and in this sense a 'religion within the limits of reason alone', to use Kant's famous title, is not something that is repugnant either to religion or to reason.

Very much the same reply might be made to objections against the inevitable esotericism of philosophical religion. It is, doubtless, very difficult to reconcile élitism or 'gnosticism' with any form of religion that emphasises the possibility of salvation for all men. But, once again, there seems to be no necessary reason why there cannot be a religion which would be accessible only to a choice few 'in the know'. There have, after all, been many esoteric religious sects, such as the various forms of Manicheism which made a sharp distinction between the 'pure' or the initiate and the ordinary second-class believers,[107] and again there have been certain forms of Buddhism that are frankly élitist.[108] The fact, then, that esotericism is at odds with religions such as Christianity, does not mean that it is at odds with religion *tout court*. Again, no matter how much importance is to be given to the requirement that religion be universally accessible, it surely cannot outweigh the requirement that it be *true*. If a religion is true and universally accessible in addition, that is all to the good; but if it is true in such a way that it is available only to the intellectual few, then, no matter how unwelcome a fact this may be to us, we cannot on that account refuse it the name of religion. The early-twentieth-century Cambridge philosopher John McTaggart has written very aptly, and very nobly, on this very point.

> No dogma – at any rate, no dogma of religion – is asserted which is not also denied by able students.
>
> It follows that a man is not entitled to believe a dogma except in so far as he has investigated it for himself. And since the investigation of dogma

is a metaphysical process, and religion must be based on dogma, it follows further that no man is justified in a religious attitude except as a result of metaphysical study. The result is sufficiently serious. For most people, as the world stands at present, have not the disposition, the education, and the leisure necessary for the study of metaphysics. And thus we are driven to the conclusion that, whether any religion is true or not, most people have no right to accept any religion as true.

We are here confronted [McTaggart goes on] with one of the great tragedies of life. Many men desire passionately to know the truth as to the great problems of religion. And no man may believe any solution of these problems to be true unless he has tested it himself. Even if he tests for himself, and comes to some conclusion, his conclusion must lack that confirmation by the unanimous agreement of inquirers which plays so great a part in knowledge elsewhere.

This is sad, and would be sad even if dogma were not essential to religion. For whether dogma is essential to religion or not, it is clear that many men do desire, and will desire, to know the truth about such dogmas as the existence of God and the immortality of man... It is sad, but I do not know why it should be thought strange. Is knowledge so easy to get that the highest and deepest of all knowledge is likely to be had for the asking? Or is everything good so common, that we should expect that religion – almost the best of all earthly things – should be never absent where it is desired?

McTaggart ends by citing Spinoza's famous apology for his own philosophical (and esoteric) religion: 'If the way which I have pointed out as leading to this result seems exceedingly hard, it may nevertheless be discovered... But all things excellent are as difficult as they are rare'.[109]

There is, finally, the question of the a-historical character of religious intellectualism. As Kierkegaard protested against Hegel, the rejection of the historical dimension of religion as irrelevant is incompatible with any religion such as Christianity which is based upon historical claims. St Paul's firm statement, 'If Christ be not risen from the dead, then all our hopes are vain',[110] is a dramatic expression of the importance of historical fact in the Christian religion. It was for this reason that Hegel's attempt to translate the substance of the central Christian doctrines – the Incarnation, the Trinity, etc. – into the categories of his own philosophy, and so to show that they really represented metaphysical necessities, seemed so outrageous to Kierkegaard and his sympathisers.

These various objections against religious intellectualism are therefore all inconclusive. However, there is a more fundamental and serious

complaint against this view, that stems not from the nature of the intellectualistic religion it proposes but rather from the conception of the nature and
scope of philosophy that it assumes. In other words, one might say that what
is wrong with this whole philosophy of religion is not so much its view of
religion as its view of philosophy, for it presupposes a high metaphysical
conception of philosophy which is formidably difficult to defend. In this
conception philosophy is held to be capable of transcending the spatio-
temporal world of our immediate experience and of providing knowledge of
immaterial and timeless entities (like Plato's Forms) or some kind of
Absolute substance (like Spinoza's God or Hegel's Spirit).

This was, of course, the kind of overweening metaphysics that Kant set
out to destroy once and for all in the *Critique of Pure Reason*, and the whole
tendency of post-Kantian philosophy – with the great exception of Hegel –
has been against this kind of 'transcendent' metaphysics, in favour of a much
more modest 'descriptive metaphysics' – a conception of philosophy which
would hardly lend itself to playing a quasi-religious role. Even before Kant,
St Thomas Aquinas in the thirteenth century had proposed a much more
limited view of the nature of metaphysics than that of his classical masters
(Aristotle and the neo-Platonists). One could say indeed that for Aquinas,
philosophy, given his conception of its nature and scope, could not plausibly
be identified with religion, in the way in which Plotinus's philosophy, for
example, could easily be so identified.

As we remarked before, the great strength and advantage of this view of
the philosophy of religion is that it makes religion into a rational enterprise
and so worthy of human beings at their best and most human. But this is
also its weakness, for it means that religion is only as good or valid as the
philosophy of which it is the issue. This point has sometimes been made in
the following way: if religion is identified with philosophy then it necessarily becomes subject to the same kind of doubting and questioning to
which any philosophical position is subject. But, so the objection goes,
whereas assent to a philosophical position is always subject to questioning
and is thus tentative and revocable, religious assent implies that we
commit ourselves absolutely and irrevocably without any doubts or
arrières pensées. In an act of religious faith I 'stake my life', whereas in an act
of philosophical assent I do nothing of the kind. Thus, Price has argued
that if the religious believer's faith is based upon arguments, then 'his faith
would have to be a kind of opinion … and if adverse evidence turns up, one
ought to feel less confidence in one's opinion or even to reject it altogether.

Now whatever religious belief may be, it is quite different from opinion. In face of adverse evidence, a man sticks to his faith, but he abandons an opinion'.[111]

There is some force to this objection; but unless some kind of philosophical relativism is being assumed, so that all philosophical positions are held to be dubitable and tentative and never capable of exacting absolute and unqualified assent, it is difficult to see that religious assent differs essentially from philosophical assent. Thinkers have, after all, staked their lives on philosophical positions just as much as on religious positions. And, from another point of view, commitment to religious faith is just as revocable and tentative in its way as a philosophical commitment. It is often said that if a person truly loves then she cannot fall out of love ('Let me not to the marriage of true minds admit impediments'); and in much the same way it seems to be implied that if one makes a religious commitment or assent then one cannot envisage the possibility of going back on it. But the notion of irrevocability is no more contained in the notion of religious assent than it is contained in the notion of love. As McTaggart has put it: 'On matters of dogma we cannot dispense with proof... This will leave all questions of dogma more or less problematic, and many quite unanswered. And this is doubtless unpleasant. But unpleasant things are sometimes true'.[112]

However, what is true in this objection is, as we have remarked, that the intellectualistic position does depend upon a certain conception of the nature and scope of philosophy being valid. And, for strictly philosophical reasons, it is difficult to see how that conception can be made valid.

Despite the general decline of this view of philosophy and of the philosophy of religion which derives from it, there are still some echoes of it in certain contemporary philosophers of religion. Apart from the influence of Hegel in liberal theology, there are hints in the philosophy of A. N. Whitehead that point towards an identification of religion with philosophy. Thus, at the end of *Process and Reality*, Whitehead considers 'God and the world' and he makes the pregnant observation that 'God is not to be treated as an exception to all metaphysical principles, invoked to save their collapse. He is their chief exemplification'.[113] Again, perhaps it is not too fanciful to see a tendency towards an intellectualist philosophy of religion in the evolutionist speculations of Teilhard de Chardin.[114]

We may conclude, then, that if this whole conception of the philosophy of religion, which has had such a long and varied and important career in Western thought, is now more or less dead, it is nevertheless not altogether lying down. It may be, perhaps, that with the movement towards rapprochement among the great world religions, it will even undergo a revival of some kind, since such a rapprochement will probably involve an emphasis on the universal and 'necessary' elements in the world-religions and a soft-pedalling of their particular and historically contingent aspects. But, as we have said, it is not easy to see how we could now reconstruct a conception of philosophy that could adequately play a religious part or assume a religious mantle.

2

PHILOSOPHY AS THE HANDMAID
OF RELIGION

An act of faith is to believe God since the formal object of faith is the Primal Truth to which we give adherence so as to assent for its own sake to whatever we believe.

ST THOMAS AQUINAS, *Summa Theologiae*

INTRODUCTION

Judaeo-Christianity is a religion, we have said, which is difficult to square with the demands of philosophical religion, since for both classical Judaism and Christianity the very concept of religion implies a God-given disclosure of truths about the divine order, as well as about the divinely ordained 'way of life' leading to salvation, inaccessible to ordinary reason. There have, of course, been many attempts within Christianity to elaborate a form of Christian intellectualism or 'gnosticism', where Christianity was made to appear as the issue of a philosophical world-view; but all these essays have involved some kind of reductionist violence being done to the Christian religion.

For the Jew or Christian of antiquity, then, wishing to give full due to the impressive tradition of the Greek philosophy of religion, while at the same time maintaining the essentially revelatory character of the Judaic Law and prophetic tradition and of the Christian Gospel, a new conception of the philosophy of religion had to be invented. Once again, the working out of this view of philosophy's relationship with religion was a long and chequered process.[1] It received its first impetus from the Jewish-Hellenistic thinker Philo of Alexandria (d. 40 CE) at the beginning of the Christian era. Philo's ideas were taken up by the early Christian Platonists Clement and Origen in the second and third centuries, and were further refined by St Augustine (350–430) and by the Boëthius (470–525) of the *Theological Tractates*. In the Middle Ages proper Peter Abelard gave the new theory more precise expression and St Anselm also contributed original elements, as did the Jewish Aristotelian Moses Maimonides. Then finally, with St Thomas Aquinas in the thirteenth century, the theory received its definitive expression. It was also in Aquinas's formulation that the difficulties of this account of the functions of philosophy with regard to religion became apparent and pressing.

PHILO OF ALEXANDRIA

Philo was a member of the Jewish community in Alexandria at the time of the founding of Christianity. Devoutly Jewish and equally devoutly committed to Greek philosophy, Philo attempted a synthesis which would enable him to have the best of both worlds. It is proof of the originality of his thought that his main ideas on philosophy and religion became common-places right through the long Judaeo-Christian tradition that culminated some 1200 years later in Maimonides and Aquinas. Clement, Origen, Augustine, Abelard, Maimonides and Aquinas all repeat in their own way the Philonic principles that govern the relations between philosophy and religion.[2]

Philo, along with his Jewish Alexandrian contemporaries, saw the Greek philosophy he knew (a mélange of Stoic ethical ideas, Platonic metaphysics and elements of Aristotelian logic) as hinting obscurely at truths that were more fully and explicitly made known in the Old Testament. It was the Jewish Alexandrians in fact who, to account for this supposed similarity, invented the legend that the Greek sages must have either had contact with Moses or been able to read his writings, an idea that retained currency right up until the Middle Ages.[3] At the same time Philo made a sharp distinction between the truths contained in the Law revealed by God through Moses, and the truths attained by human wisdom. And it was the twofold recognition that, first, divine wisdom (revelation) is of a higher order than human wisdom, and, second, that nevertheless divine wisdom is in some way continuous and reconcilable with the human wisdom of the philosophers, that led Philo to develop a tentative view of philosophy as the 'handmaid' of religion. In this view philosophy serves religion by explicating its meaning (for example, in discerning the true meaning of scriptural allegories), and by defending it against sceptical attacks. This latter defensive or apologetical role also involved for Philo the finding of rational proofs of the existence of God and of certain of his basic attributes. The classical Greek tradition had described the liberal arts as the 'handmaid' of philosophy and Philo used the analogy to describe philosophy's function with regard to the revealed wisdom of the Law.[4]

Philo presupposes that, since both human and divine wisdom come from the same God, there can be no contradiction between the Mosaic Law and philosophy. And it is this firm *a priori* conviction of the harmony of reason and revelation that causes him to give such a large and decisive role to philosophy in the interpretation of Scripture. Thus, for Philo scriptural texts have both a literal or apparent meaning and an allegorical or under-lying meaning.[5] And we know that a text is *not* to be taken literally or at its face value, if it would lead one to be 'at variance with the truth', or involve one in anthropomorphic talk about God, or compel one 'to admit anything base or unworthy of the dignity' of the inspired words of God. In all such cases we must interpret the texts 'allegorically'.[6] This would seem to imply that the sense of Scripture is to be determined (at least indirectly) by reference to human reason, for how are we to determine what in the meaning of Scripture is at variance with the truth, or what would involve anthropomorphic or unfitting talk about God, if not by extra-scriptural or philosophical means? As Wolfson has put it: 'By his allegorical method Philo found it possible to explain away any narration of incident in Scripture that seemed to him to run counter to reason or expectation or to have some similarity with Greek myths, without necessarily impugning the historicity of the essential basic fact of the story'.[7] The true sense of Scripture then is that which does not conflict with the truths of human reason. This test does not, of course, tell us positively what the true sense of any scriptural text actually *is*, but it does at least tell us negatively what the true sense is *not*, and to that extent philosophy or pure reason establishes the negative possibility of revelation.

Here we have the germ of an idea which is to be developed later in a much more sophisticated way by Moses Maimonides and Aquinas. Philo himself, however, does not bother to tease out these implications of his position. He thinks of philosophy and religion as being in harmony, even though distinct, and he sees philosophy as serving theology on the latter's terms. Theology is the mistress and philosophy the handmaid, and the mistress by definition cannot be dependent upon the handmaid.

THE CHRISTIAN PLATONISTS

Although the Christian Gospel is not wholly independent of Hellenic ideas (as witness the 'Logos' of St John's Gospel which is 'the principle of rationality and order in the cosmos and in mankind'),[8] it is not, after all, concerned to present a philosophical system. However, a number of factors forced the second- and third-century Christian thinkers to arrange an accommodation between Christian doctrine and Greek philosophy. First, there was the need to defend the Christian Gospel against the pseudo-philosophical mishmash of Gnosticism,[9] and from the charges made by anti-Christian critics, such as Origen's antagonist Celsus, that Christianity was incoherent and irrational. Thus, for instance, Celsus claimed the Christians 'do not even want to give or to receive a reason for what they believe, and they say such things as, "Do not ask questions; just believe", and "Thy faith will save thee" '.[10] The only way of meeting these objections based on philosophical argument was to use counter-philosophical arguments.

Second, although the members of the early Christian Church were for the most part simple and unlettered people, there was a sizeable and important class of Christian intellectuals who had been trained in the schools where they gained a deep respect for Greek philosophy before their conversion to Christianity.[11] Even those Christian thinkers like Tertullian who rejected philosophy's theological pretensions could not altogether get rid of this sense of respect for pure reason given them by their Greek education. Thus, Tertullian's famous piece of bravado, 'I believe because it is absurd' (*credo quia absurdum*), needs to be balanced by his remark that there is a natural or innate awareness of God in the soul (*anima naturaliter Christiana*).[12]

Justin Martyr in the second century (d. 164) is a good example of the new Christian intellectual. Educated in Greek philosophy he subsequently became a Christian, while remaining convinced of the fundamental harmony between Platonism and Christianity.[13] Justin was so impressed by the similarities between Greek philosophical ideas and the Old Testament that he repeated Philo's fanciful speculation that Socrates and Plato must

have read Moses's works and plagiarised them. At the same time he saw
Christ as the universal *Logos* or Reason,[14] in which human reason in its
various modes 'participates'. 'This Logos', it has been said, 'who is the sole
source of all man's knowledge of divine things, is also the one who in Christ
made himself wholly known to those who will believe. It follows then that in
Christ incarnate is available the full and definitive form of that truth which
the philosopher can know only in a limited way'.[15]

In very much the same vein, the third-century apologist, Clement of
Alexandria, views Christianity as fulfilling the dim and partial intuitions of
Platonism. Philosophy, Clement says, prepares for theology just as in Plato's
system mathematics prepares for philosophy.[16] Religion demands faith, for
we cannot rationally prove the truths of revelation; but religious faith is not
thereby irrational or blind since it is assent to truth on the authority of God
who is the primal Truth. Reason is not, as certain Christian anti-intellectuals
hold, the creation of the devil; it is rather the creation of God and is the
image of God in man,[17] and as such is man's highest and most noble
attribute. Faith, indeed, is inferior to knowledge in one sense, and it will
eventually give way, in the next life, to knowledge or 'true gnosis'.[18]

These tentative ideas on the relationship between philosophy and religious faith are brought together and given a more definite shape by the
great Christian thinker of the third century, Origen. Origen, apparently
educated in the Alexandrian schools, shows a close knowledge of the
various strands of Greek philosophy, in particular Platonism and neo-
Platonism. Much of his writing consists of scriptural exposition and his
views on the relationship between philosophy and religion are worked out
in the margin of his biblical exegesis. The rule of faith, Origen says, is laid
down by the Apostles and the Church, but neither of these two sources give
the rational grounds presupposed by the articles of faith. It is then the task
of the theologian to speculate about these rational grounds or presuppositions of faith. However, although reason can in this way prepare for and
defend faith, there is nevertheless a clear-cut distinction between the two
realms, for God cannot really be known in his nature as God save through
the help of divine grace. 'Human nature', Origen says, 'is not sufficient to
seek for God and find him in his pure nature unless it is helped by God who
is the object of the search'.[19] Plato may have gained some knowledge of God
but his knowledge was imperfect, as is shown by the fact that he confused
with 'the majesty of God, things which ought not to be ascribed to him'.[20]
Again, Origen's adversary, Celsus, himself admits that the philosophical

approach to God is only for the choice few. So citing Plato's *Timaeus*, Celsus says: 'To find the Maker and Father of this universe is difficult and after finding him it is impossible to declare him to all men.' And he adds: 'You see how the way of truth is sought by seers and philosophers, and how Plato knew that it is impossible for all men to travel it'.[21] But, so Origen argues, the God of faith is available to *all* mankind, and this shows the superiority of the divine *Logos* of Christianity to the human *logos* of philosophy. 'Consider', Origen says, 'whether there is not more regard for the needs of mankind when the divine word introduces the divine Logos, who was in the beginning with God, as becoming flesh, so that the Logos (of whom Plato says that after finding him it is impossible to declare him to all men) might be able to reach anybody'.[22]

Perfect or pure knowledge of God can, for Origen, only be got through theological reflection on Scripture, and this involves a distinction between the literal and allegorical meanings of the scriptural texts. Since the Scriptures 'were composed by the Spirit of God … they have not only that meaning which is obvious, but also another which is hidden from the majority of readers. For the contents of Scripture are the outward forms of certain mysteries and the images of divine things'.[23] Origen uses very much the same method as Philo in order to distinguish between the apparent and real sense of Scripture. Thus he says that where a text, taken at its face value, would involve impossibilities or anything unworthy of God, it must be interpreted in a non-literal way.[24] The bold manner in which Origen applies this method of interpretation in fact leaves very little of the literal sense of the Bible intact. Often in his exegesis the clear sense of Scripture is arbitrarily explained away and interpreted instead in terms of quasi-philosophical and moral truths, although for the most part it is taken as an allegory of Christ or the Church or the spiritual life of the soul.[25] Like Philo, Origen does not seem to be aware of the implications of his method, nor, more generally, of the problems raised by his conception of the role of philosophy with respect to religion.

ST AUGUSTINE ON FAITH AND REASON

Although in many respects St Augustine simply sums up the ideas of the Early Christian Fathers on the relationship of faith and reason, the very powerful strain of neo-Platonic religious intellectualism that was present in his thought[26] gives his position an original twist.

First of all, it is clear that for Augustine reason has a value of its own, independently of its help to faith, for by implanting reason in us God has made us superior to the rest of creation. In fact, we could not believe unless we had rational souls. And again, reason can persuade the mind to rise to faith. This function of reason is anterior to faith and is contrasted with another function of reason, posterior to the act of religious belief, seeking to understand what is believed by faith. As Augustine puts it: 'So, therefore, if it is rational that faith precedes reason in the case of certain great matters which cannot be grasped, there cannot be the least doubt that reason which persuades us on this precept – that faith precedes reason – itself precedes faith'.[27] Again, St Augustine concludes one of his sermons with the following words: 'Believe in Him whom you do not see because of the things which you do see. And do not imagine that it is I alone who exhort you thus. Listen to what the Apostle says to you: "The invisible things of God, from the creation of the world are made visible by the works He has made" '.[28]

On the other hand, St Augustine also uses frequently the celebrated formula from Isaiah, 'unless you believe, you will not understand'. So, for example, he remarks at the end of another sermon: 'Understand my word in order to believe it; but believe the word of God in order to understand it'.[29] Here Augustine seems to distinguish between the 'word' of human reason approaching God independently of faith, and the 'word' of God revealing truths about himself not accessible to human reason. Understood in this way the principle 'believe so that you may understand' is restricted to the sphere of revealed truth and does not apply to the 'preambles' of faith (the existence and attributes of God), nor, *a fortiori*, to other truths available to human reason.

We must not force St Augustine's ideas on this point too much, for he does not distinguish formally and explicitly between the different functions of 'understanding' in relation to faith. Again, it has been pointed out that Augustine does not make the assumption of Aquinas and the other medieval thinkers, based upon their Aristotelian theory of knowledge, that the human mind cannot of itself attain to direct knowledge of God. Augustine suggests that if the human mind is purified by the action of the will, its latent powers may be brought into exercise, thus enabling it to know God. In fact, the general distinction between the order of nature and the order of supernatural grace has to be made in a different way in the neo-Platonic context of Augustine's thought than in an Aristotelian perspective, for although there is in neo-Platonism a distinction between nature and the supra-sensible world of 'divinity', the former at the same time is held to 'participate' in the latter.[30] Thus, it has been said that

> while to an Aristotelian the suggestion that the vision of God is a natural possibility would imply a secret identity between the finite mind and God, Augustine's theory of knowledge proceeds in terms of the vision of luminous objects rather than an identity of knower and known; the centre of gravity is in the object rather than the mind and there is no difficulty if the object is 'above' the mind and 'greater' than the mind – indeed, that is always the case with the timeless objects of thought, which are discovered and acknowledged rather than posited by the mind. The mind, in other words, does not function according to its own *a priori* rules, but can somehow accommodate itself with elasticity to intelligibles which are somehow disclosed to the mind.[31]

Augustine uses philosophy boldly and extensively both in defending the truths of faith against anti-Christian and heretical adversaries, and also in the elaboration of Christian doctrine. For example, his work on the Trinity is permeated with Platonic and neo-Platonic themes. At the same time, as we have already suggested, Augustine is equally anxious to affirm the possibility of rational speculation about God prior to and independent of supernatural faith in God. In his own writing he devotes a great deal of attention to what were later to be called the 'preambles' of faith – the possibility of knowing God as the ground of rational certitude, the nature of the soul, freedom of the will – and it is not too much to say that he sees a 'natural theology' or a philosophical theology as an important propaedeutic to theology proper.

In the *De Libero Arbitrio*, for example, he offers a proof of the existence of God and clearly admits the possibility of a rational justification of belief in God prior to faith. The proof is of some interest since it contains the elements of the argument that St Anselm was later to outline in the *Proslogion* and that has become known misleadingly as the ontological proof of God. In the *De Libero Arbitrio*, Augustine is engaged in a discussion with Evodius and he asks him whether he is certain that God exists. Evodius answers that he does not directly know that God exists, but rather *believes* it, and Augustine remarks:

> If then one of those fools of whom Scripture writes, 'The fool said in his heart: there is no God', should say this to you, and should refuse to believe with you what you believe, but wished to know whether your belief is true, would you have nothing to do with this man, or would you think he ought to be convinced in some way of what you hold firmly –

especially if he should seriously wish to know it and not obstinately to oppose it?[32]

Evodius replies that it is sufficient to appeal to the testimony of 'all those writers who have testified that they lived with the Son of God'. Augustine agrees that, in a sense, we must believe in God in order to understand him, but he then proceeds to develop a purely rational and independent proof of the existence of God which is apparently meant to be convincing to the unbeliever. Reason, he argues, is the supreme element in human beings, but reason apprehends the existence of eternal and unchangeable truth. Now, if there is anything higher than eternal truth it is God; but if there is not, then truth itself is God. Augustine concludes his argument by saying to Evodius:

> If I showed there was something above our minds, you conceded you would confess it to be God, provided there was nothing still higher. Accepting your admission I said it was enough that I should show this. For if there is something more excellent, it is this which is God, but, if there is nothing more excellent, then truth itself is God. Whichever is the case, you cannot deny that God exists.[33]

In other words, God is defined as the 'highest' and 'most excellent' thing that we can conceive, so that to prove the existence of a highest and most excellent conceivable thing (eternal truth) is precisely to prove the existence of God. Augustine concludes that, even though we know God only in a very oblique way by rational means, we still do know him. 'God exists, and he exists truly and supremely. We not only hold this, I think, by our undoubted faith, but we also attain to it by a sure, though very tenuous, kind of knowledge'.[34]

Augustine's bold use of philosophy in his explication of theological doctrines was imitated by his later follower Boëthius (470–525), at least in his *Theological Tractates* as distinct from the *Consolation of Philosophy*. At the same time Boëthius emphasised the limits of reason and viewed his philosophico-theological analyses as giving rational support to what was already believed by faith, not as furnishing the grounds of the doctrines of faith.[35]

PHILOSOPHY AND THEOLOGY IN THE MIDDLE AGES

These various elements from Philo, the Early Fathers and St Augustine were taken up by the Christian medieval thinkers in the West and combined with the new Aristotelian ideas about the specification of the various 'sciences' (or systematic and deductively constituted bodies of knowledge) and also with the Aristotelian 'natural theology' developed in the *Physics* and *Metaphysics*. Peter Abelard is usually given the credit for being the first to use the word 'theologia' to mean the explication of the data of faith by philosophical means, in contradistinction to the older Aristotelian usage where 'theology' was a special branch of metaphysics.[36]

In his *Tractatus* Abelard makes the traditional distinction about the functions of reason with respect to faith. First, reason helps in the understanding of the meaning of Scripture; second, it helps refute the objections of the philosophers to faith; and, third, it gives rational support to what is believed on God's authority.[37] Cottiaux has described these ancillary functions of reason as 'the hermeneutical use of *ratio*, the apologetical use and the constructive use',[38] and all three are in evidence in Abelard's *Christian Theology*.[39] Although Abelard's employment of philosophical analysis in his theology gave great scandal to certain of his contemporaries, such as St Bernard of Clairvaux,[40] and caused some of his ideas to be condemned by the Council of Sens in 1141, his view on faith and reason is entirely traditional. The God of faith, he emphasises, 'exceeds what can come under human discussion or the powers of human intelligence; it would be a great slight to the faithful if God proclaimed himself as accessible to petty human arguments or as definable in mere mortal words'.[41] Again, referring to St Gregory the Great, Abelard says that he did not disdain 'defending the Resurrection against these doubting it, by suitable examples and illustrations from nature. He did not claim that we ought never to reason with regard to faith, but only that faith has no merit in the eyes of God if it rests on human argument rather than on divine authority'.[42] Again, Abelard declares that faith has no merit 'if one believes, not the God of whom the Saints speak, but human arguments'.[43] It is for this reason that the supportive proofs of what we believe by authority cannot be strictly demonstrative or 'necessary', but merely arguments of 'fittingness' (*convenientia*) and of analogy.[44]

These same views on the function of reason with regard to theology are continued in the thought of St Anselm of Bec (1033–1109). At times Anselm seems to tend towards a kind of theological rationalism according to which certain at least of the mysteries of faith could in principle be rationally demonstrated by 'necessary arguments' (*rationes necessariae*). But in his theological practice Anselm always makes the appropriate reservations and implicitly acknowledges the transcendence of the articles of faith with respect to philosophical reason.[45]

The originality of St Anselm consists in his adumbration of rational proofs of the existence of God both in the *Monologion* and the *Proslogion*. Though St Anselm does not explicitly propose these proofs of the existence of God as the ground of the Christian's faith in God, he does implicitly acknowledge that they could be the logical ground of belief for the non-believer – the fool or atheist of the Psalm (who says there is no God) and to whom the *Proslogion* is addressed. With St Anselm the problem of the non-believer who shares no presuppositions about God with the Christian believer (as distinct from the Jew and the Muslim) becomes real for the first time and the place of rational proofs of the existence of God becomes correspondingly more important. For Philo and Clement and Origen these proofs merely confirmed what we already knew by faith; but for Anselm (following in this St Augustine's hint) a systematic natural theology logically prior to faith is seen to be at least a possibility.

The traditional view of faith and reason is maintained by most theologians in the twelfth and early thirteenth century after Anselm without anything new being added to it. Thus St Bonaventure (1217–74) describes the method of theology as 'perscrutorius', that is to say, elaborated by rational means and argumentation;[46] and he declares this method to be appropriate to theology for 'the refutation of the adversaries of the faith, the support of the faith of those weak in faith, and the satisfaction of those perfect in the faith'.[47] Alexander of Hales (1186–1245) and St Albertus Magnus (1206–80) adopt the same view. Alexander, however, introduces a new note by raising the objection that theology cannot be a 'science' in the Aristotelian sense since it is based ultimately on the particular brute historical facts described by the Scriptures, and as Aristotle notes, there cannot be the universal and necessary knowledge proper to 'science' of particular contingent facts. Alexander replies, not altogether convincingly, that in Scripture particular historical facts always have a universal significance; they exemplify general and quasi-necessary truths and so in this way can be the subject of 'scientific' knowledge.[48] We have here for the first time a dim awareness of a problem that is to become important later on – how to find a place for the historical dimension of Christianity within a philosophy of religion that is, as philosophy, concerned with the universal and necessary features of religion.

MOSES MAIMONIDES

The line of thought about the relationship of faith and philosophy that we have been tracing is also discernible in the medieval Jewish tradition that culminates in Moses Maimonides (1135–1204). For Maimonides, as for Abelard, philosophy *vis-à-vis* the Law that is made known by God through Moses and the Prophets, has a hermeneutical function, an apologetical function and a properly theological function.[49] Maimonides also acknowledges the possibility of rational demonstration of the existence of God, for the most part based upon Aristotle's proofs in the *Physics*. Though he was, also like Abelard, accused by conservative Jewish theologians of rationalising away the content of the Law, it is clear that Maimonides recognised the transcendence of the realm of religious faith with respect to that of philosophical reason.

Maimonides's treatment of Aristotle's philosophical doctrine that the world was not created in time, affords a very good illustration of his view of philosophy's task with respect to faith. Thus, he says, the Aristotelian doctrine is *prima facie* opposed to the teaching of the Law which clearly states in the Book of Genesis that God created the world in time. How can we resolve this apparent conflict? First, Maimonides argues, we can demonstrate philosophically that the Aristotelian theory is not conclusive; that is, we can show that it does not prove that we must admit, under pain of contradiction, that the world is eternal. To hold that the world was created in time is therefore not impossible. As Maimonides puts it:

> All that Aristotle and his followers have set forth in the way of proof of the eternity of the world does not constitute in my opinion a cogent demonstration, but rather arguments subject to grave doubts, as you shall hear. What I myself desire to make clear is that the world's being created in time, according to the opinion of our Law – an opinion that I have already explained – is not impossible and that all those philosophic proofs from which it seems that the matter is different from what we have stated, all those arguments have a certain point through which they may be invalidated and the inference drawn from them against us shown to be incorrect.[50]

Now, it is an Aristotelian doctrine that 'where no demonstration is possible, the two contrary opinions with regard to the matter in question should be posited as hypotheses',[51] and the only way of deciding between two possible and rival hypotheses is on 'probable' grounds, that is, by analysing the kinds of consequences each hypothesis leads to. 'It should be seen what doubts attach to each of them: the one to which fewer doubts attach should be believed'.[52]

When we examine the consequences of Aristotle's hypothesis (that since everything comes to be of necessity, the world is eternal) we see that if it were true then, (i) things would not be able to come into being simply because God willed them to be; (ii) miraculous interventions by God would be impossible; (iii) contingent free acts, such as human choices, would be impossible and the rewards and punishments promised by the Law with respect to human acts would have no meaning; (iv) consequently the teachings of the Law (about God's creative power, miracles, etc.) would all have to be interpreted allegorically. As Maimonides says:

> The belief in eternity the way Aristotle sees it – that is, the belief according to which the world exists in virtue of necessity, that no nature changes at all, and that the customary course of events cannot be modified with regard to anything – destroys the Law in its principle, necessarily gives the lie to every miracle, and reduces to inanity all the hopes and threats that the Law has held out, unless – by God! – one interprets the miracles figuratively also, as was done by the Islamic allegorisers; this, however, would result in some sort of crazy imaginings.[53]

On the other hand, if we accept the hypothesis of the creation of the world in time, these various consequences are evaded and the possibility of the Law is established:

> Know that with a belief in the creation of the world in time, all the miracles become possible and the Law becomes possible, and all questions that may be asked on this subject, vanish. Thus it might be said: Why did God give prophetic revelation to this one and not to that? Why did God give this Law to this particular nation, and why did he not legislate to the others? Why did he legislate at this particular time, and why did he not legislate before it or after? Why did he impose these commandments and these prohibitions? Why did he privilege the prophet with the miracles mentioned in relation to him and not with some others? What was God's aim in giving this Law? Why did he not, if such was his purpose, put the accomplishment of the commandments and the non-transgression of the prohibitions into our nature? If this were said, the answer to all these questions would be that it would be said: He wanted it this way; or his wisdom required it this way. And just as he brought the world into existence, having the form it has, when he wanted to, without our knowing his will with regard to this or in what

respect there was wisdom in his particularising the forms of the world and the time of its creation – in the same way we do not know his will or the exigency of his wisdom that caused all the matters, about which questions have been posed above, to be particularised. If, however [Maimonides continues], someone says that the world is as it is in virtue of necessity, it would be a necessary obligation to ask all those questions; and there would be no way out of them except through a recourse to unseemly answers in which there would be combined the giving the lie to, and the annulment of, all the external meanings of the Law with regard to which no intelligent man has any doubt that they are to be taken in their external meanings. It is then because of this that this opinion is shunned and that the lives of virtuous men have been and will be spent in investigating this question. For if creation in time were demonstrated – if only as Plato understands creation – all the overhasty claims made to us on this point by the philosophers would become void. In the same way, if the philosophers would succeed in demonstrating eternity as Aristotle understands it, the Law as a whole would become void, and a shift to other opinions would take place. I have thus explained to you that everything is bound up with this problem. Know this.[54]

It is then for this kind of reason that we can say, 'The Law has given us knowledge of a matter the grasp of which is not within our power'.[55]

Maimonides thus ingeniously avoids one of the main difficulties already alluded to, namely, that if reason formally demonstrates the possibility of what we hold by faith, then the articles of faith will by that very fact be shown to be necessarily true (since the articles of faith are in themselves necessarily true, though they are not known in this way *by us*). Here Maimonides makes it clear that philosophy is restricted to showing that what the Law (or revelation) teaches is *not-impossible*. Philosophy is not concerned to establish the positive possibility of the truths of faith (as for example we can establish the possibility of a golden mountain) but rather their negative possibility or non-impossibility. Whether it is reasonable to hold that the negative possibility is actually realised or not in a particular case has to be shown probabilistically or by 'reasons of fittingness'.

So far we have been tracing the emergence of a new view of the philosophy of religion, a view in which philosophy is seen as the servant or handmaid of religious faith. Philosophy and religion are both concerned with God and the divine, but their 'formal objects' (the aspect under which they consider

God) are irreducibly distinct. In other words, the God disclosed by pure reason and the God disclosed by revelation are formally different. Similarly their modes of knowledge and apprehension are distinct, for philosophy relies upon demonstration and rational evidence, while religion relies upon faith, that is to say belief in certain matters on the authority of God. Further, whereas the God of philosophical reason is accessible only to a few sages, the God of religious faith is accessible to all men.

However, if philosophy and religion, reason and faith, are distinct, they are not wholly discontinuous. For (i) philosophical reason is just as much a part of God's creation as religious faith; in fact it is by virtue of their reason that human beings are the 'image of God'; (ii) since all truth, both philosophical and revealed, comes from God, and since God cannot contradict himself, philosophical and revealed truth likewise cannot be contradictory. The two orders of truth must be, at least negatively, harmonisable with each other, and faith and reason must complement each other; (iii) faith uses reason to express itself meaningfully and to discern the real, as opposed to the literal or apparent meaning of Scripture; (iv) faith also uses reason for apologetical or defensive purposes by showing that apparent philosophical objections to the truths of faith are not necessarily conclusive; (v) faith also uses reason to justify its presuppositions; (vi) faith uses reason to explicate the virtualities of the data of faith and to systematise them; (vii) philosophical reason is able to prove the existence of God and certain of his fundamental attributes.

It will be seen from this that the various services of philosophy with regard to faith are reducible to two main functions: the first is *within* the realm of faith, philosophy having here a hermeneutical and systematising function; the second is external to the realm of faith, philosophy in this case playing a defensive and justificatory role with regard to the presuppositions of faith. Within this second function, we have to distinguish between the role of philosophy in negatively defending the articles of faith proper by showing that apparently demonstrative philosophical arguments against them are not in fact conclusive (and thereby at the same time showing the negative possibility or non-impossibility of the truths of faith in question); and on the other hand, the role of reason in proving the existence of God. When we prove the existence of God, we are not merely showing that the concept of God is not self-contradictory or incoherent (as we do, for example, with regard to the revealed truths of faith); rather we are showing positively that the concept is both meaningful and instantiated.

This tradition of philosophico-theological thought represents a very remarkable attempt to reconcile the demands of Greek philosophy with those of the Judaeo-Christian religion without doing violence to either. The requirements of pure reason are met, while at the same time, it is claimed, the revelatory and supernatural and universalist character of the Christian religion is also given its full due.

However, the problems attending this whole conception of the philosophy of religion are hardly noticed by the thinkers we have considered. What is to happen, for example, when there is a *prima facie* conflict between a philosophical truth and a truth of religious revelation? Which is to be the *final* arbiter – philosophy or faith? The principle of the harmony of all truth (both philosophical and revealed) – itself, by the way, a philosophical principle – espoused by all the thinkers in this tradition, depends on the supposition that we know clearly in each case what the philosophical truth is and what, on the other hand, revelation declares to be the truth. But we do not know the latter without analysis and interpretation, for as both Philo and Origen acknowledge, we can only determine the *real* sense of any revelation-statement by first seeing whether or not it conflicts with truths of reason. Thus with respect to Maimonides's example of the apparent conflict between the Aristotelian thesis of the eternity of the world and the Old Testament's thesis of the creation of the world in time, we can either argue (as Maimonides does) that it can be shown on philosophical grounds that Aristotle's doctrine is not conclusive; or we can remove the apparent contradiction between Aristotle and Moses by holding to Aristotle's philosophical doctrine and interpreting the relevant Old Testament texts in a non-literal or allegorical manner. But, once again, we will only be led to do this if we first recognise that the literal interpretation of the texts would result in philosophically untenable conclusions. If philosophy and faith do not conflict, it is because philosophy so interprets the truths of faith that they cannot conflict.

Etienne Gilson, following Aquinas, remarks that 'to any believer who is at the same time a true philosopher, the slightest opposition between his faith and his reason is a sure sign that something is the matter with his philosophy. For indeed faith is not a principle of philosophical knowledge, but it is a safe guide to rational truth and an infallible warning against philosophical error'.[56] But, as we have said, revelation does not bear its meaning upon its face and the determination of what is and is not of faith inevitably involves indirect recourse to reason.

Again, if philosophy justifies the presuppositions of faith, either nega-tively as with the defence of the mysteries of faith proper, or positively as with the proof of the existence of God and his basic attributes, then this would seem to make faith logically dependent upon reason, in the sense that the meaning of the truths of faith depends, at least indirectly, upon the meaning of the truths of pure reason. To put the matter crudely, if we can give no meaning to the concept of God at the level of philosophical reason, then equally the concept of God at the level of faith must also be meaningless. God cannot give us the grace to believe in something that is unbelievable.

Philo, Origen, Augustine, Abelard, Anselm and Maimonides all speak of philosophy being the handmaid of theology humbly serving the latter on its own terms. But philosophy finds it hard to keep to its purely ancillary role and tends to usurp the role of mistress of the house. We shall see this process taking place in the thought of St Thomas Aquinas in the thirteenth century, who sums up and crystallises this whole tradition we have been considering.

ST THOMAS AQUINAS

The very first article of Aquinas's *Summa Theologiae* is concerned with the question, 'Whether, besides philosophy, any further doctrine is necessary?' The fact that Aquinas could pose this question to himself is significant enough, for it indicates that he acknowledged the plausibility of the philo-sophical religion that had been proposed by his masters, Aristotle and the neo-Platonists. The contemporary movement of 'Latin Averroism', which translated Ibn Rushd's ideas on the identity of philosophy and religion into the Christian West, had indeed virtually denied that any other doctrine save philosophy was necessary. So, in 1277, just after Aquinas's death, Bishop Étienne Tempier of Paris condemned a number of propositions such as 'there is no higher life than that of the philosophers' and 'there is no wisdom in the world except that of the philosophers'.[57]

The two objections Aquinas urges against his own position are both taken from this latter tradition of thought. First, he makes his objector say, we should not seek knowledge that goes 'beyond reason', and since knowledge that does not go beyond reason is coterminous with philosophy, 'any other knowledge is superfluous'. Second, philosophy treats of 'everything that is', including the kind of being that God is. The knowledge of God, 'theology' as

Aristotle calls it, is therefore a 'part of philosophy', so that, once again, 'there is no need of further knowledge'.[58]

Aquinas, however, rejects this position, for religious doctrine, as expressed in the Scriptures, is 'inspired by God' and thus cannot be part of philosophy which is 'the work of human reason'. There are, he goes on, truths about God which can be discovered by human reason or philosophy, and there are other truths about God which 'surpass the grasp of his reason' and which therefore need to be made known to human beings by God revealing them. This latter knowledge of God, or 'theology' in the Christian sense of the word, 'differs in kind from that theology which is part of philosophy' in the Aristotelian sense, both with respect to the truths about God which it knows and to the mode of its knowledge. God's revelation discloses truths of a different order from the truths disclosed by pure reason, and again, whereas we know the former by faith – assenting to them because of the authority and trustworthiness of the one (God) who reveals them, and not because we see them to be evidently or demonstrably true – we know the latter by virtue of their intrinsic rational evidence.[59]

This clear-cut discussion between religion (dependent on God's revelation and our faith in that revelation) and philosophy (dependent upon pure reason and rational evidence) is blurred by Aquinas's further contention that certain philosophical truths about God (for example, that God is one and non-material)[60] can also be made known by revelation and believed by faith. This is because religious salvation depends upon the knowledge of all the basic truths about God, and since philosophical truths about God can be known only by philosophical experts and are also subject to the fallibilities of human reason, it is practically necessary that these truths should be made known to the majority of men by revelation, otherwise 'the truth about God which human reason could discover, would be only known by a few, and that after a long time, and with the admixture of many errors'. Presupposed to Aquinas's argument here is the idea that religious salvation must be accessible to all men, with the consequence that knowledge of the essential truths about God on which salvation depends, must also be universally accessible.[61]

It remains true, however, that if I know a truth about God by reason then I do not, *ipso facto*, know it by faith since the motive of my assent in both cases is quite different. 'Rational knowledge and faith cannot be in the same subject and about the same object', although one person may believe by faith what another knows rationally.[62] It remains true also that there is a sharp distinction between those truths about God that are *in themselves* rationally *knowable* and those that are merely religiously *credible*.

Philosophy (in so far as it is concerned with God) and theology proper both have God as their 'material object', but they consider God under different 'formal objects'.[63] Supernatural theology, or 'sacred doctrine', 'essentially treats of God viewed as the highest cause – not only in so far as he can be known through creatures in the same way the philosopher knows him ... but also in so far as he is known to himself alone and revealed to others'.[64] Since it has its own formal object and its own 'principles' (the data of faith) from which 'conclusions' may be deduced, it may therefore be considered in its own right as a systematic body of knowledge or a 'science' in the Aristotelian sense.[65]

It is of great importance to note here that Aquinas uses the notion of 'faith' in a technical and exact way that goes far beyond its common-sense connotation of believing on the authority of God. First, for Aquinas faith is primarily a matter of *assent* to truths about God, and for him it is not, as it is for many contemporary theologians, a practical attitude of commitment, or trust, or 'belief in'. However, the assent of faith is not motivated by the evidence of the truths to which it assents, as my assent to the truth 'two plus two equals four' is so motivated by its evidence. No doubt the truths of faith are evident in themselves (God, so to speak, would see *why* they were true and had to be assented to, and we will see and be compelled by their evidence later in the next life when we enjoy the vision of God), but we cannot now in this life appreciate that evidence and see why they are true. Instead we assent to them because they are revealed by God who is the Primal Truth. 'An act of faith', Aquinas says, 'is to believe God since ... the formal object of faith is the Primal Truth, to which man gives his adherence, so as to assent for its sake to whatever he believes'.[66] And this belief in God as the author of revelation is aided by a special grace from God; 'since man, by assenting to matters of faith, is raised above his nature, this must needs be supplied to him from some supernatural source moving him inwardly, and this is God'.[67]

It will be seen from this that Aquinas's account of faith is based upon his philosophical analysis of the intellectual act of assent. The intellect is motivated to assent to the truth of a proposition because of the *evidence* of the proposition. The evidence does not strictly *cause* one to assent, since for Aquinas assenting, like all mental acts, is an intentional act; but equally I do not decide or will to assent, for assenting is not a voluntary act. For Aquinas, following Aristotle's deductive model, propositions are either self-evident (*per se nota*) or they derive their evidence from propositions which are self-evident.

In the case of religious faith, the intellect assents to certain propositions as true, but the assent is not motivated by the evidence of the propositions, since this evidence is not available to us – the truths in question belonging to the supra-rational realm of revelation. The assent of faith needs then some other kind of extra-intellectual motivation and this, according to Aquinas, is supplied by the will. Here, in contrast with ordinary assent, I do have to *decide* or *will* to assent. And I decide or will to assent on the authority of someone whom I take as the guarantor of the truth of the propositions I assent to, and whose guarantee in this way supplies for the evidence that is lacking to me.

There are then two distinct moments in faith: first, my assent to God as the guarantor of the truth of the propositions of revelation; and second, my willed assent to the truth of revelation which is motivated by this first assent to God as guarantor of the truth of revelation. The first moment of assent obviously cannot be an assent based upon evidence, for the only evidence I have here is that God, the author of revelation, is negatively possible, and this is insufficient to motivate my assent to an actual God of revelation actually revealing truths (e.g. the Judaeo-Christian God). Again, it cannot itself be a willed assent motivated by assent to the authority of God. It must therefore be a willed assent motivated by a special grace from God.

For Aquinas the grace of faith does not give us any special cognitive 'insight' into the objects of faith, as though by faith we were empowered to know, directly or intuitively, things that we could not know by ordinary reason. Rather, the grace of faith acts upon the will in that it enables me to will to believe propositions (since revealed by God) which I do not see to be true,[68] and which therefore do not of themselves command my assent. Aquinas takes St Paul's remarks about faith being a dark and enigmatic way of knowing very seriously[69] and he makes it clear that religious faith is not in any way what Rudolf Otto calls 'a non-rational knowledge of God', or bound up with 'religious experience'. God can, no doubt, miraculously intervene in the normal processes of human knowledge to give certain people special 'prophetic visions', but these miraculous and extraordinary interventions are not to be confused with the grace of faith. Since the grace of faith perfects and complements man's rational nature and does not involve a suspension of the ordinary operations of that nature it is clearly distinct from any miraculously endowed religious experiences. As a contemporary Thomist philosopher has put it: 'For St Thomas, at least in his later writings, faith is not a distinct kind of apprehension due to some sort of sixth sense; it is not a knowledge of superior rank in which, thanks to a new light given by God, our intelligence might grasp supernatural meanings and truths. Despite what the term "light" naturally suggests, the *lumen fidei* or the "light" given by grace to the believer, does not directly or properly concern the order of intelligence. This light does not enable us to discover in the object of faith new aspects that would not have been discovered without it, nor to "see" this object, nor to grasp it as present, through "supernatural evidence" '.[70]

It will also be clear from this account of the act of faith that, although for Aquinas religious faith is primarily a matter of intellectual assent, and only secondarily a practical attitude involving the affective side of human beings, the assent of faith is at the same time motivated by the will. It is therefore, in this respect, very different from ordinary evidential assent. The grace of faith orients me practically to assent to God as the author of revelation, and so to accept him as guarantor of the truth of revelation. For Aquinas, then, the modern debate over whether faith is 'belief that' or 'belief in' is misconceived, for the act of faith can be seen both as 'belief that' (propositional assent) and as 'belief in' (practical attitude or disposition) and we cannot have the one without the other.

We may also remark the fundamental continuity, for Aquinas, between the God of philosophy and the God of revelation and faith. Certainly, as we have seen, revelation and philosophy are essentially distinct and so are faith and reason, but they are not thereby discontinuous, for just as grace perfects nature and does not contradict it, so also the truths of revelation complement and perfect the truths of philosophy about God. In a certain sense even, grace cannot function without nature as its basis nor can faith function without reason as its basis: 'faith presupposes natural reason, even as grace presupposes nature ... and perfection supposes something that can be perfected'.[71]

The great early-twentieth-century French Catholic thinker Maurice Blondel has complained that Aquinas's account of the relationship between natural reason and supernatural faith simply juxtaposes the one against the other and does not show how they really complement each other. For the Thomist tradition, he says, the natural and supernatural orders were placed one above the other, but in touch, in an ascending hierarchy. There were three zones, as it were, on different levels: on the lowest, reason was in sole charge; on the highest, faith alone revealed to us the mystery of divine life and that of our summons to the feast of God; between the two was a meeting ground where reason discovered in an incomplete way the more important of natural truths, and these were confirmed and later explained by faith. By thus bearing upon certain common *objects*, these two currents, flowing from different sources, mingled their waters without losing their identities. But there was hardly any thought of examining in a critical spirit what might be called the subjective possibility or the formal compatibility of these two orders.[72]

However, as we have said, Aquinas himself sees that the order of nature and the order of the supernatural cannot simply be juxtaposed, for he insists that the supernatural 'perfects' and 'elevates' the natural, so that consequently the natural must be in itself perfectible or elevatable by supernatural grace in a quasi-dispositional way and not just in a merely passive way. What is true in Blondel's objection is that Aquinas did not work out fully the implications of what are, in themselves, very bold ideas.[73]

It is at all events this general view of the complementarity of grace and nature that lies behind Aquinas's account of the role of philosophy *vis-à-vis* religious faith. First, philosophy helps faith to express and systematise its truths; second, philosophy justifies the preambles or presuppositions of faith; and, third, philosophy defends the truths of faith from sceptical objections. With regard to the first, Aquinas emphasises that philosophy's role is a purely ancillary one and that religious faith does not really depend upon philosophy, at least in this respect. Theology, he says,

> can in a sense depend upon the philosophical sciences, not as though it stood in need of them, but only in order to make its teaching clearer... Therefore it does not depend upon other sciences as upon the higher, but makes use of them as of the lesser, and as handmaidens (*ancillae*). That it thus makes use of them is not due to its own defect or insufficiency, but to the defect of our intelligence, which is more easily led by what is known through natural reason ... to that which is above reason.[74]

Regarding the external role of philosophy with respect to faith, Aquinas's position is much less clear-cut. At times he appears to suggest that both the justification of the preambles of faith and the defence of the articles of faith are also merely confirmatory of faith and do not involve any kind of dependence of faith upon reason. But at other times he clearly thinks that faith is, at least in these respects, dependent upon reason. Thus, on the one hand, he holds that the merit of faith is diminished if it depends in any way upon rational argument;[75] while on the other hand he acknowledges that 'faith presupposes natural knowledge'. So in his discussion of the rational proofs of the existence of God,[76] Aquinas proposes the following objection to himself: 'It seems that the existence of God cannot be demonstrated. For it is an article of faith that God exists. But what is of faith cannot be demonstrated, because demonstrations produce scientific (i.e. deductive) knowledge, whereas faith is of the unseen (Heb. 11:1). Therefore it cannot be demonstrated that God exists.' Aquinas replies to this as follows: 'The existence of God and other like truths about God, which can be known by natural reason, are not articles of faith, but are preambles to the articles: for faith presupposes natural reason, even as grace presupposes nature, and perfection supposes something that can be perfected.' This seems clearly to make faith dependent upon philosophy in the sense that the concept of God, as used in a specifically religious realm of discourse, only has meaning if we can first show that it is *philosophically* meaningful.

We must distinguish here between the logical dependence of faith on reason, as just described, and the psychological dependence of faith upon reason. It may very well be the case, as a matter of psychological fact, that a person may come to understand the concept God in a context of religious faith, without explicitly adverting to its philosophical presuppositions. But this does not imply that the religious concept of 'God' is not logically dependent upon the philosophical concept of God, in the sense that if no meaning can be given to the latter then no meaning can be given to the former.[77]

Much the same considerations apply, *mutatis mutandis*, to the role of philosophy in defending the articles of faith against sceptical attacks, since although Aquinas does not discuss the matter in any detail, the meaning of the articles of faith for him indirectly depends upon the philosophical demonstration of their non-impossibility. Aquinas adopts here the position of Maimonides and argues that, while we cannot demonstrate the truth of the articles of faith (as distinct from the preambles of faith), we can at least show that supposed arguments against them, purporting to prove that they are incoherent or self-contradictory, are themselves inconclusive. As he puts it: 'Since faith rests upon infallible truth, and since the contrary of a truth can never be demonstrated, it is clear that the arguments brought against faith cannot be demonstrated, but are difficulties that can be solved'.[78]

Aquinas's position with regard to revelation and philosophy, faith and reason, is in its essentials the same as that we have traced from Philo through the early Christian thinkers and Augustine, to Abelard and Maimonides – though with Aquinas the position is systematised and made more rigorous by his use of the Aristotelian theory of knowledge and his reference to Aristotle's natural theology. With Aquinas's formulation also the difficulties of this position become much more obvious, for Aquinas sees, at least in part, that if philosophy is a handmaid to faith it is a logically indispensable handmaid. Aquinas dimly discerns the price that has to be paid for the reconciliation of philosophy and faith, but he is hesitant in drawing out the full consequences that are implicit in his own position. Let us then look at some of those consequences, and the difficulties that they raise.

We remarked before that, for Aquinas, there are three main functions of philosophical reason with regard to religious faith – one internal to faith, expressing and elaborating the data of faith, and the other two external to faith, justifying the preambles of faith and defending the articles of faith.

With regard to the first, Aquinas appears at times to think that we can in some way understand the truths of faith as contained in the Scriptures independently of natural reason, so that reason only comes in later and secondarily when we want to explicate those truths and to see their relations with one another. But, on Aquinas's own premises, it is difficult to see how this can be so, for, as we have seen, he does not hold that faith is a special kind of knowledge with its own peculiar 'logic'. God's revelation to human beings must be expressed in ordinary human concepts and propositions that retain their own ordinary use and obey the ordinary logical laws. Unless we can understand at least the meaning of the propositions that we believe by faith, then we cannot believe them, for otherwise we could not say *what* we were believing. It may well be that we do not *fully* or *completely* understand what we believe (Aquinas himself draws a distinction between understanding and 'comprehending'),[79] but we must understand at least that what we believe is not gibberish or conceptually incoherent. Again, no doubt the content of revelation inevitably transcends the capacity of any human conceptual system, but it has to be expressed in ordinary concepts, for in what other way could it be expressed? As a recent English writer has put it:

> Christian doctrines are said to be *mysteries*. It is necessary to explain in what sense they are such in a way that leaves enough, but not too much room for faith... If faith is a kind of belief, and a virtue because it is exercised in circumstances where knowledge is impossible for us, it seems

that on the one hand it is a minimum condition that it should be possible to understand what is believed, and on the other a maximum condition that it should be impossible for us to understand *how* it is true. To take a parallel example from physics, we can attach a sense to, and hence know the truth-conditions of, saying that light is particles, and that light is waves; but we do not (as yet) understand how anything can be both particle and wave. It is in the sense given by this latter condition that Christian doctrines are mysteries, for were it impossible for us to understand what it is we believe, it is difficult to see how we could be said to believe it. To be sure, there are degrees of understanding, and it is enough here to be able to show that the propositions in which we express our beliefs can be given a sense, and that they are not self-contradictory. If we cannot do either of these things, we are as yet unable to explain to non-Christians what Christian doctrine consists in, and they are accordingly not in a position to assess its relevance.[80]

In the sense, then, that the propositions expressing our beliefs have to be given a meaning, faith depends on reason. As we saw before, very much the same point comes up apropos Philo's and Origen's theory of the allegorical meaning of Scripture, for we only know that Scripture is to be interpreted allegorically when we see that a literal interpretation would lead to absurdity at the level of philosophy and natural reason.

Similar remarks may be made about the third or defensive function of philosophy with respect to religious faith. Even though philosophy is here restricted to showing that objections against the truths of faith are not cogent, and so to showing that the truths themselves are negatively possible or non-impossible, this is still to admit that the conditions of meaning of the truths of faith are established by philosophy. It is also to admit that, if a given article of faith is to be meaningful, some philosophical positions must implicitly be rejected or denied. For example, if the notion of the supernatural is to have any meaning, then the philosophical position of radical empiricism must be rejected as false, since this latter denies the very possibility of any meta-empirical order of reality. Again, if the notion of personal immortality is meaningful, then the philosophical position of materialism must be denied, since this latter also denies the possibility of any real distinction between the mind (and personality) and the body. Aquinas himself holds, for instance, that belief in the Trinity involves the denial of the philosophical doctrine of nominalism;[81] that the doctrine of the Eucharist involves the denial of any quasi-Humean account of things as simply the sum of their accidental properties (so that the notion of 'substance' as distinct from 'accidents' has no meaning); and that the doctrine of the Incarnation involves the rejection of any philosophical position that refuses to distinguish between 'person' and 'nature'. Religious belief or faith therefore involves one willy-nilly in philosophy, at least in this indirect and negative way. It does not, of course, involve one in having positively to espouse a particular philosophical position, but it does require that one deny certain positions as false and that one be able to show their falsity by philosophical argument.

Thus, to believe in the meaningfulness and truth of an article of faith is *ipso facto* to believe, on the authority of God, that no particular argument will ever actually succeed in showing conclusively that the article of faith is necessarily self-contradictory. Or put in another way, to believe in an article of faith is to hold implicitly that we will always be able to counter successfully, *on the philosophical level*, any such arguments by showing that they are not philosophically cogent. Is this position intelligible? Can we have a *general* belief that we will always be able to show *ad hoc* that any *particular* argument against the meaningfulness of an article of faith will not be cogent? Perhaps it might be possible to strike an analogy here with Wittgenstein's conception of philosophy, for Wittgenstein had a general philosophical belief that it is possible to show *ad hoc* that all philosophical problems are as a matter of fact 'dissolvable' and so not substantive problems. Again, another Wittgensteinian, Norman Malcolm, has this to say:

> With respect to any particular reasoning that is offered for holding that the concept of seeing a material thing, for example, is self-contradictory, one may try to show the invalidity of the reasoning and thus free the concept from the charge of being self-contradictory *on that ground*. But I do not understand what it would be to demonstrate *in general* and not in respect to any particular reasoning, that the concept is not self-contradictory.[82]

This logical dependence of faith upon reason is seen at its most flagrant in Aquinas's philosophical proofs of the existence of God and of certain of his basic attributes – the 'preambles' of faith as he calls them. Thus the God that emerges from Aquinas's 'Five Ways'[83] is boldly equated by him with the Yahweh of *Exodus*. Aquinas blandly takes Yahweh's description of himself as 'I am who I am'[84] as equivalent to his own Aristotelian philosophical definition of God as one whose essence and existence are identical.[85] Again, the obvious intent of the long and complex philosophical discussion of the attributes of God in the first twenty-six questions of the *Summa Theologiae* is to provide a rational justification of the God of revelation discussed in the various parts of the rest of the *Summa*. And Aquinas assumes without question that the God of the Five Ways and of the beginning of the 'Prima Pars' of the *Summa* coincides perfectly with the God of Judaeo-Christian revelation.

We might ask, however, what right we have to assume that the God of natural reason and the God of Christian faith do so nicely coincide. There are, after all, many profound differences between the Old Testament conception of Yahweh and Aquinas's Aristotelian God. It has, for instance, been remarked that in the prophetic literature in the Old Testament 'the character of Yahweh is more and more intimately revealed, not as the lord of nature, but as the lord of human life, who imposes moral obligations'.[86] Thus, instead of seeing God in a cosmological perspective, as Aquinas does, the Old Testament sees him primarily as the ground of the moral life of man.[87]

The Old Testament view of God is, in fact, philosophically speaking, a very loose and imprecise one, and it contrasts in this respect with the clear and distinct and highly technical conception of God that Aquinas (relying upon Aristotle's ideas on contingency and necessity and potentiality and actuality) develops.[88] Again, it has often been noted that the whole perspective of the Old Testament is an historical one, so that 'the God of the Bible is the God of a people's historical experience'.[89] Of course, truths of universal import emerge through the historical record of Yahweh's dealings with Israel, but the whole atmosphere of the Bible is still predominantly historical, whereas of course Aquinas's approach to God is severely philosophical. Like his Greek mentors, Aquinas has very little sense of history, for it is the universal and necessary and eternal that is of main interest to him and not the particular and contingent facts that constitute 'historia'.

Much the same could be said of the discrepancy between the God of the New Testament on the one hand, and the God of the 'Five Ways' and the 'Prima Pars' of the *Summa Theologiae* on the other. As Rahner has put it: 'The essential point of view of the New Testament is not that of metaphysical contemplation of the elements that necessarily belong to the concept of God – elements that risk remaining impersonal and abstract. The New Testament is mainly interested in a personal God and in his free and concrete action'.[90]

It may well be that Aquinas's philosophical conception of God is reconcilable with the biblical view of God in that it can be shown that the latter presupposes the former; but this in turn would involve subjecting the God of the Bible to philosophical analysis and showing that, as it stands, the biblical concept of God is incomplete. Aquinas himself simply assumes without question that the two concepts of God are complementary because he has already implicitly interpreted the God of revelation in philosophical categories. Philosophy and faith cannot conflict over their respective concepts of God because philosophy has already pre-arranged their harmony.

Aquinas's basic position on faith and reason was given a special and favoured place in the theological teaching of the Roman Catholic Church after the Council of Trent in the sixteenth century, and, at least until the Second Vatican Council, it represented the typical (if by no means the only or exclusive) Roman Catholic view. Thus, in the so-called Thomist tradition that runs through Cajetan in the sixteenth century, and John of St Thomas in the seventeenth century, to twentieth-century Catholic philosophers such as Garrigou-Lagrange, Gilson and Maritain, the essentials of Aquinas's theory on the relations between philosophy and religious revelation are maintained.[91] There is also an interesting Thomistic stream within Anglicanism that runs from the great Anglican divines of the seventeenth century to contemporary thinkers such as E. L. Mascall and A. Farrer[92] who also adopt, with modifications, Aquinas's philosophy of religion.

TWO CRITICS OF AQUINAS'S POSITION

As we have noted, Aquinas's position on faith and philosophy has had a long history in Roman Catholic thinking due to the special place given to the Saint within the Catholic Church. The neo-Thomist revival in the late nineteenth century, associated with the names of the German philosopher-theologian Joseph Klutgen, the Belgian scholars Maurice de Wulf and Cardinal Desirée Mercier, and in the early twentieth century with the French philosophers Etienne Gilson and Jacques Maritain, gave Aquinas's thought a privileged place in the Roman Catholic Church. Pope Leo XIII's encyclical letter *Aeterni Patris* in 1879, extolling the virtues of the Angelic Doctor's philosophy and theology, set the seal on this process. Again, the bowdlerised version of Thomism used in the teaching of Catholic seminaries ('seminary scholasticism') also increased the monopoly of Thomism in the Catholic world almost until the middle of the twentieth century.[93] As a result, the conclusions of Aquinas's natural theology came to be seen by some Catholics almost as a matter of faith, so that, for example, for a Catholic scholar to impugn Aquinas's philosophical 'Five Ways' of proving the existence of God was tantamount to denying the existence of the God of faith!

However, in the late nineteenth and early twentieth century a number of Catholic philosophers – Maurice Blondel, Edouard Le Roy, John Henry Newman and others – reacted against what they saw as the excessive intellectualism and implicit élitism of Aquinas's natural theology. It will be useful to consider two of these thinkers, Newman and Le Roy.

John Henry Newman

Although Newman does not advert directly to Aquinas's views there is no doubt that the *Grammar* is directed against 'seminary scholasticism' – 'the subtlety', as Newman puts it, 'the aridity, the coldness of mere scholastic science'.[94] Newman says that he is attempting to 'prove Christianity in the same direct and informal way in which I can prove for certain that I have been born'.[95] And in the *Essay* he sets out what he conceives to be this direct and informal way.[96]

As we have seen, a crucial assumption that lies behind the *Grammar* is that the truths of religion must be easily accessible to everyone and so cannot depend on abstruse philosophical reasoning available only to a few experts. In one of his Oxford University sermons in 1853 Newman said that his 'most original insight' was 'how you can convert factory girls as well as philosophers'[97] and this is certainly his intention in the *Grammar*. (It is worthwhile remembering that the quotation from St Ambrose on the title page of the *Grammar of Assent* is 'It is not by dialectics that God has decided to save his people'.) Just as moral or ethical truths must be easily accessible to everyone so that every person of good will can apprehend them by his or her 'conscience', so religious truths are apprehended by a 'sense' which everyone of good will possesses. Later in the *Grammar* Newman calls this the 'illative sense' but it is clear that Newman sees it as part of 'conscience'. A commentator on Newman puts it as follows: 'By examining the soul and its nature, we begin to discern reflections from beyond the veil. For if we look inward we find conscience ... we find a law which is not the law made by societies. It is an ultimate law'.[98] In an eloquent passage in the *Grammar* Newman has this to say: 'Our great internal teacher of religion is ... our Conscience. Conscience is a personal guide, and I use it because I must use myself; I am as little able to think by any mind but my own as to breathe with another's lungs. Conscience is nearer to me than any other means of knowledge. And as it is given to me, so also is it given to others; and being carried about by every individual in his own breast, and requiring nothing besides itself, it is thus adapted for the communication to each separately of that knowledge which is most momentous to him individually – adapted for the use of all classes and conditions of men, for high and low, young and old, men and women, independently of books, of educated reasoning, of physical knowledge, or of philosophy. Conscience, too, teaches us, not only that God is, but what he is; it provides for the mind a real image of Him as a medium of worship, it gives us a rule of right and wrong, as being his rule, and a code of moral duties.'[99]

It would seem then that for Newman 'conscience' is able to adumbrate a complete natural theology and that it goes far beyond what we ordinarily mean by conscience, the judgement of what means to adopt to secure an end in these particular and concrete circumstances. Newman mentions Aristotle's notion of *phronesis*, or right judgement about what decision one should make in particular circumstances, but Aristotle's *phronesis* has nothing to do with the apprehension of religious truths and it seems as though Newman is willy-nilly committed to some form of religious intuitionism. Newman is very much a child of his time and of his social class and he simply assumes that a 'civilised' person would see immediately that there is a God who rewards the good and punishes the wicked and exercises a providential care of his creatures. Newman was, as he said, concerned to make assent to religious truths available to the 'factory girl' as well as the philosopher but it is difficult to believe that a 'factory girl' in nineteenth-century England would spontaneously 'see' without any kind of argument that there is a just and merciful God. Again, we might ask what Newman would say to the religious sceptic like Nietzsche who holds that the whole idea of a religious order is meaningless and that the idea of God is simply, as Freud says, an illusion.

A second objection to Newman's view is that it is difficult to see what role theology has to play in religious belief if theology, like philosophy, is confined to the realm of the 'systematic and general' and never capable of exacting 'real' and imaginative assent to religious beliefs. Nevertheless, there is a valid and important point in Newman's view that if religious belief is based upon a sophisticated philosophical justification then it becomes élitist and accessible, at least in its fullness, only to the philosopher and not to the factory girl. This is an objection that Aquinas's natural theology has to meet.

Edouard Le Roy

Edouard Le Roy was an early-twentieth-century French philosopher and well known Catholic thinker. His essay *What is a dogma?* was published in

1905.[100] If dogmas or religious statements such as 'God is a person', 'Jesus is risen', are taken as being speculative or 'intellectualistic' or descriptive in function then, so Le Roy claims, it would be impossible to prove that they were true. We know how to verify scientific and mathematical statements but we do not know at all how to verify religious statements. Reasoning in theology and the religious realm is completely unlike the reasoning used in the sciences and philosophy. In the sphere of religion, so Le Roy argues, 'no Authority can make me find, or prevent me from finding, a train of reasoning solid or weak, nor that such and such a notion has or has not meaning for me... And how would I obey the Authority if it should impose on me that I should understand a given formulation that I do not understand? One might just as well ask me not to think any more at all. No *reason* can be of *faith*, this is a matter of identity pure and simple. There is no such thing as a revealed logic'.[101]

The traditional Catholic view of religious faith is that it depends indirectly on abstruse and contestable philosophical ideas. For example, the doctrine of transubstantiation (that in a eucharistic ritual the bread and wine are changed into the body and blood of Christ) depends upon a philosophical distinction between the 'substance' of the bread and its 'accidents' or perceptible properties so that one can speak of the colour, taste, etc. of the eucharistic bread remaining the same even though its substance has changed. It looks and tastes like bread but after the words of consecration it is not *really* bread. Does it make sense to distinguish between substance and accidents in this way? This is a purely philosophical position which can be understood, if it can be understood at all, only by a small group of believers and not by everyone.

According to Le Roy, then, so long as we conceive of religious statements as having a speculative or intellectualistic function, we are faced with insoluble problems. But if we see those statements as being 'practical' in function, these problems disappear. Le Roy gives a number of examples of how apparently speculative or intellectualist religious statements may be translated into the practical mode. ' "God is personal" means "Believe in your relations with God as you would in your relations with a human person". Likewise "Jesus is risen" means "Be in your relations with Him as you would have been before his death, as you are before a contemporary of yours".'[102] In general then, Le Roy concludes, 'Christianity is not a system of speculative philosophy, but a source and rule of life, a discipline of moral and religious action, in short a set of practical means for obtaining salvation. It is not surprising then that its dogmas are concerned with conduct rather than with pure reflective knowledge.'[103] This is why, Le Roy adds, assent to dogmas is always 'an act of the will, not the inevitable result of a logically compelling train of reasoning'.[104]

Once we see religious statements in this light 'we understand ... how dogmas are common to everyone, accessible to everyone, despite the inequality of men's intellects, whereas when they were conceived in the intellectualistic mode we were inevitably led to make them the exclusive property of a select group'.[105] 'Again, the content of dogmas or religious statements being relative to practice alone, is not relative to peoples' variable degrees of intelligence and knowledge; it remains exactly the same for the scholar and the unlettered man, for the clever and the lowly, for the ages of high civilisation and for races that are still barbarian'.[106]

A major difficulty for Le Roy is to explain how we judge whether the practical attitudes we adopt in religious matters are appropriate or justified or not. No doubt, when the Christian believer says 'I believe in God' he or she is adopting a practical attitude to the world and to life, but this attitude is only justified and appropriate if there really exists a being we all call 'God'. Again, if we say that 'Jesus Christ has risen from the dead' and that a practical translation of this is something like 'I believe that the way of life that Jesus espoused is still alive and relevant and I carry on my life accordingly', this is only appropriate if there really exists a 'historical Jesus'. Unless our practical attitudes have some reference to the real world it is difficult to see how religious statements can have any real practical meaning for us. Plausible as it is, then, Le Roy's account needs filling out to meet these kinds of objections. One might perhaps discern a similarity here between religious and ethical statements. Notoriously, it is difficult to see what 'objective' realities (either about the world or about ourselves) make our ethical statements and attitudes justified or relevant, and yet of course there is in practice a wide measure of experiential agreement about which ethical attitudes are meaningful.

As is the case with Newman, Le Roy assumes that Catholic Christianity is a kind of religious paradigm and he does not consider how his theory (if one may call it that) would work with other religious systems. Most Muslims, for example, refer all religious statements to the words of the Prophet in the Qur'an and since it is believed by Muslims that these are the very words of God himself dictated to the Prophet, there is no way to translate the statements in the Qur'an into the practical mode. The apparently descriptive statements in the Qur'an have to be understood literally as descriptive statements.

The important point, however, in both Newman's approach to religious assent and Le Roy's account is that if religious faith depends, directly or indirectly, on philosophical presuppositions (as in Aquinas's account) then we end up with some form of religious intellectualism and élitism.

CRITIQUE AND CONCLUSION

The tradition of thought which Aquinas sums up and systematises is a very bold and remarkable attempt to have the best of both the world of Greek philosophical theology and the world of Judaeo-Christian religion. On the one hand, it insists with the Greek religious intellectualism that, if religion is a worthwhile human enterprise, it must be within the realm of reason, or at least not contrary to reason. If the realm of divinity is mysterious, that mysteriousness must be due to its excess of intelligibility and not to its irrational unintelligibility. Or again, if religious faith goes beyond reason, it must at the same time build upon and complement reason. As grace perfects nature and does not destroy it, so faith perfects reason and raises it to a higher power and does not contradict or nullify it. As we have seen, for Aquinas's faith is not a miraculously given kind of religious insight or intuitive experience which suspends or interrupts the ordinary course of the natural processes of reason; rather it presupposes nature and in a certain sense requires it as its basis. Reason, this whole tradition holds, is just as much God's work as his revelation, and the truths of pure reason about God are just as valid, in their own way, as the truths of revelation. Reason can no more be denied or slighted for the sake of faith than faith can be denigrated for the sake of reason. For, as Augustine says, if human beings are saved by the truths of revelation it is equally by their reason that they are *imago Dei*.

On the other hand, by restricting philosophy to proving the preambles or presuppositions of faith, and to the negative task of showing the non-impossibility of the articles of faith, this tradition of thought allows room for an order of revelation and faith transcending the order of philosophy and pure reason. It insists, as we have seen, that the truths of revelation are essentially distinct from the truths of philosophy about God, and that religion and philosophy cannot be identified. Religion and philosophical theology both have the same 'material object', namely God, but they have different 'formal objects' in that the one considers God under the aspect of author of revelation, and the other considers him under the aspect of author of nature or cosmological First Cause. In this context Aquinas emphasises the 'remotive' or 'negative' character of our philosophical thinking about God – we know what God is mainly by knowing what he is not.[107] This is, indeed, implicit in his theory of analogical predication which plays a central role in his philosophical theology, for, as we have seen, although we know that predicates such as 'exists', 'is the cause of the world', 'is good', 'is a person' apply properly to God and not merely metaphorically, we do not know *how* they apply to God. All that we know is that such predicates do not mean apropos of God what they mean when they are applied to created things within our experience. Their meaning in the two cases is not univocally similar but analogously similar.[108]

At the same time, for Aquinas there is no doubt that we can rationally prove the existence of God and, albeit in an analogical way, what basic properties or attributes he has.[109] And again, no matter how indirect and negative the role of reason *vis-à-vis* faith may be, reason is in some sense always the final arbiter. This does not mean, as the Reformation theologians were to complain later, that the admission of reason inevitably results in the rationalising away of faith, the violation of the autonomy of faith, and the denial of its gratuitousness in that, so far as belief is made to depend upon man's reason, to that extent it does not depend upon the pure grace of God. The objections of the Reformers in fact neglect the negative role of reason with regard to faith, and they also presuppose a radically different view of grace and nature from that of Aquinas. However, it remains true that both for its own expression and elaboration, as well as for the justification of its preambles and its defence, faith is dependent, in the sense explained, upon reason. Neither Philo, Origen, Augustine, Maimonides nor Aquinas is altogether clear about the nature of this dependence, but it follows nevertheless from the logic of their position and, as we have seen, is especially obvious in Aquinas's formulation.

Although this conception of the philosophy of religion escapes the full force of the objections that we saw could be brought against the position of religious intellectualism which identified philosophy and religion, it is nevertheless subject to those same objections in an oblique form. First, it does involve a predominantly intellectualist or speculative view of religion, the practical side of religion being secondary. Indeed, man's final happiness for Aquinas consists in the contemplative vision of God, the love of God being consequent upon this vision.[110] And religious faith is, as we have seen, primarily a matter of *assent*, even if that assent is not of an ordinary kind but has to be willed in lieu of rationally compelling evidence.

For Aquinas, then, religious belief consists essentially in intellectual assent to the truth of certain propositions. Although practical conclusions as to how believers should live their lives follow these acts of assent, they do not constitute religious belief. To put it crudely, one is defined a religious believer if one assents to certain propositions; whereas, if one does not adopt the practical policies or attitudes consequent upon those beliefs, one may be classed as an inconsistent or hypocritical believer, but one will still be a believer. For Aquinas it is therefore at least possible to say without contra-diction, 'I believe in God but this belief makes no difference to the way I live my life', and in this sense there is for him a logical gap between religious belief and religious practice. For Kant and the neo-Kantians, of course, this furnishes grounds for a conclusive objection to the whole intellectualist position represented by Aquinas. Religious belief, they claim, is of its very nature practical so that to say, 'I believe in God' is precisely to commit oneself to live in a certain way.

Second, the understanding of the mysteries of faith involves, at least negatively, the use of philosophical reason; for example, I can only take in and believe what is involved in the mystery of the Eucharist if I can under-stand (at least implicitly) that no formal contradiction is involved in supposing that the 'substance' of the bread and wine can change while the 'accidents' remain the same. And to this extent Aquinas's position does involve some degree of esotericism. Aquinas attempts to evade this objection by arguing that the majority of non-philosophical believers can believe by faith the presuppositions of faith, although the latter are in themselves capable of being known philosophically or by pure reason. But, given his view of the nature of faith, it is difficult to see how we can believe by faith truths that are presupposed by faith. Third, as we have remarked, Aquinas's theological perspective is largely a-historical, in the manner of the whole Greek tradition of philosophical religion.[111] It is also an impersonal and 'objective' view that leaves aside altogether the dimension of what Pascal calls 'the heart' and Kierkegaard 'subjectivity' and Newman 'real and im-aginative assent'.

Kierkegaard's strictures against St Augustine could also be applied here to Aquinas. 'He resuscitated the Platonic–Aristotelian definition, the whole Greek philosophical pagan definition of faith … a concept which belongs to the sphere of the intellect.' 'From the Christian point of view', Kierkegaard continues, 'faith belongs to the existential: God did not appear in the character of a professor who has some doctrines which must first be believed and then understood... Faith expresses a relation from personality to personality'.[112] This objection depends, of course, on the philosophical validity of the notion of 'personal knowledge' – a non-intellectual mode of apprehension that, it is claimed, is typical of personal relationships: a 'belief in' that is essentially distinct from 'belief that'.

The fundamental difficulty, however, with Aquinas's whole approach is that it makes religious belief dependent upon the success of particular philosophical arguments, and indeed upon the viability of a specific conception of philosophy, so that the religious believer is, by his belief, exposed to philosophical dispute. This view of the philosophy of religion depends, for instance, upon a 'transcendentalist' conception of the role of philosophy according to which philosophy can go beyond what Kant calls the limits of our immediate experience. It must be admitted that Aquinas's conception of the nature and scope of philosophy is certainly more restricted and more modest than that of the Platonic/neo-Platonic tradition, since he insists that we can only know God and the other beings outside our experience by *a posteriori* inference. In other words, we do not know God directly or self-evidently and we have no innate knowledge of him; rather the concept of God only emerges after we have reflected upon our experience of the material world and have been led to seek a causal explanation of it. Further, as we have seen, even this indirect and inferential and postulatory knowledge of God is largely negative and 'analogical' in its mode. We know much more what God is *not* than what God *is*.

However, it remains true that Aquinas does see philosophy as having a 'transcendent' role and that his conception of philosophy is, to speak anachronistically, an anti-Kantian one. And, in turn, this means that his whole view of the philosophy of religion rests upon the validity of this contestable, or at least arguable, conception of the nature and scope of philosophy. For the philosopher who is convinced by Kant's radical criticism of this view of philosophy, this is a conclusive objection to Aquinas's whole position. And for the Reformation theologians also with their insistence upon the pure autonomy of faith, this represents the fatal flaw in Aquinas's philosophy of religion. But for Aquinas, of course, this is the inevitable risk that has to be run by any position that wants to emphasise the continuity and complementarity of the realms of grace and nature, faith and reason – a position of 'both/and' rather than 'either/or'. For him there cannot be an order of pure faith where we can escape making any rational or philosophical commitments and be safe from argument. Unless religious faith has some repercussions in the realm of reason and makes some philosophical demands upon us, it is empty. For Aquinas, if nothing is ventured in philosophy, nothing is won in faith.

3

PHILOSOPHY AS MAKING ROOM
FOR FAITH

Rousseau put me back on the right road. Rousseau is another Newton. Newton completed the science of external nature: Rousseau that of the internal universe.

IMMANUEL KANT, *Philosophical Correspondence*

AGNOSTICISM IN THE SERVICE OF FIDEISM

'If we submit everything to reason, our religion will have no mysterious or supernatural element'.[1] Pascal's statement very aptly expresses the persistent fear and suspicion of philosophy within the Christian tradition that has existed alongside the religious intellectualism we have just been discussing. Once philosophy is allowed a foothold within the domain of religious faith, it inevitably ends, so it is claimed, by rationalising away the mysterious and supernatural dimension of faith, and by making religion appear as our own work and achievement instead of being a free gift and gratuitous disclosure from God. Again, the philosophising of religious faith makes it into a kind of speculative assent, so that the practical or moral or personal dimension of religion becomes secondary; or, put in another way, philosophical religion is necessarily 'objective' in the sense that it is concerned with impersonal truths that are available to all, and the 'subjective' or 'personal' or 'inward' character of religious faith is neglected. The God of the philosophers, as Pascal says again, is not the God of Abraham and Isaac and Jacob.[2]

85

This anti-intellectualist or fideist trend has had a long and complex history, and it has usually been supported by St Paul's dark warnings against philosophy and worldly wisdom, as well as by other scriptural texts. St Paul's denunciation of 'philosophy and vain deceit'[3] was in fact directed against the Gnostics who claimed to have a special kind of knowledge superior to that of faith, but his strictures were exploited in a general and undiscriminating way, and the other Pauline doctrine to the effect that we could come to know God by reason[4] was conveniently neglected. In the same way, the saying of Jesus that the kingdom of heaven is hidden from the wise and the prudent and revealed to babes[5] came to be generalised into an anti-intellectualist canon. As McTaggart tartly put it: 'Such a principle is sure to be popular, for it enables a man to believe that he is showing meekness and humility by the confident assertion of propositions which he will not investigate and cannot prove'.[6]

Among certain of the early Christian thinkers, this fear of philosophy (at least in religion) was coupled with what has been called an 'absolute conviction in the self-sufficiency of Christian Revelation'.[7] Tertullian, for instance, rejects the 'foolishness' of philosophy and of 'unhappy Aristotle' since all that the Christian needs to know is in the Gospel.

> What indeed has Athens to do with Jerusalem? What concord is there between the Academy and the Church? What between heretics and Christians? Our instruction comes from the porch of Solomon who himself taught that the Lord should be sought in simplicity of heart. Away with all attempts to produce a mottled Christianity of Stoic, Platonic and dialectic composition! We want no curious disputation after possessing Christ Jesus, no inquisition after enjoying the Gospel! With our faith, we desire no further belief. For this is our palmary faith, that there is nothing which we ought to believe besides.[8]

Elsewhere Tertullian makes his famous, or notorious, statement: 'I believe because it is absurd',[9] meaning that what is taken (wrongly) to be absurd by philosophy is nevertheless seen to be true by the eyes of faith.

Tertullian's rejection of philosophy, it is important to note, is not inspired by a 'know nothing' obscurantism backed up by a simple-minded religious fundamentalism, for Tertullian makes extensive use of the instruments of reason in order to show the limits of reason in the religious domain. As Pascal will remark later on, there are two kinds of ignorance – 'natural ignorance', and 'learned' or 'educated' ignorance (*docta ignorantia*)[10] – and it is this latter kind of philosophical ignorance which Tertullian argues is proper to the Christian.

In the same way, certain medieval thinkers, such as the eleventh-century St Peter Damian and St Bernard of Clairvaux in the twelfth century, themselves use dialectics to argue against the pretension of the dialecticians in theology.[11] Neither Peter Damian nor St Bernard is an intellectual barbarian, for both make free use of the dialectical and rhetorical arts they condemn so vociferously. Thus in St Bernard's letter to the Pope indicating Abelard's 'errors', he claims that Abelard presumptuously applies dialectics to theology, and he asks, 'what could be more against reason than to attempt to go beyond reason by means of reason?'[12] But he sees nothing paradoxical in his own procedure, for in his view he is using reason in order to delimit reason and to show its incompetence in matters of religion and thus, in turn, to safeguard the autonomy of the realm of faith. Exactly the same position is taken up within the medieval Islamic tradition by the great and remarkable Al Ghazzali who sees it as the task of philosophy to show the 'inconsistency' of the philosophers' views of religion. Philosophy ends inevitably in antinomies if it attempts to touch upon religious issues, and by showing this we make a place for the supernatural religion of the Qur'an and for personal religious experience. As we shall see, Al Ghazzali is the first to attempt to formalise this whole position.

In later medieval philosophy, William of Ockham and the Ockhamist school also emphasise very strongly the limits of philosophy with respect to supernatural faith. Ockham is certainly not in any way a philosophical sceptic, but he is concerned to emphasise the omnipotence of God and this, in turn, leads him to take a fairly agnostic view of philosophy's capacities with regard even to the preambles of faith. Thus, for Ockham, while we can prove by reason that God exists, we cannot prove that there must necessarily be one and only one God. Again, while it can be shown that the intellectual soul is distinct from the body, we can neither prove nor disprove the immortality of the soul. It is through faith alone that we come to know that God is one and that the soul is immortal. God can do anything save what involves self-contradiction, and this means that we can be certain only of those truths guaranteed by the principle of non-contradiction. All other truths are contingent, and that they are as they are is dependent upon the free will of God[13] whose acts of course cannot be known demonstratively or necessarily by reason. One might say that there is much more scope and play for God's free will in Ockham's world than in Aquinas's, so that there is much greater scope for faith and correspondingly less scope for reason in the religious order.

Ockham's agnosticism, as we have called it, is even more pronounced in certain of his followers such as Nicholas of Autrecourt (1300–60). For Nicholas the principle of causality is not an absolutely certain truth since it can be denied without contradiction, and this means of course that all arguments relying upon the principle of causality – such as the arguments for the existence of God and the immortality of the soul – can claim neither certainty nor even probability.[14] Once again, Nicholas's intention is not in any way a sceptical one, for what he takes away from philosophy he gives to faith. His agnosticism, like that of Ockham, is very much in the service of faith and is meant to safeguard its independence and autonomy. Ockham and the later Ockhamists, such as Gabriel Biel (Luther's mentor), however, remain within the medieval scholastic tradition, and they do not ever carry their philosophical agnosticism *vis-à-vis* religion to the extreme to which subsequent post-Reformation thinkers will later take it.[15]

All these various tendencies receive a powerful addition through the ideas on faith and reason set in train by the Reformation. The interests of the Reformers, Luther and Calvin, are exclusively theological, and they are content to make their theological points about revelation and faith and to leave philosophy to cope with them as best it can. No doubt, they assume implicitly that there cannot be any real conflict between the conclusions of philosophy and the demands of religious faith, and that therefore we must be able to show at the philosophical level that philosophy does in fact allow room for the conception of religious faith they propose. In other words, they tacitly presuppose that some such conception of the scope and limits of philosophy as that put forward later by Kant is philosophically viable. But they do not themselves argue for such a conception and in this sense they do not have a philosophy of religion. However, the ideas of the Reformers have been so influential within the stream of thought we are considering that something must be said about them.

Luther does not deny that reason has a proper place in the ordering of human affairs – law, government, the arts, science – nor even that we can in principle have a general knowledge of God and of his moral law. However, after the Fall, human reason has a fatal tendency to pride; it refuses to accept its creaturely status and sets itself up as the final judge of everything, including God's Word. 'This is the vice of human nature,' Luther says, 'it does not consider these things to be creatures and gifts but rather says, "This I have made". Instead it should rather say: "I have received and the Lord has given", not "man has made".'[16] Luther apparently thinks that this Pelagian tendency of human reason is inevitable and that, although theoretically reason and philosophy can come to a knowledge of God, in the actual state in which we humans finds ourselves this is practically impossible. A natural theology would have been possible for Adam, but it is no longer possible for us. Our only knowledge of God comes through God-given faith which we cannot merit by our own human efforts in any way. 'Reason is a whore', Luther says, for it seduces the believer from his trusting acceptance of God's Word and leads him to think himself self-sufficient.[17] Luther's rejection of reason in matters of faith is thus principally motivated by his theological stress on the wholly gratuitous nature of God's grace, including the grace of faith, and his corresponding view of the inevitable Pelagian tendencies of human reason. Reason always tends to set itself up over-weeningly as the arbiter of God's revelation so that the creature becomes the judge of the Creator. For Luther, grace does not build on nature and perfect and complete it, as it does for Aquinas; rather grace stands in for 'corrupt nature' and supplies for its deficiencies. In the same way, faith supplies for the deficiencies of reason and does not presuppose it or complement it.[18]

Calvin likewise emphasises the theoretical possibility of human reason coming to know God. Indeed, in the first part of the *Institutes of the Christian Religion*, he argues that 'the knowledge of God has been naturally implanted in the minds of men'.[19] If this were not so then men would be able to claim that they were ignorant of God and they would not be culpable for refusing to acknowledge him. However, 'since men one and all perceive that there is a God and that he is their Maker, they are condemned by their own testimony because they have failed to honour him and to consecrate their lives to his will'.[20] Men are then capable of knowing God, but in actual fact they refuse to know him because of their 'proud vanity and obstinacy'. 'They do not therefore apprehend God as he offers himself, but imagine him as they have fashioned him in their own presumption'.[21] The God of reason is thus 'a figment and dream' of man's own making; it is in fact a 'dead and empty idol' that has nothing to do with the true God,[22] a 'shadow deity' that displaces the true God 'whom we should fear and adore'.[23]

> It is therefore in vain [Calvin concludes] that so many burning lamps shine for us in the workmanship of the universe to show forth the glory of its Author. Although they bathe us wholly in their radiance, yet they can of themselves in no way lead us into the right path. Surely they strike some sparks, but before their fuller light shines forth these are smothered. For this reason, the apostle, in that very passage where he

calls the world's creatures the images of things invisible, adds that through faith we understand that they have been fashioned by God's word.[24] He means by this that the invisible divinity is made manifest in such spectacles, but that we have not the ideas to see this unless they be illumined by the inner revelation of God through faith. And where Paul teaches that what is to be made known of God is made plain from the creation of the universe,[25] he does not signify such a manifestation as men's discernment can comprehend; but rather, shows it not to go farther than to render them inexcusable.[26]

It is interesting in this passage to see Calvin's interpretation of the Pauline texts which, *prima facie*, seem to suggest the possibility of a natural knowledge of God. For Aquinas, these texts were direct support of his thesis that faith presupposed such a natural theology; but for Calvin, Romans 1:19 simply means that humans are culpable if they reject God, since they are capable of knowing him at least in a minimal way.

For Calvin the only real way of knowing God is through his revelation in the Scriptures. And we know in this way both what Aquinas calls the preambles of faith – God as creator and 'sole Author and Ruler of all that is made'[27] – and the articles of faith about God as Mediator and Redeemer: 'Seeing that it is impossible for us men ever to come to the true knowledge of God, God has revealed himself to us in his Word. The incarnate Word attested in Scripture, the Son of God himself, has entered into the breach between God and ourselves'.[28]

For both Luther and Calvin therefore philosophy is, for theological reasons, forbidden to enter into the domain of faith. To admit the possibility of a natural theology, through which our reason could come to know God merely as the author of nature, would be to impugn the doctrine of God's transcendence with respect to his creatures as well as the doctrine of the pure gratuitousness of his dealings with us. It would also be to impugn the theological doctrine of our sinfulness and corruption, manifested above all in our over-weening pride which even causes us to fashion God in our own image. To the extent that a natural theology is possible we can save ourselves by our own efforts and to that extent we are independent of God and do not need God's grace. But, Luther and Calvin claim, no Christian can believe that we can save ourselves (even partially) by our own efforts – that is the heresy of Pelagianism – nor that we can be independent of God's grace. 'All is a gift of God, even the faith by which we appropriate the gift'.[29] Therefore we must deny the possibility of a natural theology.

It is within this theological context that both Kant and Kierkegaard attempt, in their different ways, to work out a new conception of philosophy's role with regard to religion. It is too facile to call Kant 'the philosopher of Protestantism', for Kant's own conception of religion is highly complex and not simply reducible to the basic Protestant position. Nevertheless his view of the philosophy of religion, like that of his great sceptical mentor David Hume, chimes in with Luther and Calvin's theological position. Thus, in the *Critique of Pure Reason*, philosophy demonstrates its own limits with respect to the objects of religion, and so makes room for faith. And then in the *Critique of Practical Reason* religion is shown to be a phenomenon that belongs to, or is solely approachable through, the practical or moral or 'subjective' realm. For Kierkegaard also, reason makes room for faith by showing its own limitations. The whole tendency of Kierkegaard's thought is to destroy the pretensions of the 'objective' thinking that is typical of philosophy (or at least of one kind of philosophy), and thereby to show that religion belongs to the realm of 'subjectivity'. As it has been said, for Kierkegaard 'God cannot be proved, because what can be proved, if it could be proved, cannot be God'.[30] And of course this same position is maintained in modern Protestant philosophy of religion, profoundly influenced as it has been by both Kant and Kierkegaard.

Outside the Protestant theological context, the position we have been characterising is represented also (though with its own highly original twist) in the thought of the great French Catholic thinker Pascal (1623–62). 'The last proceeding of reason', Pascal says, 'is to recognise that there is an infinity of things which are beyond it'.[31] God is approachable only through 'the heart' and not through Cartesian reason; the personal God of authentic religion has nothing to do with the abstract and impersonal God of the philosophers.

We have here a distinct view of the philosophy of religion. Even though in this view philosophy is excluded from the religious realm, it is philosophy itself which effects this exclusion by a kind of self-denying ordinance. As in the other two traditions we have already considered, this position involves its own conception of the scope and nature of philosophy, and its own conception of religion. Again, as a specific form of the philosophy of religion it has its own credits and its own debits, its own insights and its own deficiencies. Let us then attempt to analyse the structure and 'logic' of this position by looking at some typical formulations of it.

AL GHAZZALI: THE INCONSISTENCY OF THE PHILOSOPHERS

Although the tradition of philosophical agnosticism in respect of religion had, as we have seen, very ancient origins, the first attempt in Western thought to formalise this position is to be found in the philosophical theology of the remarkable Islamic thinker Al Ghazzali (1058–1111). Al Ghazzali in his own way anticipates most of the moves that Kant was to make later in the *Critique of Pure Reason* concerning the antinomies of speculative reason with respect to the subjects of 'God, freedom and immortality', and it is worthwhile looking briefly at his ideas.[32]

In his autobiography of his own intellectual and spiritual career, *The Deliverance from Error*,[33] Al Ghazzali recounts the story of his conversion to philosophy and of his subsequent disillusionment in that, first, it did not lead him to the knowledge of God, and, second, it came to conclusions that were directly contrary to the religious teachings of the Qur'an, particularly concerning the resurrection of the body, God's providential knowledge of particular events, and the beginning of the world in time.[34] However, instead of totally rejecting philosophy like the Islamic fundamentalists, 'loyal to Islam but ignorant, who think that religion must be defended by rejecting every science connected with the philosophers',[35] Al Ghazzali attempts to show the religious limitations of philosophy from within philosophy itself and by using philosophical means. Al Ghazzali's purpose is not a sceptical one, for he clearly acknowledges that philosophy has its rightful place; but in respect of the religious order generally, his aim is to show the necessary agnosticism of philosophy. It has been said that the import of his teaching is that 'intellect should only be used to destroy trust in itself',[36] and this is true if it is understood with respect to the intellect's attempt to intervene in the religious domain. It is the task of philosophy to show that religious truths can be neither proved nor disproved, and thus to clear the way for faith.

This is, in effect, the thesis of Al Ghazzali's great work *The Inconsistency of the Philosophers* (*Tafahut al-Falasifa*).[37] In this work Al Ghazzali attempts to show that the philosophico-theological speculations of Al Farabi and Ibn Sina either end inevitably in antinomies or involve false philosophical assumptions. Thus, for example, he attacks the view of Ibn Sina, that since the universe is governed by causal laws, therefore everything takes place by deterministic necessity so that, in turn, God's free will can have no exercise in the world and miracles are impossible. But, argues Al Ghazzali, we can show by a philosophical analysis of the notion of causality that it does not entail necessity. 'In our view,' he says, 'the connection between what are believed to be cause and effect is not necessary'.[38] No self-contradiction is involved in denying the truth of a causal proposition and this shows that it is not logically necessary. In fact, causal connections are based upon observation of the succession or conjunction of events. Thus the fire is not the cause of the effect of burning; rather 'observation shows only that one is *with* the other and not that it is *by* it'. In other words, the burning happens *with* the fire and not *by* it or because of it.[39] Al Ghazzali further anticipates Hume by arguing that the apparent necessity of causal connections derives from our psychological expectations: 'It is only when something possible is repeated over and over again (so as to form the norm) that its pursuance of a uniform course in accordance with the norm in the past is indelibly impressed upon our minds'.[40] Given this idea of causality, we can see that miracles are not impossible, for there is nothing self-contradictory involved in supposing that God might suspend the natural order of so-called cause and effect. God may then by his free will bring about the resurrection of the body in the next life and effect all the other things that are promised in the Qur'an and which 'elude the discernment of human sensibility'. As with William of Ockham later on, the only restriction on God's omnipotence is the law of contradiction, for God cannot of course effect what is logically impossible. Apart from that we cannot set any limits to the power of God.

For Al Ghazzali, the space that philosophy clears for religion is to be filled by a direct and immediate kind of religious experience. Al Ghazzali adopted the religion of Sufi mysticism which emphasises direct experience of God – the 'sinking of the heart completely in the recollection of God and ... complete absorption in God'.[41] This is accompanied by revelations and visions, and it culminates in an ecstatic state which is 'hard to describe in language'. As he says:

> What is most distinctive of mysticism is something which cannot be apprehended by study, but only by immediate experience or tasting, by ecstasy and by a moral change. What a difference there is between *knowing* the definition of health and satiety, together with their causes and presuppositions, and *being* healthy and satisfied... Similarly there is a difference between knowing the true nature and causes of the ascetic life and actually leading such a life and forsaking the world.[42]

It is the personal or subjective dimension of religion that is all-important for Al Ghazzali and that necessarily escapes the grasp of reason and philosophy, inevitably concerned as the latter is with knowing *about* things in an

'objective' way. As we shall see, this combination of philosophical agnosticism with a personalistic or 'subjectivistic' view of religion is a constant
feature of the strain of philosophy of religion of which Al Ghazzali is the first
systematiser.

PASCAL: THE REASONS OF THE HEART

Pascal's *Pensées* are merely the rough notes for a projected apologetical work
on the Christian religion, so that his ideas are expressed in a fragmentary and
aphoristic style without much argument or detailed development. We can,
however, discern in this religious classic a well-defined position on the relations of philosophical reason to religious faith.

Pascal admits that it is theoretically possible to prove the existence of
God by reason,[43] and, for all his suspicions of philosophy and philosophers,
he is not in any sense an irrationalist. Thus he says that man's dignity
consists in the fact that one is capable of thinking (a person is a 'thinking
reed'),[44] and he holds firmly that religion cannot flout the principles of
reason: 'If we offend the principles of reason our religion will be absurd and
ridiculous'.[45] But, these admissions having been made, the main drift of
Pascal's thought in the *Pensées* is to expose the limitations and impotence,
even dangers, of philosophy and reason in the domain of religion. This is
shown in a number of different ways and from different points of view,
which we can set out summarily as follows: (i) Man is a finite creature and is
therefore a 'Nothing in comparison with the Infinite'.[46] And since he is finite
he can only comprehend what is finite and cannot comprehend the Infinite:
'the end of things and their beginning are hopelessly hidden from him in an
impenetrable secret; he is equally incapable of seeing the Nothing from
which he was made, and the Infinite in which he is swallowed up'.[47] In fact,
'there is an unconquerable opposition between us and God' which cannot be
overcome by human reason.[48] In this view our inability to have any natural
rational knowledge of God derives from our ontological finitude. And it
would seem that not only is knowledge of the actual existence of the supernatural order excluded by the argument, but also knowledge of the *possibility*
of the supernatural. (ii) Pascal, however, also offers another argument to
show that, while reason can admit the *possibility* of a supra-rational order, and
so of a supernatural order, it cannot in any way demonstrate whether that
possibility is in fact realised or not. Such a demonstration would presuppose
that there is some common ground or 'affinity' between the rational and

supra-rational, or between the natural and supernatural orders. But of course there cannot be any such affinity or likeness. 'If there is a God,' Pascal says, 'he is infinitely incomprehensible, since, having neither parts nor limits, he has no affinity to us. We are then incapable of knowing what he is or if he is. This being so, who will dare to undertake the decision of the question. Not we, who have no affinity to him'.[49] And he goes on, 'God is, or he is not. But to what side shall we incline? Reason can decide nothing here. There is an infinite chaos which separates us'.[50]

It is this situation which is the basis of Pascal's famous 'wager', for given that we cannot decide certainly about the actuality of God's existence, the best we can do is to calculate the advantages and disadvantages of adopting one or the other of the two possibilities. According to Pascal's very dubious 'games strategy' argument, it is a better bet to believe that the possibility that there is a God is actually realised, rather than to believe the opposite.[51] But he admits that the purpose of the wager is not so much to convince the non-believer as to shake his religious indifference. (iii) Apart from these *a priori* arguments purporting to show the necessary agnosticism of the human mind with respect to the supernatural order, Pascal employs a number of subsidiary arguments which are meant to prove the practical inability of human reason to understand anything about God. Thus human knowledge, he says, is subject to error and deception of all kinds with regard to mundane objects,[52] the implication being that *a fortiori* we can hardly have any certain knowledge of religious realities since they are so much more remote than mundane realities. And again, he remarks that the evidences in Nature of the existence of God are all of them ambiguous. Nature does not unequivocally testify to the existence of God, nor does it unequivocally testify against the existence of God.[53] 'It is incomprehensible that God should exist, and it is incomprehensible that he should not exist'.[54] (iv) Pascal also uses an argument based upon the theological doctrine of the Fall. In the actual existential state in which we find ourselves, our knowledge is so distorted by pride and vanity that we find it difficult to see and accept the truth. Rather we tend to see what we want to see and to invent the kind of God we want. This is exactly what the deists do, and it is because of this that, so Pascal claims, the God of deism (a 'great, powerful and eternal being') has nothing to do with the God of religion. Indeed, deism is 'almost as far removed from the Christian religion as atheism'.[55] (v) In any case, even if the proofs for the existence of God were cogent, they are of their very nature remote and abstract and impersonal, so that the God they produce is likewise remote and impersonal. But 'it is the heart which experiences God, and not the reason', and faith is 'God felt by the heart, not by the reason'.[56] In other words, religious faith is a personal commitment to God involving a direct experiential contact with God: 'The heart has its reasons, which reason does not know'.[57] By 'the heart' Pascal means the capacity for direct, intuitive, affective, personal knowledge ('spiritual insight'),[58] as contrasted with the inferential, abstract, objective and impersonal knowledge of philosophy. And there is no doubt that when he speaks of God being felt by the heart Pascal always has in mind his own overwhelming experience of God on 23 November, 1654.[59] Again – an important point – whereas we are not free to refuse assent to the necessary truths of philosophy, faith is of its nature a free acceptance of God.[60]

Pascal insists that it is reason itself which shows us these limits of reason, and so demonstrates its necessary agnosticism with regard to the supernatural order. In this sense reason is indispensable to faith, even if its sole function is a self-abnegating one. It is worthwhile citing Pascal at length on this point, since he himself views it as of central importance.

> The last proceeding of reason [he says] is to recognise that there is an infinity of things which are beyond it. It is but feeble if it does not see so far as to know this. But if natural things are beyond it, what will be said of supernatural things?... We must know where to doubt, where to feel certain, where to submit. He who does not do so, understands not the force of reason... Submission is the use of reason in which consists true Christianity... Reason would never submit, if it did not judge that there are some occasions on which it ought to submit. It is then right for it to submit, when it judges that it ought to submit... Wisdom sends us to childhood. *Nisi efficiamini sicut parvuli.* There is nothing so conformable to reason as this disavowal of reason.[61]

Pascal unfortunately does not develop this position in any detail. Above all, he does not explain what he means by the knowledge of 'the heart', by which alone, according to him, we can apprehend the God of Abraham and Isaac and Jacob. Is there a distinctive mode of knowledge proper to 'the heart'? Does it have its own logic? How is this 'subjective' or experiential knowledge of God related to philosophical and 'objective' knowledge of God? Is it really the case that there is nothing in common between the God of religion apprehended by 'the heart' and the God of the philosophers? Is this subjective knowledge communicable in any way? Is it 'self-authenticating' or infallible, or does it admit the possibility of error? If the latter, what tests are there for distinguishing between veridical and non-veridical experiences or intuitions of 'the heart'? Nevertheless, although Pascal does not argue for this position, he does sketch its outline in firm strokes: reason showing its own agnosticism with regard to the religious order, and so allowing space for revelation and faith; the relation of religious faith to the knowledge of 'the heart' as against the remote and abstract character of philosophical religion; and the necessary freedom of religious faith which is incompatible with the 'necessitarianism' of philosophy logically exacting the mind's assent.

DAVID HUME: SCEPTICISM AND FAITH

In the Preface to his *Prologomena to Any Future Metaphysics*, Kant testifies that it was David Hume's *Philosophical Essays* that first interrupted his 'dogmatic slumbers' and set him on a new path that led to his 'critical philosophy'. Hume's influence also seems to have been of central importance in the profound change that came over Kant's philosophy of religion in its development from its 'pre-critical' to its 'critical' phase. Kant's early essays in the philosophy of religion were for the most part in the traditional Wolffian mould. In his thesis of 1735, for instance, he admitted the possibility of proving the existence of a being which exists with 'absolute necessity', and in the short work *The Only Possible Proof of the Being of God*, written in 1763, he set out a proof of an 'unconditionally necessary being' and of its basic attributes.[62] In all these proofs Kant assumes that 'the world as given is an object for which we are bound by the principle of causality to seek an explanation'.[63] It was, however, both these assumptions – that the world as a whole is an 'object' needing an explanation of its existence, and that we can extrapolate the principle of causality 'outside' the world of our experience – that Hume was concerned to attack both in the *Enquiry Concerning Human Understanding* (1751) and in the later *Dialogues Concerning Natural Religion* (1779), and there seems little doubt that Kant's philosophy of religion was radically changed as a result of his reading of Hume. We know, in fact, that Kant read the *Dialogues* in translation in 1780, the year before the publication of the *Critique of Pure Reason*, and that Hume's powerful criticism of the teleological argument for the existence of God caused him to revise his ideas on philosophical theology in the forthcoming *Critique*.[64] But Hume's influence on Kant's philosophy of religion shows in other more fundamental ways. First, Hume rejects any use of the principle of causality 'beyond the reach of human experience'.[65] Second, Hume attempts to show that irresolvable problems arise when reason tries to grapple with religious topics: 'All religious systems ... are subject to great and insuperable difficulties'.[66] Third, the notion of God as 'a necessarily existent Being' is dismissed by Hume as meaningless on the ground that 'whatever we conceive as existent, we can also conceive as non-existent'.[67] Fourth, Hume allows the possibility that philosophical scepticism about religious matters may encourage men to 'fly to revealed truth with the greatest avidity',[68] although it is clear enough that this is not Hume's personal position or the intention behind his own scepticism. Fifth, Hume emphasises the persistence and quasi-inevitability of religious belief, despite its irrationality. For Hume, it has been said, 'neither the experience of evil nor the lesson of scepticism entirely eliminates a post-critical residual belief in a divine mind beyond nature'.[69]

All of these points are taken up by Kant in the *Critique of Pure Reason* and become essential features of the philosophy of religion developed in the latter part of that work. To understand Kant on religion, then, we have to look briefly at Hume's own philosophy of religion, even though, no doubt, Hume would be very amused to see his radical religious scepticism dignified as a 'philosophy of religion'.[70]

At the conclusion of the *Dialogues*, Philo (Hume's *alter ego*), after showing the sterility of 'natural theology', comes to the following ironic conclusion:

> Believe me ... the most natural sentiment which a well-disposed mind will feel on this occasion, is a longing desire and expectation, that Heaven would be pleased to dissipate, at least alleviate, this profound ignorance, by affording some more particular revelation to mankind, and making discoveries of the nature, attributes, and operations of the divine object of our Faith. A person, seasoned with a just sense of the imperfections of natural reason, will fly to revealed truth with the greatest avidity: while the haughty dogmatist, persuaded that he can erect a complete system of theology by the mere help of philosophy, disdains any further aid, and rejects this adventitious instructor. To be a philosophical sceptic is, in a man of letters, the first and most essential step towards being a sound, believing Christian.[71]

This pretended alliance of philosophical scepticism with revelation and faith was, in fact, a constant feature of Hume's philosophy of religion. Thus, in his conclusion to the essay *Of Miracles* Hume has this to say: 'I am the better pleased with the method of reasoning here delivered, as I think it may serve to confound those dangerous friends or disguised enemies to the Christian Religion, who have undertaken to defend it by the principles of human reason. Our most holy religion is founded on Faith, not on reason; and it is a sure method of exposing it to such a trial as it is, by no means, fitted to endure'.[72] Again in the essay *Of the Immortality of the Soul* which is, as Kemp Smith nicely says, 'quite definitely negative of any such belief', Hume writes: 'By the mere light of reason it seems difficult to prove the immortality of the Soul... But in reality, it is the gospel, and the gospel alone, that has brought life and immortality to light'.[73] And, finally, there is the celebrated passage in the *Enquiry Concerning Human Understanding* where Hume couples his own scepticism with the Calvinist view of faith as a miraculous supplanting of reason:

> We may conclude [says Hume with malice aforethought] that the Christian religion not only was at first attended with miracles, but even at this day cannot be believed by any reasonable person without one. Mere reason is insufficient to convince us of its veracity. And whoever is moved by Faith to assent to it, is conscious of a continued miracle in his own person, which subverts all the principles of his understanding, and gives him a determination to believe what is most contrary to custom and experience.[74]

Hume's general position here is primarily a tactic, which he learned from Pierre Bayle, of cutting the rational ground from under religion while pretending to be concerned with preserving its autonomy. But it is also a direct expression of his view of the scope and limits of philosophy, and of its necessary agnosticism with regard to questions that are 'beyond the reach of human experience'. Thomas Huxley invented the word 'agnosticism' to describe Hume's position, and it does so very exactly. In the realm of religion, Hume says, we are 'quite beyond the reach of our faculties'.[75] 'We are', he goes on, 'like foreigners in a strange country, to whom everything must seem suspicious, and who are in danger every moment of transgressing against the laws and customs of the people with whom they live and converse'.[76] And later he concludes: 'A total suspense of judgement is here our only reasonable resource'.[77] It is also this conviction that led Hume to adopt the dialogue form for his main work on religion, for, as he puts it, 'any question of philosophy ... which is so obscure and uncertain, that human reason can reach no fixed determination with regard to it; if it should be treated at all, seems to lead us naturally into the style of dialogue and conversation'.[78]

Whether or not this philosophical agnosticism, despite its plausible air, is really possible, is a question that will have to be discussed later. How can philosophical reason draw its own limits without being able to stand 'outside' the limits? How, in other words, can we *know* that there is a possible order of things that we cannot in principle know? This, as we shall see, is a problem that Hume bequeathes to Kant.

However, Hume admits at least the possibility that religious faith may be erected on philosophical scepticism. Certainly Hume himself does not think that this possibility is actually realised, and he would not have wanted religious believers to have used his position in this way so as to guarantee the autonomy of faith by making it invulnerable to rational criticism. He is, indeed, very sarcastic about those 'sagacious divines' who use reason or deny reason as it suits them: 'Thus, sceptics in one age, dogmatists in another; whichever system best suits the purpose of these reverend gentlemen, in giving them an ascendant over mankind, they are sure to make it their favourite principle, and established tenet'.[79] But it remains true that his position is able to be exploited by the fideist wishing to deny reason in order to make room for faith. It is a final irony (that the great master of irony would perhaps not have altogether appreciated) that Hume is thus the precursor of Kant and Kierkegaard.[80]

KANT: RELIGION AND PRACTICAL REASON

Everything turns to complexity in Kant's hands and his philosophy of religion is no exception to this rule. At first sight, perhaps, Kant's views on the relationship of philosophy and religion seem to be simple enough; but when we probe more deeply his position is seen to be much more intricate and, it might be said, much more ambiguous. To help us to thread our way through the Kantian maze it may be useful to set out in a very general way the main theses of Kant's philosophy of religion.

1. Speculative or theoretical reason – reason in so far as it is concerned to know what is true and false about the world of our experience, and about the conditions of possibility of such knowledge – cannot either prove or disprove that there is a God, or indeed establish anything at all positively about the religious order. Of its very nature speculative reason is agnostic about God, and for that matter any other realities that transcend our ordinary experience. This is a purely philosophical thesis derived from a 'critical' analysis of the scope and limits of speculative reason.

2. Religion is in any case not a speculative phenomenon but a practical or moral one. To be religious, for Kant, is not to assent to certain truths, but rather to direct or orient one's life in a certain way. Religion, in other words,

is a matter of the will – it being understood that for Kant the will is identified with practical reason, that is to say, reason in so far as it is concerned with recognising that certain acts ought to be done or that certain attitudes ought to be adopted. Religion, one might say, is one of the practical conditions of morality, or at least an important dimension of morality, and the concept of God becomes meaningful to us only through morality, that is to say through the lived experience of the moral life. Rousseau's ideas on religion had a very great influence on Kant in this respect.

3. An analysis of practical reason – reason in so far as it is concerned with prescribing how we ought to act, and not with describing what is the case – allows us to conclude to the existence of God (along with the immortality of the soul) as a 'postulate' or presupposition of its own adequate exercise. We do not *know*, speculatively or theoretically, that there *is* a God; but our analysis of practical reason shows the real possibility of God, and then the reality of God becomes clear to us in the living out of the moral life. God is that which justifies our hope of attaining the highest moral good and of becoming morally perfect and happy. Or, put in another way, which Kant sometimes suggests, to believe that moral perfection is ultimately attainable and that virtue and happiness will finally coincide, is in effect to believe in God.

4. Kant speaks on occasion as though the essence of religion is identical with morality, in the sense just mentioned. To believe in God just is to take up certain fundamental moral attitudes. This involves, of course, the denial of any supernatural or revelatory dimension to religion and the de-emphasising of the particular and historical aspects of Christianity. At other times, however, Kant speaks as though God exists in a 'transcendent' way quite independently of any moral attitudes we may have. And in this vein he allows some place for the supernatural dimension of Christianity and also for its historical and particular aspects.

It will be seen from this brief summary that there are two quite distinct strands in Kant's philosophy of religion. If we see religion within the context of speculative reason, then philosophy's task *vis-à-vis* religion is a purely negative or agnostic one. Its function is simply to make room for faith by delimiting the scope of speculative reason in such a way that both speculative proofs and disproofs of God come to be seen as illusory. If we cannot prove the existence of God, equally we cannot disprove it. On the other hand, within the perspective of practical reason, both the possibility and reality of God become manifest to us, and philosophy, in so far as it is concerned with the presuppositions or postulates of practical reason, has therefore a positive task with respect to religion. In fact, if we adopt one of the alternative readings of Kant's position here, philosophy (in the sense just described) does not simply prepare the way for religion but is, in effect, identical with religion. To acknowledge certain of the postulates of practical reason – those conditions without which the operations of practical or moral reason would be 'unjustified' – is *ipso facto* to acknowledge the existence of God and to be a religious person.

With this general plan before us, let us look in more detail at Kant's position.

In one of his letters, Kant tells us that the *Critique of Pure Reason* was written in order to resolve the antinomies that confront reason as soon as it tries to engage in any 'transcendent' speculation: 'That is what first aroused me from my dogmatic slumber and drove me to the critique of reason itself, in order to resolve the scandal of ostensible contradiction of reason with itself'.[81]

Kant's answer to this problem in the *Critique of Pure Reason* rests upon what has been called 'the principle of significance', namely, that

> there can be no legitimate, or even meaningful, employment of ideas or concepts which does not relate them to empirical or experiential conditions of their application. If we wish to use a concept in a certain way, but are unable to specify the kind of experience-situation to which the concept, used in that way, would apply, then we are not really envisaging any legitimate use of that concept at all. In so using it, we shall not merely be saying what we do not know; we shall not really know what we are saying.[82]

For knowledge, both sense perception and understanding are necessary, and we can no more have understanding without sensibility than we can get knowledge from sensibility without understanding. 'Without sensibility no object would be given to us, without understanding no object would be thought. Thoughts without content are empty, intuitions without concepts are blind... The understanding can intuit nothing, the senses can think nothing. Only through their union can knowledge arise'.[83] It follows from this that any attempt to use understanding in a 'transcendent' way outside the bounds of sensibility, or beyond our experience, is doomed to futility since in such a situation understanding would have no object; there would be nothing to understand. Nevertheless we are led, almost irresistibly, to attempt to use reason in this way. Thus, it is a natural tendency of the mind to see the world of experience in a unified and connected way, as a 'systematic unity', and to this end we suppose that it originated 'from an all-sufficient necessary cause' or God. This is innocent enough if it is seen for what it is – a methodological supposition or heuristic device, or as Kant calls it, 'a regulative principle of reason'. But if it becomes hypostatised and taken for a real objective entity, then we fall into illusion.[84]

All attempts to prove the existence of God, either 'cosmologically' by way of the principle of causality, or 'ontologically' by analysis of the concept of God, are therefore rejected by Kant since they inevitably involve either the fallacy of taking the world as a totality or whole which requires explanation for its existence,[85] or they involve an illicit extension of the principle of causality beyond the world of experience,[86] or they involve an illicit transition from the conceptual to the real order. Kant shows with great brilliance how we are fatally tempted to use understanding beyond all possible experience, and how plausible this 'transcendent' use of reason can seem, particularly with respect to the concept of God. He is not solely concerned to expose the illusory character of this kind of reasoning, but he also wishes to show the pathological structure of the illusion and so of all attempts at speculative religion where, it is claimed, God is attained by speculative reason. One might say indeed that Kant is trying to answer Hume's mystified query as to how belief in God persists despite all the evidence to the contrary.[87]

At the end of his discussion of the speculative proofs of the existence of God, Kant sums up his 'critique of all theology based upon speculative principles of reason'. 'All attempts', he says, 'to construct a theology through purely speculative reason, by means of a transcendental procedure, are without result'.[88] And he goes on: 'Through concepts alone, it is quite impossible to advance to the discovery of new objects and supernatural beings; and it is useless to appeal to experience, which in all cases yields only appearances.[89] As far as speculative reason is concerned, God cannot be known, and necessarily cannot be known, and 'there is not one shred of evidence for believing in the existence of God or in a future life'.[90] If, however, it is impossible for us – given the constitution of the human mind – ever to know God speculatively or ever to be able to affirm the proposition 'God exists' as true, Kant certainly does not want to say that the concept of God is *in itself* meaningless. If it were meaningless, then of course we could neither affirm it nor deny it; but this is not what Kant means when he says that we can neither affirm nor deny the existence of God by speculative reason. We can neither affirm nor deny the existence of God because God is beyond the reach of speculative reason; but for Kant what is beyond the reach of speculative reason is not thereby beyond the reach of *all* reason and so meaningless. How does speculative reason know that there is another realm of reason in which objects of thought may be meaningful, even if they are not meaningful (though this does not mean that they are therefore meaningless) for speculative reason? Or, put in another way, how does speculative reason see both sides of the limits that circumscribe it, so that it is able to know that there is a sphere that it cannot know? This, as we shall see presently, is a difficulty which Kant never satisfactorily resolves.

Kant supposes that, by showing the limits of speculative reason, we also show that all purported *dis*proofs of the existence of God are equally illusory, and in addition that deistic and anthropomorphic conceptions of the nature of God are without foundation. We can thus purify the idea of God, so to speak.

> Such critical treatment [Kant says] is, indeed, far from being difficult inasmuch as the same grounds which have enabled us to demonstrate the inability of human reason to maintain the existence of such a being must also suffice to prove the invalidity of all counter-assertions. For from what source could we, through a purely speculative employment of reason, derive the knowledge that there is *no* supreme being as ultimate ground of all things, or that it has none of the attributes which, arguing from their consequences we represent to ourselves as analogical with the dynamical realities of a thinking being, or (as the anthropomorphists contend) that it must be subject to all the limitations which sensibility inevitably imposes on those intelligences which are known to us through experience. Thus, while for the merely speculative employment of reason the supreme being remains a mere *ideal*, it is yet an *ideal without a flaw*, a concept which completes and crowns the whole of human knowledge. Its objective reality cannot indeed be proved, but also cannot be disproved, by merely speculative reason.[91]

The benefit of Kant's agnosticism is that religion is removed from any dependence upon philosophy and so is not exposed to philosophical doubt and refutation in the way in which all forms of religious intellectualism are.

In the case of Maimonides and Aquinas we saw that they distinguished sharply between the functions of philosophical reason with respect to the existence and attributes of God on the one hand, and with respect to the 'revealed' articles of faith on the other hand. Philosophical reason could prove the former, but it could only show the negative possibility or non-impossibility of the latter. Kant, however, denies any positive demonstrative function to philosophy apropos of God and his attributes, and holds that its only function is the negative one of showing the non-impossibility of God and of any other objects of religious faith. In other words, he extends the negative or defensive role of philosophy with regard to religion even to what Aquinas calls 'the preambles of faith'. But, as we have seen, it is not at all clear how speculative reason can be aware that even this negative possibility of the existence of God obtains, since in order for it to know that it is limited (so that there is thus 'room for faith') it must, so to speak, be able to stand outside the limits. As we remarked before, although agnosticism appears to be a plausible position, it is in fact difficult to make sense of it. 'I have found it necessary', Kant says in the famous passage in the *Critique of Pure Reason*, 'to deny knowledge, in order to make room for faith',[92] meaning by this that speculative knowledge of God (and of freedom and immortality) is to be denied in order to allow us to become aware of his reality (not to 'know' him in the strict sense) through practical reason and morality.[93] But how can we deny that we do have knowledge of a realm of objects, and at the same time know that they are apprehensible in another non-speculative way? We can know that our sense knowledge is limited by the nature of our sense organs and that there are sensible objects that *we* are unable to sense; but it is paradoxical to hold that our intellectual knowledge is limited in an analogous way by 'the constitution of the mind' and that there are objects which are in principle unknowable.[94]

These questions will come up anew when we examine Kant's theory of practical reason and its implications for religion. But before we go into that topic we must say something of Kant's own personal view of religion. Though it boggles the imagination to think of the stern sage of Königsberg avidly reading the fervent prose of Jean-Jacques, Kant was in fact an enthusiastic admirer of Rousseau and there is little doubt that the latter's ideas about religion made a deep impression on him. Thus in the remarkable 'Confession de foi d'un vicaire savoyard' that forms the latter part of Book IV of *Émile*, Rousseau advanced a view of religious belief that radically changed Kant's early Wolffian rationalism. For Rousseau the essence of religion consists in its moral dimension and not in 'subtle dogmas'. Religious belief is not a matter of speculation but an affair of 'the heart'. 'Consult your heart while I speak', says the Savoyard priest to Émile, 'that is all I ask'.[95] The idea of revelation and of the Church as custodian of the truths of revelation are both rejected, and the relevance of miracles is likewise denied. The Gospel, Jean-Jacques says through his simple priest, is full of incredible things, things repugnant to reason, things which no natural man can understand or accept... This is the unwilling scepticism in which I rest; but this scepticism is in no way painful to me, for it does not extend to matters of practice, and I am well assured as to the principles underlying all my duties. [And he concludes:] I serve God in the simplicity of my heart. I only seek to know what affects my conduct. As to those dogmas which have no effect upon my actions or morality, dogmas about which so many people torment themselves, I give no heed to them.[96]

For Rousseau it is through the conscience above all that we become aware of God, and since the voice of conscience is innate in every man learned and unlearned, whether they be philosophers or non-philosophers, both morality and religion are available to all men and not just to a few scholars:

Conscience! Conscience! Divine instinct; immortal voice from heaven; sure guide for a creature ignorant and finite indeed, yet intelligent and free; infallible judge of good and evil, making man like to God. In thee consists the excellence of man's nature and the morality of his actions; apart from thee I find nothing in myself to raise me above the beasts, nothing but the sad privilege of wandering from one error to another, by the help of an unbridled understanding and a reason which knows no principle. Thank heaven we have now got rid of that alarming show of philosophy; we may be men without being scholars.[97]

Again, Rousseau's parish priest warns of the dangers of philosophy regarding religion:

The abuse of knowledge causes incredulity. The learned always despise the opinions of the crowd and each of them must have his own opinion. A haughty philosophy leads to atheism just as much as blind devotion leads to fanaticism.[98]

Rousseau's point here about the universal accessibility of moral and religious truth, as contrasted with the exclusivism of philosophy, greatly impressed Kant, as he himself testified: 'I am a seeker by nature,' Kant wrote in 1764, two years after the publication of *Émile*,

avid for knowledge. I sincerely thought that the greatness of man lies there and that in this way the cultivated man is to be distinguished from the plebs. Rousseau put me back on the right road. Rousseau is another Newton. Newton completed the science of external nature, Rousseau that of the internal universe or of man. Just as Newton laid bare the order and regularity of the external world, so Rousseau discovered the hidden nature of man. It was imperative to recover a true conception of the nature of man. Philosophy is nothing but the practical knowledge of man.[99]

Rousseau, it might be noted, had in *Émile* proposed a striking anticipation of Kant's argument for the immortality of the soul in the *Critique of Practical Reason*. God is supremely just and therefore supremely good. He would not be good if people lived just lives and were not made happy as a consequence. In the present condition of things, however, this conjunction of justice and happiness does not obtain, so that if man's life ended with the death of the body God would be guilty of deception and injustice and so not good. Therefore man must survive the death of his body in order that justice and happiness may coincide. 'If the soul is immaterial, it may survive the body; and if it so survives, Providence is justified'.[100]

Kant's personal views on religion are expressed in their clearest and frankest form in a letter written in 1775. This is such an important confession of faith that it is worthwhile citing it at some length:

> I distinguish the *teachings of* Christ [he writes] from the *report* we have of those teachings. In order that the former may be seen in their purity, I seek above all to separate out the moral teachings from all the dogmas of the New Testament. These moral teachings are certainly the funda-mental doctrine of the Gospels, and the remainder can only serve as an auxiliary to them. Dogmas tell us only what God has done to help us see our frailty in seeking justification before him, whereas the moral law tells us what we must do to make ourselves worthy of justification... Our trust in God is unconditional, that is, it is not accompanied by any inquisitive desire to know how his purposes will be achieved or, still less, by any presumptuous confidence that the soul's salvation will follow from our acceptance of certain Gospel disclosures. That is the meaning of the moral faith that I find in the Gospels, when I seek out the pure, funda-mental teachings that underlie the mixture of facts and revelations there. Perhaps, in view of the opposition of Judaism, miracles and revelations were needed, in those days, to promulgate and disseminate a pure religion, one that would do away with all the world's dogmas. And perhaps it was necessary to have many *ad hominem* arguments, which would have great force in those times. But once the doctrine of the purity of conscience in faith and of the good transformation of our lives has been sufficiently propagated as the only true religion for man's salvation (the faith that God, in a manner we need not at all understand, will provide what our frail natures lack, without our seeking his aid by means of the so-called worship that religious fanaticism always demands) – when this

true religious structure has been built up so that it can maintain itself in the world – then the scaffolding must be taken down. I respect the reports of the evangelists and apostles [Kant continues] and I put my humble trust in that means of reconciliation with God of which they have given us historical tidings – or in any means that God, in his secret counsels, may have concealed. For I do not become in the least bit a better man if I know this, since it concerns only what God does; and I dare not be so presumptuous as to declare before God that this is the real means, the only means whereby I can attain my salvation and, so to speak, swear my soul and my salvation on it. For what those men give us are only their reports. I am not close enough to their times to be able to make such dangerous and audacious decisions. Moreover, even if I could be sure, it would not make me in any way more worthy of the good, were I to confess it, swear it, and fill up my soul with it, though that may be of help to some people. On the contrary, nothing is needed for my union with this divine force except my using my natural God-given powers in such a way as not to be unworthy of his aid or, if you prefer, unfit for it.

Kant goes on to emphasise that it is 'moral faith' that is of the essence of religion, all else – confessions of faith, appeals to holy names, rituals and observances, veneration of the person of Jesus, the Gospel stories – being secondary and dispensable. 'I seek in the Gospels not the ground of my faith but its fortification', he says; and again, 'the essential and most excellent part of the teachings of Christ is this: that righteousness is the sum of all religion and that we ought to seek it with all our might'.[101]

From this it is clear that for Kant, as for Rousseau, the essence of religion lies in 'moral faith', the 'unconditional trust in divine aid', 'the striving for purity of conscience and the conscientious conversion of our lives toward the good'. The Judaeo-Christian revelation, the gospels, miracles, religious observances and rituals, prayer, theological dogmas, historical reports about Jesus, are all adventitious and dispensable devices, though they may be of some help in bringing simple people to see 'the necessity of moral faith'. Again, even if the latter are not the 'ground' of religious faith they may nevertheless fortify it. At the same time, while rejecting religious revelation in any speculative or theoretical sense – that is, as the disclosure of certain truths about the divine order – Kant seems to admit that there is a place for God's grace supporting and fortifying the human will in the pursuit of the good: 'God, in a manner we need not at all understand, will provide what our frail natures lack'; 'God will supplement our efforts and supply the good that is in our power'. We could then speak of a 'practical' revelation, a supernatural supplement to the will. However, we cannot merit this divine help through specifically religious means – prayers, religious ceremonies, rituals, belief in miracles and revelations: 'No confession of faith, no appeal to holy names nor any observance of religious ceremonies can help – though the consoling hope is offered that, if we do as much good as is in our power, trusting in the unknown and mysterious help of God (without meritorious "works" of any sort) we may partake of this divine supplement'.[102]

The task of the *Critique of Pure Reason* is, as we have seen, to display the limits of pure reason. But for Kant this negative task was simply the preparation for the more positive one of making room for practical reason, or showing the negative possibility of the whole order of morality. 'On a cursory view of the present work,' Kant says, 'it may seem that its results are merely *negative*, warning us that we must never venture in speculative reason beyond the limits of experience'. But, he goes on, the *Critique of Pure Reason* also shows by the same stroke that these limits are established by the nature of sensibility and not by reason, so that the scope of speculative reason is not coterminous with reason as such, nor are 'the bounds of sensibility co-extensive with the real'. There can possibly be another kind of employment of reason, and there can possibly be other kinds of 'realities'. This other kind of exercise of reason is what Kant calls practical reason and these other kinds of 'realities' are disclosed within the sphere of practical reason. The argument of the *Critique of Pure Reason*, Kant says, 'removes an obstacle which stands in the way of the employment of practical reason, nay threatens to destroy it', and in this way has a 'positive and very important use'. 'At least this is so', Kant goes on, 'immediately we are convinced that there is an absolutely necessary *practical* employment of pure reason – the *moral* – in which it inevitably goes beyond the limits of sensibility. Though practical reason, in thus proceeding, requires no assistance from speculative reason, it must yet be assured against its opposition that reason may not be brought into conflict with itself'.[103] In order fully to understand Kant's doctrine here, we have to take account of his distinction between things as they appear to us in experience and things as they are in themselves. 'All possible speculative knowledge of reason', he says, 'is limited to mere objects of experience'.[104] But at the same time the objects of our experience also exist as things in themselves ('otherwise we should be landed in the absurd conclusion that there can be appearances without anything that appears'). We cannot, of course, *know* speculatively things as they are in themselves, but we can *think* them in the sense that we can see that they are not self-contradictory, or are logically possible. Kant's argument here is very difficult to follow, for he seems to imply that although we cannot know things in themselves or even their 'real possibility', we can nevertheless have some kind of cognitive apprehension of them in that we see them to be logically possible. But even to think something as logically possible presupposes that I know it in some minimal sense; I must at least have a *concept* of it, even if I do not know that it is instantiated or has what Kant calls 'objective validity'.

At all events, Kant seems to think that speculative reason leaves the way open for practical reason without in any way delimiting or specifying what is really possible within the latter realm. All that we know speculatively is that the law of causality applies only to the phenomenal world of our experience, so that there would be nothing self-contradictory in supposing some kind of noumenal agency (e.g. the will) that was not subject to causality but was free. But we do not as yet *know*, prior to an analysis of practical reason, that the human will is *in fact* free. In the same way, we apprehend that there would be nothing self-contradictory in supposing the existence of God, but we do not *know* that the concept of God has objective validity until we follow out the implications of practical reason or morality. It is only within the sphere of morality that the concept of God comes to have 'real possibility' for us, and not merely logical possibility, though Kant does not explain how the category of possibility, which belongs to the sphere of speculative reason, can also apply within the sphere of practical reason.

It is here that we must turn to the *Critique of Practical Reason*.[105] The idea of God, Kant argues, arises when we analyse what is implied in our moral willing of the highest good. All human beings cannot but desire perfect happiness, and they equally cannot but hope that if they fulfil their moral obligations they will attain happiness. But, Kant argues, the existence of God is a condition of this hope being justified, for it is only God who can secure an 'exact coincidence of happiness with morality'. As he puts it:

> The postulate of the possibility of a highest derived good (the best world) is at the same time the postulate of the reality of a highest original good; and it is not merely our privilege but a necessity connected with duty as a requisite to presuppose the possibility of this highest good. This presup-position is made only under the condition of the existence of God, and this condition inseparably connects this supposition with duty. Therefore it is morally necessary to assume the existence of God.[106]

Kant emphasises that the existence of God is not the condition of morality or obligation as such, but of morality in so far as it is concerned with bringing about the highest good:[107] 'Through the concept of the highest good as the object and final end of pure practical reason, the moral law leads to religion'.[108]

What kind of assumption is involved in postulating the existence of God as the condition of achieving the highest moral good? Or, put in another way, what is the 'moral necessity' of which Kant speaks as attaching to the existence of God? At times Kant speaks as though the assumption is of a speculative kind, and that the necessity that belongs to the postulation of the existence of God is the same as that which belongs to any explanatory hypothesis. The final end of morality would not be attainable unless God exists; but the final end of morality must be attainable; therefore God must exist. As Kant puts it in the *Critique of Pure Reason*: 'Reason finds itself constrained to assume' the existence of God, 'otherwise it would have to regard the moral laws as empty figments of the brain, since without this postulate the necessary consequence which is itself connected with these laws could not follow'.[109] This is a piece of speculative reasoning, even though the 'facts' it is attempting to explain or save are facts about morality. Instead of arguing to the existence of God from facts about the world (God being postulated as an explanatory hypothesis to account for the mutability or contingency of things in the world), we argue here to the existence of God from facts about our moral life (God being postulated to explain the fact that we have an obligation to seek to further the highest good).[110]

At other times, however, Kant argues that the 'inference' that leads us to assume the existence of God is wholly practical in mode. We find ourselves under an obligation to promote the highest good, and we adopt the practical attitude that this can be effectively realised, and that, despite appearances, it will coincide with happiness. If God is a postulate of the practical reason, then our knowledge of God must be couched in terms of practical reason – not in terms of 'is' but in terms of 'ought'; not in indicatives but in imperatives. As Kant notes, practical reason cannot be concerned with postulating the existence of hypothetical entities, 'since such a supposition concerns only the theoretical use of reason'.[111] 'God exists' therefore would have to be rendered in practical terms as follows: 'Act with confidence or firm hope that the highest good may be secured, that happiness and morality will coincide, and that nature and morality come into harmony'. From this point of view, to believe in God is to take up a fundamental moral attitude, an attitude presupposed to other moral attitudes. What this involves may be seen, Kant suggests, by looking at other forms of morality that do not make this presupposition, or adopt this attitude about the ultimate coincidence of virtue and happiness. Thus the Epicureans had based their morality upon happiness, without expecting any coincidence between happiness and obligation, while on the other hand the Stoics based their morality on obligation without expecting any coincidence between obligation and happiness. In both cases morality was distorted, for in the one case it became sub-human (arbitrary inclination taking the place of duty), and in the other it became supra-human ('something which is contradicted by all our knowledge of men').[112] To believe in God, then, is to adopt an attitude that helps us to avoid these distortions and to make a truly human morality possible. Put in another way, it is the practical conviction that the *apparent* diseconomy between nature and morality is not final or absolute. This is in fact the gist of Christianity:

> The moral law does not of itself promise happiness, for the latter is not, according to the concepts of any order of nature, necessarily connected with obedience to the law. Christian ethics supplies this defect ... by presenting a world wherein reasonable beings single-mindedly devote themselves to the moral law; this is the Kingdom of God, in which nature and morality come into a harmony, which is foreign to each as such, through a holy Author of the world, who makes possible the derived highest good.[113]

If we were to follow out this vein of Kant's reasoning we would have to say that all talk about God would have to be translated into the practical mode, that is in terms of obligations and imperatives; or, in other words, that the existence of God has to be translated into terms of human needs, attitudes, actions. And in this sense religion would be coterminous with a truly human morality which respects the conditions of the moral will. Kant almost says this in a number of passages:

> Religion [he says] is the recognition of all duties as divine commands, not as sanctions, i.e. arbitrary and contingent ordinances of a foreign will, but as essential laws of any free will as such.[114] [And again] Granted that the pure moral law inexorably binds every man as a command (not as a rule of prudence) the righteous man may say: I will that there be a God, that my existence in this world be also an existence in a pure world of the understanding outside the system of natural connections... I stand by this and will not give up this belief, for this is the only case where my interest inevitably determines my judgement because I will not yield anything of this interest.[115]

In other words, my practical interest in promoting the highest moral good 'determines' my judgement that there is a God.

The consequence of this, however, is that we cannot in any way know that God exists, nor indeed can we speak of God existing apart from human needs and attitudes and action. If God is a postulate of the practical reason, then we cannot make any truth claims about him, nor about the religious sphere at all. As we have already said, to believe in God will not be to assent to the existence of an entity, but rather to adopt a certain fundamental moral attitude or to make an act of practical faith about the ultimate attainability of moral perfection and the coincidence of happiness and virtue.[116] Kant, however, sees the difficulties that attend this position and he tries to argue that, although God is a postulate of the practical reason, we can nevertheless speak about the existence of God and make truth claims about the religious order in general. We can, that is, *know* through practical reason that God exists, and further that he exists apart from human practical interests.

But this is surely a case of wanting to have your cake and eat it. For either this knowledge of God's existence is speculative in mode, that is inferred by speculative reason as an explanatory hypothesis to account for the 'facts' of morality;[117] or it is in the practical mode and so expressible only in terms of moral imperatives. The first alternative falls foul of the same objections that Kant urges against the cosmological proofs for the existence of God, for even if the moral 'facts' are not the same as sensible facts from which the cosmological proofs start, we still have to extrapolate the principle of causality beyond the world of sense experience in order to account for them, and this of course for Kant is quite illicit. More generally, as H. L. Mansel says, if Kant is right:

> it follows indeed that the infinite is beyond the reach of man's arguments, but only as it is also beyond the reach of his feelings or volitions. We cannot indeed reason to the existence of an infinite Cause from the presence of finite effects, nor contemplate the infinite as a finite mode of knowledge; but neither can we feel the infinite in the form of a finite affection, nor discern it as the law of finite action.[118]

The second alternative, as we have seen, has the consequence that we cannot make any truth claims about God or the religious order, and if this is so then it is difficult to see how we can in any sense 'know' God or have any religious knowledge. Practical reason, on Kant's own account, cannot tell us what is or what exists, or make truth claims; it can only formulate imperatives commanding us to do certain things, what attitudes to take up, what we ought to do. Its whole purpose is not to describe what *is* the case but to prescribe what *ought* to be done and in this sense it cannot give us any knowledge about reality. We can, however, by *speculative* reflection on practical reason and morality, attempt to show its presuppositions – what reality must be like in order for there to be the phenomenon of morality and all that it implies – and in this sense we can (if we allow that Kant's argument is valid) gain a *speculative* knowledge of God as an explanatory hypothesis. We cannot, however, as Kant suggests, have a *practical knowledge* of God even in the minimal sense he gives to such a 'knowledge'.[119]

> We shall make no progress [a Kantian scholar writes] in our under-
> standing of Kant's conception of practical reason unless we recognise the
> basic paradox which lies at the heart of any discussion of practical reason.
> Practical reason is reason at work in the field of action. A *discussion* of
> practical reason is an example of speculative reason at work... Knowing
> or proving freedom would be an activity of theoretical reason and in
> making freedom an object of knowledge we should have converted it into
> something other than itself; in fact, as Kant seems to be fully aware, we
> should have converted it into the only category of knowledge which
> could be relevant, namely, natural causality... Freedom is not and cannot
> be known. Freedom is acted or directly experienced in action or, to put
> the point paradoxically, freedom is known in action.[120]

Precisely the same point could be made about the other 'postulates of practical reason', God and immortality. If God is a postulate of practical reason
then God is not and cannot be known. Knowing God would be an activity of
theoretical reason and in making God an object of knowledge we would
convert him into something other than himself, for the concept of God only
has meaning in and through moral action.

We are therefore forced to conclude that Kant's strenuous attempt to
provide a systematic basis for Pascal's and Rousseau's appeal to the 'heart' in
matters of religion as against theoretical reason, does not succeed. The heart
cannot have 'reasons' that reason knows nothing of; and practical reason
cannot 'know' things that are inaccessible to speculative reason.

The ambivalence in Kant's thought that has been already remarked,
continues in his later philosophy of religion. Thus in his work *Religion within
the Limits of Reason Alone* (1791) Kant appears to identify religion with
morality and he offers a very bold and comprehensive reductionist account
of religious doctrines as disguised moral prescriptions.[121] As it has been put:

'Kant sees in religion neither an enlargement of our speculative knowledge, nor yet a collection of special duties towards God distinct from those to our neighbour, but a peculiar way of regarding the latter'.[122] Similarly in *The Dispute of the Faculties* (1798) Kant defines true religion as 'that faith which finds the essential feature of all honour paid to God in human morality'.[123] Again he says in the same work that 'the God who speaks through our own Practical Reason is an infallible and universal interpreter of this work of his and there can indeed be no other.[124] This apparent identification of religion with morality is expressed in even more extreme terms in Kant's last writings, the so-called *Opus Postumum* (1800–03). 'God is not', he says, 'a Being outside of me, but merely a thought within me. God is the morally practical reason giving laws to itself'. And again, 'The proposition, "There is a God", means no more than: "There is in human reason, determining itself according to morality, a supreme principle which perceives itself determined and necessitated to act without cessation in accordance with such a principle" '.[125] God therefore is not a transcendent being distinct from our practical reason confronting us with moral duties. 'There is a God,' Kant says, 'for there is a categorical imperative of duty, before which all knees do bow, whether they be in heaven or in the earth or under the earth; and whose Name is holy, without our having to suppose a substance which represents this Being to the senses'.[126]

Kant, however, did not follow out this train of thought to its final conclusion so as to deny absolutely the existence of God conceived apart from morality. Thus, alongside the passages just cited from the *Opus Postumum* there are others that speak of God as an actual entity existing externally to us,[127] and in the famous letter to Friedrich Wilhelm II (1794) after the official censure of *Religion within the Limits of Reason Alone*, Kant claims that his philosophy of religion is perfectly in accord with the traditional doctrines of Christianity.[128] Again, in *The Dispute of the Faculties* Kant admits that there is a modest place for theology, narrowly conceived as the study of the historical representation of God in the Bible (as distinct from the God revealed through 'moral faith' or practical reason), and he says 'the biblical theologian proves that God exists by means of the fact that he has spoken in the Bible'.[129]

There is no doubt, however, that Kant's dominant view is that propositions about God, and indeed all religious propositions, are only fully meaningful if they are translated into the practical mode, that is, into the form of moral imperatives or prescriptions. But Kant shrinks from the consequences of this view, namely that we can no longer speak of God or other religious realities existing apart from morality or make any truth claims about them, nor can we *know* God in any adequate sense. The best we can say is that God is experienced in moral action in its highest and most complete form; or rather, more exactly, we should have to say that God is experienced as a dimension of moral action. In this context to believe in God and to be a religious person *just is* to act in the confident hope that the pursuit of the highest moral good is not vain and that the apparent disharmony between the world of nature and the world of human morality is apparent only. To evade these consequences Kant tries to show that practical reason discloses the existence of God as a presupposition of its own exercise with respect to its pursuit of the highest moral good. But, as we have seen, this leads Kant into paradox, for to know the existence of God as a presupposition of practical reason is an exercise of *speculative* reason, and for Kant God can never be known by speculative reason.

Kant's monumental attempt to combine philosophical agnosticism with religion defined in terms of the 'heart' or morality or the practical reason, is thus beset by fatal difficulties. For, first, it is hard to see how a position of pure agnosticism with regard to the existence of God is philosophically viable. The concept of God must either be logically possible or meaningful, or logically impossible or meaningless, and if it is known to be logically possible (in whatever way this might be done) then, to that extent, we must have some speculative knowledge of it. Whether or not the concept of God is actually instantiated or not is of course a further question, though, as St Anselm in his *Proslogion* saw very acutely, the question as to the logical possibility of the concept God and that of the instantiation or non-instantiation of the concept cannot really be separated in the same way as with ordinary concepts. I may very well have the concept of a unicorn and yet remain agnostic about whether that concept is instantiated or not; but, St Anselm argues, I cannot in the same sense have the concept of *God* and remain agnostic about whether there is an actual instance of that concept or not. The debate between the theist and non-theist is not really over whether or not there is actually an instance of the concept of God, but rather over whether the very concept of God is logically possible or meaningful. In this sense God either necessarily exists or necessarily does not exist and there is no place left for agnosticism, at least of the Kantian kind. Second, as we have seen, Kant's ingenious attempt to define God and religion in practical or moral terms leads him into deep waters. We cannot have a practical knowledge of God, for the notion of 'practical knowledge' is, on Kant's own premisses, a paradoxical one. Again, the faith for which philosophy makes room is no longer religious faith in any recognisable sense, for it is identified (albeit tentatively) with morality itself.[130]

KIERKEGAARD: SPECULATION AND SUBJECTIVITY

Kierkegaard (1813–55) was above all a theologian, or rather a religious prophet attempting to awaken us to the need for unconditional religious commitment. And it is mainly for this reason that his typical style was that of rhetorical exaggeration and paradox and irony. Kierkegaard used any dialectical means that would jolt readers out of their complacency and self-conceit and conventional behaviour, and into a realisation of the need for opting vitally for themselves and for making the 'leap' of faith. Again, Kierkegaard's thought was elaborated largely by way of exasperated reaction against the 'System' of his arch-enemy Hegel.[131] In countering the extravagances of Hegel's religious rationalism ('there is no philosophy so harmful to Christianity as the Hegelian'),[132] Kierkegaard was led into equal and opposite anti-rational extravagances, so that he appears to exalt the ir-rational and absurd and paradoxical at the expense of the rational and intelli-gible. If we took Kierkegaard's thought on the relationship between philosophy and religion at its own face value, we would be tempted to dismiss it as sheer and wilful obscurantism – a deliberate denial of reason and a perverse glorying in the irrationality and absurdity of religious faith, as though Kierkegaard held that it was precisely *because* religious faith was paradoxical and flouted reason that it was thereby believable.

Both Kierkegaard's friends and his enemies have indeed often inter-preted his thought in this way – as though for him irrationality were the *ground* of religious faith. However, if we take the trouble to look beneath the surface of his rhetoric and his prophetic exaggerations, and if we make allowance for the fact that for him Reason is equated with Hegel, we can no longer see Kierkegaard as an obscurantist. We can, in fact, discern the outlines of a philosophy of religion of a Pascalian and Kantian type, even if its metaphysical and epistemological underpinnings are not fully developed.

All honour to philosophy [Kierkegaard says in the *Concluding Unscientific Postscript*], all praise to everyone who brings a genuine devotion to its service. To deny the value of speculation (though one might wish that the money-changers in the forecourts of the temple could be banished as profane) would be, in my opinion, to prostitute oneself. It would be particularly stupid in one whose energies are for the most part, and in proportion to aptitude and opportunity, consecrated to its service; especially stupid in one who admires the Greeks. For he must know that Aristotle, in treating of what happiness is, identifies the highest happiness with the joys of thought, recalling in this connection the blessed pastime of the eternal gods in speculation. And he must furthermore have some conception of, and respect for, the fearless enthusiasm of the philosophical scholar, his persistent devotion to the service of the Idea.[133]

It is only when philosophy, and reason in general, attempt to play a positive role in the religious sphere – pretending to explain and prove and justify the objects of religious faith – that it is to be rejected, though even this rejection is in part the work of philosophy itself. Philosophy itself sees that faith has an object and mode of exercise other than and beyond its own. The Christian 'believes against the understanding', and 'also uses understanding to make sure that he believes against the understanding'.[134]

Kierkegaard's basic position is in fact very similar to that of Kant. But Kierkegaard is more consistent than Kant in that he pushes his philosophical agnosticism *vis-à-vis* faith and the religious order to its logical conclusion – a conclusion that Kant himself baulked at. By reason, Kierkegaard argues, we understand that there is a limit to reason and that there is at least the possibility of objects existing that we do not and cannot know – the 'Unknown' as he calls it.[135] But for reason, this 'Unknown' remains strictly unknown and unknowable and it cannot be specified or determined in any way. Kant held that speculative reason could at least apprehend the logical possibility of God and to that extent specify or determine what was beyond the reach of speculative reason. And he also held that this logical possibility could be shown through practical reason to be a real possibility. Kierkegaard, however, argues that if there is an 'Unknown', then we cannot know it in any positive or determinate way. 'What then is the Unknown? It is the limit to which the Reason repeatedly comes, and in so far ... it is the different, the absolutely different. But because it is the absolutely different, there is no mark by which it could be distinguished'.[136] In particular, we certainly have no right to identify the Unknown with God. Dr Johnson once remarked of Jacob Boehme that if he had really experienced the Unutterable he ought not to have tried to utter it; the Unutterable is not something that can be uttered by some special or extraordinary means of expression, but it is that which is precisely beyond the limits of intelligible utterance. In the same way, for

Kierkegaard the Unknown is that which lies beyond the limits of knowledge of any kind – though even this way of putting it is misleading in that it suggests that the Unknown is a determinate realm of (knowable) objects.

Philosophical reason, therefore, knows that there is the possibility of objects existing that we do not and cannot know by philosophical reason. And reason also knows that there is a difference between its own 'objective' and speculative mode of apprehension and what Kierkegaard calls 'subjectivity' – a special mode of non-speculative, 'personal' apprehension (if indeed we can call it apprehension, since it is not a form of cognition but rather a form of willed commitment).

It is in this way that philosophy allows room for religious faith, for religious faith is concerned with objects that are beyond the range of reason, and its mode of apprehension also differs from that of philosophy in that it is a species of 'subjectivity'. The first point is obvious enough, for God is infinite, whereas the reason can know only what is finite: 'The understanding is related to the dialectic of finitude'.[137] Again, the objects of faith are 'paradoxical', for Christianity claims that God (the infinite) became man (the finite) in the person of Christ so as to do away with the 'absolute unlikeness (between God and sinful man) in absolute likeness'.[138] Further, the objects of religious faith are such that they demand a vital and personal response and commitment from us, and not merely speculative assent: 'Faith belongs to and has its home in the existential, and in all eternity it has nothing to do with knowledge… Faith expresses a relation from personality to personality.[139] God is not an object we assent to, or contemplate; he is a person who invites a personal interest and response from us. To the extent that we speculatively contemplate God we cannot be interested in him, for speculation means that we put the object at a distance from us and judge it in an impersonal way, whereas my interest in God implies that I, this individual person, see him and respond to him as the source of my own eternal happiness.[140] For Kierkegaard this is a strict either/or; *either* we are infinitely interested in God, *or* we are convinced speculatively of his truth.

> The inquiring subject [he says] must be in one or the other of two situations. Either he is in faith convinced of the truth of Christianity, and in faith assured of his own relationship to it; in which case he cannot be infinitely interested in all the rest, since faith itself is the infinite interest in Christianity… Or the inquirer is, on the other hand, not in an attitude of faith, but objectively in an attitude of contemplation and hence not infinitely interested in the determination of the question.[141]

The object of religious faith, we have said, is such that it demands a practical commitment from us, not speculative assent. But how are these objects proposed to us in the first place? They are, Kierkegaard says, proposed by God's grace. However, before we consider this point we must examine Kierkegaard's difficult and ambiguous notion of 'subjectivity' in more detail, since religious faith is a species of subjectivity. Kierkegaard says a number of quite different things about subjectivity and it is not easy to reconcile all of them; however, we may try to systematise his ideas by considering the mode of subjectivity, its object and its ground. As to its mode, it goes without saying that for Kierkegaard subjectivity has nothing to do with subjectivism in the sense that belief is equated with feeling or emotion or pure psychological experience. Rather it denotes personal appropriation of an object, as against impersonal assent to, or contemplation of, it. As such, it implies that I have personal interest in or 'passion' towards the object; that I value it as being important for me and my life; that I make a practical commitment to, or choice or option of, the object. This last is an important point for Kierkegaard, for whereas the objects of reason necessitate our assent by their evidence, the objects of subjectivity require that we freely choose them, that we take a 'risk', that we make a 'leap'. As with Pascal, the freedom of the act of faith is of its essence for Kierkegaard. An object of faith that necessitated our response to it would precisely not be an object of faith, any more than a personal relationship that was imposed on us or exacted from us by force would be an authentic personal relationship. 'Freedom is the true wonderful lamp; when a man rubs it with ethical passion, God comes into being for him'.[142]

As to its object, subjectivity is concerned with the individual existent, as against the general and universal and ideal and systematic, since it is only the individual existent that can invite practical interest and 'passion' from us. Existence is always individual existence, whereas reason is always concerned with the universal or the ideal, and that is why we cannot reason systematically about existence.

> I always reason from existence, not toward existence, whether I move in the sphere of palpable sensible fact or in the realm of thought. I do not for example prove that a stone exists, but that some existing thing is a stone. The procedure in a court of justice does not prove that a criminal exists, but that the accused, whose existence is given, is a criminal. Whether we call existence an *accessorium* or the eternal *prius*, it is never subject to demonstration.[143]

Again, the object of subjectivity is typically 'paradoxical'; 'it is a sign, an enigma faced with which reason can only say: "I cannot resolve it; for me that is not intelligible". But it does not follow therefrom that the paradox is in fact nonsense'.[144]

Finally, as to the ground of subjectivity, for Kierkegaard it is ultimately the will that posits any act of subjectivity. In Kantian terms, it is an act of the practical reason. To the extent that my assent is 'necessitated' by evidence, Kierkegaard seems to suggest, *I* do not believe, it is not *my* act any more than an act of the will is *my* act (or even an *act* in any real sense) if it is necessitated.[145]

This, then, is subjectivity, a mode of 'apprehension' that is at every point contrasted with speculative knowledge. And religious faith is subjectivity at its highest and most intense. In religious faith the interest at stake is an 'infinite interest', for my relationship with God concerns my eternal welfare, and for this reason it demands the greatest degree of personal response and commitment from me. At the same time, both the existential and 'paradoxical' features of the object of subjectivity are, in religious faith, intensified to the maximum, for God is both the supreme existent and the absolute paradox. And for the same reason, the role of the will is, in religious faith, at its most pronounced. The 'risk' and the 'leap' involved are of the most dramatic kind, and the introduction of reason and of any kind of rational proof or justification here is correspondingly at its most irrelevant or, as Kierkegaard likes to say, at its most comical.[146]

It is God's grace that ultimately moves the will to believe in God and that sustains us in a relationship of subjectivity towards him. 'God gave to his disciple the condition that enables him to see Him, opening for him the eyes of faith'.[147] We can, of course, prepare ourselves for the grace of faith. In fact, faith would be impossible for one who had not entered upon what Kierkegaard calls the 'ethical' plane of living and realised the importance of subjectivity and its irreducibility to the speculative. As Kierkegaard puts it: 'One does not prepare oneself to become attentive to Christianity by reading books, or by world-historical surveys, but by immersing oneself deeper in existence'.[148] Again, the consciousness of guilt and willingness to engage in 'self-annihilation' are necessary conditions of religious faith.[149] But, in the last resort, it is God's grace that motivates the will to believe, even if that grace works through man's freedom and is not to be conceived of as a quasi-miraculous suspension of man's 'natural' powers. 'To be a Christian means to accept thankfully this infinite grace of having to be a follower of Jesus Christ here in this life and thus being eternally saved by grace'.[150]

For Kierkegaard, therefore, religious faith is defined by its opposition at every point to philosophy, and it might be thought that, for this reason, it is nonsense to speak of him having a philosophy of religion. But despite this, and despite Kierkegaard's continual and savage denigration of philosophy and all its works, he does nevertheless have an implicit philosophy of religion. For him it is through philosophy that we know that there is the logical possibility of a realm that cannot be apprehended by philosophy or speculative reason. And again, it is through reason that we appreciate the difference between its own 'objective' mode of exercise and that of subjectivity. One might say, indeed, that Kierkegaard *depends* upon the contrast with philosophy in order to make his points about 'subjectivity' and religious faith. If we did not know first what the object and mode of philosophy was, we would not know what subjectivity and faith were. Or put in another way, we will only realise fully the true meaning of subjectivity if we have first been seriously tempted by the attractions of philosophy and 'the speculative view', as indeed Kierkegaard himself undoubtedly was. Thus, even though the functions of philosophy with respect to religion are all of them quite negative, they are nevertheless in a certain sense necessary to a right understanding of religious faith, and we can in this sense speak of Kierkegaard's philosophy of religion.

In *The Works of Love*, Kierkegaard indeed speaks of philosophical reflection as having a quasi-apologetical function in that it shows the impossibility of any rational justification of faith. Reflection helps us to understand that we cannot understand Christianity:

> People have always thought that reflection would destroy Christianity, and is its natural enemy. I hope I have shown, with God's aid, that religious reflection can retie the knot which a superficial reflection has unravelled for so many years. The authority of the Bible, and all that belongs to it, have been abolished, and it looks as if one were only waiting for the ultimate stage of reflection to clear up everything. But see how, on the contrary, reflection is going to render service by putting springs under Christianity again, and in such a way that it is able to hold out against reflection. Christianity of course remains completely unchanged; not a jot has been altered. But the struggle has become different: previously it was only between reflection and immediate simple Christianity; now it is between reflection and simplicity armed by reflection... The real task is not to understand Christianity but *to understand that one cannot understand it*. That is the sacred cause of faith, and reflection is sanctified by being used for it.[151]

The advantages of this view of philosophy's relations with religion are obvious enough. First, the autonomy of religious faith is guaranteed in that it has no kind of dependence upon philosophy or reason at all, so that its certainty cannot be affected by changes in philosophy. As a recent commentator has put it apropos of Kierkegaard: 'The point that he grasped so surely was that faith begins when its certainty is inward. If it were a certainty that resulted from a metaphysical scheme then it could be held only as long as that metaphysics is held. Now this is patently not true of faith'.[152] In fact, Kierkegaard transposes on to the religious plane Kant's fundamental position about the autonomy of morals. Just as for Kant any attempted justification or explanation of the moral order necessarily meant that it was explained away and reduced to other, non-moral, terms, so for Kierkegaard any 'explanation' or justification of the religious order would mean that it was being explained away in non-religious terms. The only kind of explanation that is in place here is that of showing that religious faith is religious faith and not another thing. It is the 'function of an explanation to render it evident that the something in question was this definite thing, so that the explanation took the obscurity away but not the object. Otherwise the explanation would not be an explanation but something quite different, namely, a correction'.[153]

The second advantage of this position is that it does full justice to the 'practical' character of religious belief. For Kierkegaard, to believe religiously is not to give assent to doctrines but to act in a certain way, to orient one's life in a certain way. 'Christianity is not a doctrine but an existential communication expressing an existential contradiction. If Christianity were a doctrine it would *eo ipso* not be an opposite to speculative thought, but rather a phase within it. Christianity has to do with existence, with the act of existing; but existence and existing constitute precisely the opposite of speculation'.[154]

The price that has to be paid for these advantages is, however, prohibitively high. For first, by placing faith beyond reason this position severs the religious order completely from philosophy and history and science and the entire realm of human culture – in fact from the whole of God's natural creation. Kierkegaard accepts this consequence. 'If it were God's aim to make a splendid world out of this world, then mankind would be without a guide. For the New Testament, the message of Christ, is based upon the principle that this is an evil world'.[155] But it is clear that it is a very drastic consequence. In any case, the severance between faith and reason cannot be complete, for, as Kierkegaard admits, there are rational limits to what is believable by faith. Faith cannot believe the nonsensical or the purely irrational[156] and to this extent at least it is subject to reason, for we must have some criteria for distinguishing between the 'paradoxical' – which is the object of faith – and the nonsensical or contradictory.[157]

Second, although Kierkegaard accounts for the practicality of faith, the dichotomy he sets up between speculation and 'subjectivity' makes it difficult to see how we can specify the object of faith. If to have faith is to be interested, to act in a certain way, to adopt a particular, 'existential' and personal point of view; and if to speculate is precisely to be disinterested, to disengage oneself from the particularity of existence and to adopt a general or universal or impersonal point of view – then by definition there can be no speculation within the realm of faith. We cannot, that is, know the object of faith or specify it in any way; all that we can do is to act with 'infinite passion' without knowing to what we are committing ourselves.[158] Thus it would seem that merely to act in a certain way or to have certain fundamental attitudes to life (e.g. to act in imitation of Christ), would constitute faith. Kierkegaard himself almost suggests this when he says that what is important in subjectivity and faith is the 'how' and not the 'what': 'The objective accent falls on WHAT is said, the subjective accent on HOW it is said... It is in the passion of the infinite that is the decisive factor, and not its content, for its content is precisely itself. In this manner subjectivity and the subjective "how" constitute the truth'.[159] Kierkegaard goes on to say that a heathen who prays in spirit and in truth, even though the object of his prayer is a false god, in fact believes in the true God; while on the other hand the Christian who prays to the true God, but does not pray truly, is in reality believing in an idol![160] However, we cannot really make even this distinction, for we cannot adopt one attitude to life rather than another without some principle of discernment; we cannot say *how* we ought to act without specifying *what* the object is of our action or attitudes. We cannot just *believe* in something without knowing anything about *what* we are believing in.

If we were to take Kierkegaard's account at its face value, faith would be completely blind and objectless and inexpressible not just to others but even to the believer himself. 'As soon as I speak I express the universal, and when I remain silent, no one can understand me'. In fact, I cannot even understand myself. Again, if Kierkegaard is right in his commendation of the sincere idolator over the insincere Christian, then, as a recent writer has put it, 'truth is being estimated by the standards of sincerity'.

> It might well be said [the same critic goes on] that the fervent idolator is the better man; he makes the utmost of what he has, while the self-deceiving Christian has everything and lets it slip. But is it nothing to have a *true* conception of God? If so, intensity of devotion is the whole of religion, and intensity of devotion may be shown in the pursuit of what is false and even wicked. If we reject this consequence, there must be *some* place in religion for an *objectively* true conception of God.[161]

On the other hand, if subjectivity and faith have a cognitively specifiable object – as indeed Kierkegaard seems at times to suggest – then the hard-and-fast distinction between speculative knowledge and subjectivity will have to be abandoned and some kind of philosophical justification of religion will be in order.[162]

The particular philosophy of religion delineated here can be given very different expressions both in so far as the ground of the philosophical agnosticism, which is an essential part of this position, is susceptible of being established in different ways, and in so far as the 'faith', for which room is made through this agnosticism, is also susceptible of different interpretations.

Kierkegaard's Anglican contemporary H. L. Mansel, for example, used Sir William Hamilton's 'philosophy of the Unconditioned' to establish the possibility of a sphere of existence beyond the reach of our finite and determinate knowledge. If there are realities that are finite or conditioned, Mansel argues, then there must be an Infinite or Unconditioned. But human thought is limited to the determinate and finite, and so the Infinite or Unconditioned is 'incognisable and inconceivable', and 'we are thus taught the salutary lesson that the capacity of thought is not to be constituted into the measure of existence, and are warned from recognising the domain of our knowledge as necessarily co-extensive with the horizon of our faith'.[163] We must postulate *that* there is an Infinite, but we cannot in any way *know* this Infinite, for an infinite object of consciousness would be a contradiction in terms. 'The condition of consciousness is distinction; and the condition of distinction is limitation. We can have no consciousness of Being in general which is not some Being in particular: a *thing*, in consciousness, is one thing out of many. In assuming the possibility of an infinite object of consciousness, I assume, therefore, that it is at the same time limited and unlimited'.[164] For Mansel the identification of the Unconditioned with God, and with the Christian God, is effected by faith. 'In this impotence of Reason', he says, 'we are compelled to take refuge in Faith, and to believe that an Infinite Being exists, though we know not how',[165] although Mansel also admits the relevance of 'evidences' or probable 'presumptions' to the determining of the truth of Christianity.

It is, however, within twentieth-century Protestant thought that the Kantian–Kierkegaardian account of philosophy's relations with religion has had its most important expression. Within this tradition the transcendence and 'otherness' of God, and of the whole order of revelation, is dramatically stressed, while the finiteness of human beings and their knowledge, and the effects of their sinfulness upon them, are correspondingly emphasised. Calvin's saying, *finitum non capax infiniti*, the finite is not capable of comprehending the infinite, exactly expresses this position. In this perspective religious belief is possible only as a freely given grace from God, and any attempt by philosophy or human reason to prepare positively for faith is seen as an attempt by the creature to judge the Creator – a means 'whereby the rational creature may reverse the order of being and advance towards God in terms not first provided by the Creator'.[166]

This whole conception of religion chimes in perfectly with the Kantian and Kierkegaardian philosophy of religion – philosophy demonstrating its own limits and thus its powerlessness in any supra-rational sphere, and thus in turn allowing room for a 'practical' faith that is not subject to rational justification or criticism in any way. Indeed this philosophy of religion harmonises so nicely with radical Protestantism that it is commonly taken for granted by contemporary Protestant thinkers and no need is felt to justify it in any systematic way.

Rudolf Otto's celebrated and influential work *The Idea of the Holy*, for example, limits the sphere of rational and conceptual thought very drastically so as to make room for non-rational modes of awareness. Otto places the primary religious object, the 'numinous', in the sphere of the 'non-rational', and this means of course that it is 'inexpressible'. We can, however, have a quasi-intuitive 'experience' of the numinous; indeed, Otto suggests that there is a special mode of consciousness – quite apart from speculative rationality and moral consciousness – proper to religion. Just as for Kant we have a special moral consciousness which cannot be 'justified' (since justification could only be in non-moral terms), so for Otto there is a distinct mode of religious consciousness which cannot be justified in other, non-religious, terms. The religious mode of consciousness, or the 'faculty of divination', is 'an original and underivable capacity of the mind'.[167]

At the same time Otto claims that reason can in various ways provide helpful analogies or 'ideograms'[168] of the inexpressible numinous, though he does not explain how we are able to judge which 'ideograms' are more revealing and enlightening than others. Again, if the numinous is, as Otto claims, so wholly 'other', how can mere reason even indicate or suggest analogies of it? As Paul Tillich has put it: 'It must be shown in what essential relationship this "wholly Other" stands to the other forms of consciousness. For if it stands in no relation, or even in a supplementary relation, it splits the unity of consciousness and it would not be *we* who experience the holy'.[169]

Again, with the great twentieth-century Protestant thinker Karl Barth, Kant's philosophical agnosticism is welcomed,[170] as is Kierkegaard's dichotomy between the speculative and the 'subjective'.[171] Barth was deeply influenced by Kierkegaard and like the latter is concerned to show the 'abyss' between the sphere of philosophical reason and that of religious faith. His attack on all kinds of 'natural theology' and on every attempt to justify religion rationally, is so vehement and uncompromising that at times he seems, like Kierkegaard, to be embracing irrationalism of the wildest kind and making a virtue out of obscurantism.[172]

However, despite his rhetorical exaggerations, Barth does have an implicit philosophical position of a quasi-Kantian kind on the limits of reason; and, moreover, he admits that reason can play a part in the theological elaboration of the Word of God.[173] So long as philosophy does not pretend to prove or justify the objects of faith (and so violate the autonomy of the order of faith), it can be used for theological purposes. Rudolf Bultmann, who differs from Barth in many ways, also allows philosophy a role in the theological explication of the data of faith. But although Bultmann has used Heidegger's early philosophical thought in the service of his own theology, he insists that his theology does not thereby become 'dependent upon a philosophical system by ... seeking to make fruitful use of the concepts of the so-called philosophy of existence, particularly of Heidegger's analysis of existence in *Being and Time*'. 'I learned from him', Bultmann continues, 'not *what* theology has to say, but *how* to say it, in order to speak to the thinking man of today in a way he can understand'.[174] Despite Barth's fear that Bultmann might be leading theology back into 'an Egyptian bondage in which a philosophy lays down what the Holy Spirit is permitted to say', Bultmann denies that his use of philosophy injures the autonomy of faith. 'Philosophy', he says, 'leaves fundamentally free the possibility of a word spoken to man from beyond. It offers, however, the possibility of speaking of Christian existence in a language which is comprehensible today'.[175] Philosophy, he argues elsewhere, cannot determine either the meaningfulness or the meaninglessness of human existence and it cannot lead to 'absolute knowledge'. Questions about the meaning of existence can only be answered by 'the concrete man' or by what Kierkegaard would call 'subjectivity',[176] and this is the realm in which faith has its proper place. For Bultmann, as for Barth, the Word of God is presented directly to man by God, and it is only by the faith that God also provides that we can apprehend the religious meaning and import of that Word. God provides both the object of belief and also the motivation of the act of belief itself.

The complex thought of Paul Tillich also in its own way implicitly relies upon a Kantian–Kierkegaardian philosophy of religion. Though Tillich is very much concerned, as against Barth, to bring faith and philosophy into contact and a dialectical relationship, he accepts that Kant has shown once and for all the impossibility of demonstrating the idea of God in 'positive rational terms'.[177] We can, according to Tillich, apprehend the reality of the 'Unconditioned' (which is not an entity, but the 'ground' of the being and value of everything, a little like Plato's Form of the Good), but the Unconditioned is not comprehensible by theoretical reason, save 'symbolically'. Once again, the main task of philosophy is to know what we cannot know by philosophical reason and so to allow a place for an 'original decision' of the individual person in response to God's grace.[178]

As we have seen, the strong points which this tradition of the philosophy of religion emphasises and exploits are, first, that religious faith is made autonomous and so independent of any direct reliance upon disputable philosophical premises; second, the transcendence of the religious order is guaranteed; and, third, the 'practical' mode of religious faith and its personal and 'inward' character ('the reasons of the heart') are given primacy. In other words, all the disadvantages of the intellectualist position are compensated for in the Kantian–Kierkegaardian position. Indeed, this latter view of the philosophy of religion depends for a good deal of its plausibility upon its exposure of the difficulties of the intellectualist position, and its own claims to have overcome them.

However, as we have already remarked, this philosophy of religion faces formidable difficulties of its own. First, in order to draw the limits of reason, so as to make room for faith, we have to rely upon philosophical argument.

Thus Kant's criticism, in the latter part of the *Critique of Pure Reason*, of any attempt at philosophical proof or disproof of the existence of God, involves the highly disputable philosophical doctrine of the rest of the *Critique of Pure Reason*; and Kierkegaard's theory of subjectivity likewise involves the assumption of a particular and very contentious epistemological doctrine. In this way then Kant's and Kierkegaard's philosophical agnosticism with respect to the order of faith, is just as much dependent upon philosophical premisses as is the intellectualist position of Aquinas, and it is just as vulnerable and open to philosophical dispute as the latter. Philosophy, both Kant and Kierkegaard say, can neither prove nor disprove the objects of religious faith; but this view of philosophy's limits itself depends upon philosophical argument and cannot merely be taken for granted because it happens to harmonise conveniently with a certain view of religion.

Second, it is difficult to see how reason can establish the limits of reason and so show the possibility of a transcendent 'supra-rational' order. Kant and Kierkegaard both want to claim that what is beyond the reach of speculative reason may nevertheless be meaningful for 'practical reason' or 'subjectivity', so that, as Pascal says, the heart may have its own reasons beyond the reach of ordinary reason. For them, that which is beyond the limits of reason is not thereby strictly irrational or unintelligible or meaningless.

This conception of the limits of reason derives its plausibility from its apparent analogy with the limits of sense perception, for in the case of the latter we can quite meaningfully know that our senses are limited and that there are sensible objects that we cannot sense because of the structure or constitution of our sensory equipment. Given the kind of eyes we have, for example, there are many visible things that cannot be seen by us. Kant supposes that, in the same way, the mind is limited by its structure or constitution. As Mansel puts it: 'My conclusions ... are not deduced from any necessary axiom concerning the condition of the finite in all possible states of existence, but from certain facts of human consciousness in the present life'.[179] But this view of the limits of the mind is clearly incoherent, for to draw the limits of the mind we would, so to speak, have to be able to see both sides of the limits and so to be able to transcend the limits. We would, that is, have to know by our minds what it is that we are precluded from knowing by virtue of the constitution of our minds. Certainly, there are many things that we cannot *in fact* know; but it is paradoxical to argue that we can know that there are things we cannot *in principle* know.

It follows from this that there cannot really be any kind of non-rational or non-conceptual form of knowledge or cognition with its own peculiar 'logic', other than ordinary rational knowledge. Kierkegaard virtually admits this when he says that 'subjectivity' cannot have for its object that which is formally self-contradictory or nonsensical for speculative reason. Something cannot be meaningless for speculative reason and yet meaningful for practical reason, or 'subjectivity', or 'the heart', or for 'faith'. If there are reasons of the heart, they must nevertheless be judged by the reason of the head.

The objects of religious faith therefore cannot be wholly transcendent, wholly 'other', without any kind of relation to reason. If they were without any such relation then, as Tillich himself says, we could not be aware of them at all.

Finally, although this philosophy of religion stresses the practical character of religious faith, so that to believe means not to assent to truths but rather to engage oneself or to commit oneself to certain fundamental attitudes, the separation of the practical realm and of the realm of faith from the speculative means that it is impossible to specify the *object* of faith. The faith that philosophical agnosticism makes room for is necessarily a blind faith. Faith then, as with Kierkegaard, tends to become a matter of purely practical attitude and the *object* of faith ceases to be important. As Kierkegaard says, it is *how* and not the *what* of faith that is of its essence. To believe means that you adopt an attitude of ultimate concern, or an agapeistic attitude, or an attitude of confidence in the coincidence of virtue and happiness. In this way, the philosophical agnosticism which was supposed to guarantee the autonomy and transcendence of faith, leads eventually to a reductionist position where that autonomy and transcendence is effectively denied.

AGNOSTICISM AS A RELIGIOUS ATTITUDE

Recently some philosophers and theologians have employed Kant's theory of knowledge to propose a form of agnosticism about religious realities (where we cannot say, for example, whether God exists or not) while at the same time re-interpreting traditional religious discourse in a secular mode. The function of religious statements, according to this view, is to emphasise certain fundamental human values about personal autonomy, the importance of community relationships and so on. Some indeed speak of a 'religionless Christianity'.

The American philosopher–theologian Gordon Kaufman, for example, uses a quasi-Kantian argument to show that the concept of God has no reference in reality. So he says, 'If nothing within our experience can be directly identified as that to which the term "God" properly refers, what meaning can or does the word have?'[180] Again, Kaufman argues that 'the real referent for "God" is never accessible to us or in any way open to our observation or experience. It must remain always an "unknown X" '. All talk about God is a 'human construction that we have invented'.[181] And as we have constructed the concept of 'God' it can be reconstructed to advance 'human fulfilment and meaning'.[182] So, in his work *The Theological Imagination*[183] Kaufman says that 'speech about the Christian God as "real" or "existent" expresses symbolically the conviction that free and loving persons-in-community have a substantial metaphysical foundation, that there are cosmic forces working towards this sort of humanisation'.[184] One is reminded here of Plato's 'noble lie' in the *Republic* where the philosopher rulers propagate mythical ideas about the foundation of city states by the Gods because those ideas are (though false) valuable in that they foster a sense of community. However, one can question Kaufman's assumption that we cannot say, after Kant, that it is impossible to know anything about God as an 'unknown X' since this is beyond our experience. Unless this is interpreted in a positivist sense where 'experience' is defined as what is accessible to empirical verification, as in the natural sciences, then it makes no sense to say that the concept of God 'goes beyond' human experience. Whether or not God exists is a metaphysical question and if it can be proved by metaphysical reasoning (as in, say, Aquinas's 'Five Ways' or Ibn Sina's proof from the contingency of the world) that God exists, then Kaufman's assumption no longer holds. In fact, Kaufman does not attempt a philosophical disproof of the existence of God and he simply refers rather vaguely to religion being no longer in tune with the 'new consciousness'.

Similar views to those of Kaufman have been espoused by certain English philosophers and theologians such as Don Cupitt and others in the so-called 'Sea of Faith' network.[185] Cupitt was formerly an Anglican priest and Dean of Emmanuel College, Cambridge. He became involved in 1984 with the 'Sea of Faith' network (the title is derived from a passage in Matthew Arnold's poem *Dover Beach* which laments the retreat of religious faith in face of the nineteenth-century world-view). Cupitt seems to take up Nietzsche's position that it is necessary to bring about the 'death of God' in order to allow certain human values to flourish and that this is a quasi-religious act. He clearly thinks that his critique of certain traditional religious ideas leads to agnosticism and even atheism but, as with Kaufman, he also seems to think that this agnosticism has a quasi-religious value. So he speaks of a 'religionless Christianity'. Kantian agnosticism, however, does not erect agnosticism into a kind of religious value, for Kant of course saw morality (derived from the 'practical reason') as taking the place that traditional metaphysics had vacated *vis-à-vis* religious realities. For Kant it is through the moral 'conscience' that we indirectly apprehend the existence of God. It is only speculative reason that is condemned to agnosticism about God. For Kaufman and Cupitt, however, their agnosticism is a quasi-positive state. One is reminded here of certain interpretations of Wittgenstein's *Tractatus*: all the propositions of traditional philosophy, says the *Tractatus*, are 'nonsense', but the philosophical propositions of the *Tractatus* itself are (so the interpretation goes) 'important nonsense' which make us aware of the fact that philosophy, defined as the pursuit of deep and fundamental truths, is a meaningless exercise. But this is clearly an incoherent position and so also is the idea that agnosticism is a quasi-religious state. The early sixth-century BCE Chinese Buddhist teacher Hsuang Tsang once remarked that 'Unreality is unreal', and similarly not knowing whether God and the religious order in general is meaningless is simply a state of unknowing and not a paradoxical way of (religious) knowing.

4

PHILOSOPHY AS THE ANALYSIS OF
RELIGIOUS LANGUAGE

An honest religious thinker is like a tightrope walker. He almost looks as though he were walking on nothing but air. His support is the slenderest imaginable. And yet it is possible to walk on it.

WITTGENSTEIN, *Culture and Value*

PHILOSOPHY OF RELIGION WITHOUT METAPHYSICS

This chapter and the next discuss two distinct attempts by contemporary thinkers to elaborate a philosophy of religion without the help of traditional metaphysics. They represent, in different ways, minimalist forms of philosophy of religion. This chapter considers the English–American movement of linguistic analysis, both in its Logical Positivist form and in the form associated with the work of Ludwig Wittgenstein, and chapter 5 deals with the contemporary Continental movement (or movements) loosely called 'Postmodernism'.

Kant, as we have seen, introduced a wholly new direction into classical philosophy of religion. The *Critique of Pure Reason* purported to show that the traditional metaphysics, which his predecessors had relied on to undergird their 'natural theology', was untenable. Pure or speculative reason was effectively imprisoned within the world of sensory 'experience' processed by the categories of the understanding, and any attempt to transcend that world and to speak of the religious realities beyond our experience was doomed to failure. However, by reflection on 'practical reason' which governs human action and morality, we can, according to Kant, fill the space left by the discredited metaphysics of the older philosophers of religion like Plato, Plotinus and the medieval Aristotelians such as Ibn Sina, Maimonides and Aquinas.

Kant's rejection of metaphysics, and of any philosophy of religion based on metaphysics, has had an enormous influence on modern thought and for many thinkers it is almost taken for granted without any need for justification. Some philosophers of religion (for example, John Henry Newman and Edouard Le Roy in the late nineteenth and early twentieth centuries) have developed Kant's ideas on morality being the only possible entry into the religious order, while others (like the Logical Positivists discussed below) have, in their own way, embraced Kant's dismissal of metaphysics in the *Critique of Pure Reason* while rejecting the escape offered by Kant in the *Critique of Practical Reason*. One might also see the various attempts, mentioned above, to formulate what might be called a religious agnosticism – allowing believers to enjoy, so to speak, the benefits of religion without making a theistic metaphysical commitment – in this light.

LINGUISTIC ANALYSIS

In twentieth-century thought the rejection of metaphysics has been especially marked in the movement of Logical Positivism associated with the philosophers belonging to the so-called Vienna Circle in the 1920s and 1930s – Neurath, Schlick, Waissman, Carnap and others – and with the English philosopher A. J. Ayer and his followers in England. What linguistic analysts of this persuasion have in common is, so they claim, not a philosophical doctrine but rather a method of dealing with philosophical doctrines or 'puzzles'. The task of the philosopher is not to invent speculative systems, or syntheses, or world-views, in the fashion of the classical metaphysicians, but rather to clarify what we mean and how we mean by the locutions we use. Many, if not all, of the traditional philosophical problems have arisen, so the analysts says, from logico-linguistic confusions about meaning, and when we analyse the conditions which various kinds of locution – empirical, mathematical, scientific, ethical etc. – must satisfy in order to have meaning, then these problems or puzzles simply evaporate. Philosophical problems are solved by being 'dissolved' and the function of philosophy is wholly 'therapeutic' in character. This does not involve us in making any metaphysical or epistemological assumptions of the kind made by traditional philosophers since a criterion of meaningfulness can be formulated in purely logical (metaphysically and epistemologically neutral) terms, and by using this criterion we can dissolve many of the traditional philosophical problems. This applies also to ethics or moral philosophy. Moral philosophers can, by 'meta-ethical' analysis of the 'logic' of ethical propositions and reasoning, clarify the conditions of ethical discourse, but they cannot help us to make a positive and specific option of a moral 'way of life' or concrete moral decisions.

For the analytical philosophers, as we shall see, religious propositions – 'God is all-powerful', 'God is just', 'God is merciful' – are not verifiable in the way in which the propositions of the natural sciences are, and they are thereby 'meaningless' or 'nonsense'. They *appear* to be meaningful and to state something to be the case, but in reality, after analysis, it is seen that they are vacuous. We do not need to prove this since, simply by analysing the logical structure of religious propositions (and indeed of all metaphysical propositions), it can be shown that they do not, despite their appearance, meet the requirements for meaning. In other words, they do not assert falsehoods: rather they simply do not make sense.

Faced with the logical positivist denial that truth and falsity could apply to religious (and all metaphysical) propositions, some later philosophers (Richard Hare, R. B. Braithwaite and others) argued that religious propositions were not (despite their appearance) descriptive in function, but that they could nevertheless be meaningful if they were seen as having a non-descriptive 'practical' or quasi-ethical function prescribing what we ought to do, or as having an expressive function indicating our basic attitudes, or even as having an emotive function. This reductivist approach (reducing religious propositions to other, non-religious, terms) enjoyed some popularity in the 1940s and 1950s and we shall discuss it later.[1]

Another, more important, version of linguistic analysis and of its implications for the philosophy of religion is that associated with the name of Ludwig Wittgenstein (1889–1951), an Austrian thinker who spent most of his life as Professor of Philosophy at the University of Cambridge in England. Wittgenstein is a central, if rather ambivalent, figure in this variety of analysis. At first it was thought that his early book, the celebrated *Tractatus Logico-Philosophicus* (1921) was a kind of eccentric logical positivist tract and that the enigmatic end of the work mentioning 'the mystical' (*das mystische*) – the inexpressible sense of the world as a bounded or limited whole viewed *sub specie aeternitatis*[2] – was itself simply a piece of mystification. This sense or 'experience' cannot be expressed in propositional form since propositions picture 'facts', and 'the totality of facts', or the world, is of course not a 'fact' about the world.[3] It can, however, be 'shown'.

Many of Wittgenstein's associates – Russell, the philosophers of the Vienna Circle and A. J. Ayer (the future author of the influential *Language, Truth and Logic* (1936)) – neglected the latter part of the Tractatus and interpreted the book as a logical positivist tract. As it has been put: 'By his theory of language, it was thought, he [Wittgenstein] had nailed down once and for all the coffin of metaphysics which Kant had built with his critical method'.[4] However, it now seems clear that for Wittgenstein himself the cryptic remarks in the last four pages of the *Tractatus* on ethical and religious matters were meant to be the whole point of the book. Apparently, the *Tractatus* was meant to be the first half of a two-part treatise where the second (unpublished) part would deal with questions of ethical value and religion.[5] In his later work, *Philosophical Investigations* (1953) and the collection *Culture and Value* (1980), Wittgenstein developed new ways of expressing his thought on religious issues, above all through the idea of 'language-games' and 'forms of life'. Some of his followers have interpreted him as holding that there was a discrete religious language-game which was part of an autonomous religious form of life or quasi-culture, but as the British Wittgensteinian D. Z. Phillips notes, it would be more precise not to speak of 'the religious language game since religious belief involves many language games', and not to speak of religion as being a 'form of life' but 'as existing in a form of life'.[6]

VERIFICATIONISM AND RELIGIOUS LANGUAGE

After these general remarks it may be useful to examine the positions mentioned in more critical detail. First, with respect to Logical Positivism, the views put forward by the English philosopher A. J. Ayer in his celebrated book *Language, Truth and Logic* (1936) were enormously influential. The heart and soul of Ayer's version of the doctrines of the Vienna Circle philosophers is the so-called 'Verification Principle' which states that a proposition is only factually or descriptively meaningful if it is able to be verified by reference to the real (empirical) world, that is, in the way scientific propositions are verifiable. The propositions of logic and mathematics may be meaningful as conventional rules which we lay down for our own pragmatic purposes, but they do not tell us anything about the real world.

All other metaphysical propositions about God, the soul etc. are 'nonsense', that is, they are locutions that, despite their grammatical appearance, violate the logical conditions required for any such locution to have sense or meaning. In effect the only meaningful propositions are the propositions of the natural sciences.

It is obvious enough, however, that Ayer's verifiability principle is not a purely formal or logical principle but depends upon the surreptitious assumption that the only legitimate kind of verification is that used in the physical sciences. It is worth noting in parenthesis that not only are all metaphysical principles (including those that are presupposed to scientific knowledge such as the principle of causality) declared *a priori* to be nonsense, but that moral or ethical judgements are equally nonsensical since they are of course not scientifically verifiable. Ayer's answer to this latter point is that moral locutions do not describe 'facts' of any kind but are rather 'emotive utterances' evincing our approval or disapproval of certain forms of conduct.

Thus 'stealing is wrong' can be analysed as having a factual component, 'taking another person's property without his or her consent', and an accompanying emotive component expressed by an exclamation, 'No!', 'Ugh!'. A consequence of this extraordinary doctrine is, as Ayer admits, that 'there can be no way of determining the validity of any ethical system and, indeed, no sense in asking whether any such system is true. All that one may legitimately enquire in this connection is what are the moral habits of a given person or group of people, and what causes them to have precisely those habits and feelings'.[7] As Ayer puts it: 'The presence of an ethical symbol in a proposition adds nothing to its factual content. Thus if I say to someone, "You acted wrongly in stealing that money", I am not stating anything more than if I had simply said, "You stole that money" in a peculiar tone of horror, or written it with the addition of some special exclamation marks. The tone, or the exclamation marks, adds nothing to the literal meaning of the sentence. It merely serves to show that the expression of it is attended by certain feelings in the speaker'.[8] A consequence of this contentious doctrine is, as Ayer admits, that 'there can be no way of determining the validity of any ethical system and, indeed, no sense in asking whether any such system is true. All that one may legitimately enquire in this connection is what are the moral habits of a given person or group of people, and what causes them to have precisely those habits and feelings'.[9]

A later and more sophisticated version of Ayer's position has been put forward by those who exclude religious statements as meaningless on the grounds that we do not know what would falsify them, that is, what would count against them being true. This so-called 'falsifiability principle' has been exploited by the great philosopher of science Karl Popper in his account of scientific knowledge. But a number of philosophers of religion have also used the falsifiability principle to support their reductionist accounts of religious language. The English philosopher Anthony Flew, for example, argues that there is 'no conceivable event or series of events the occurrence of which would be admitted by sophisticated religious people to be a sufficient reason for conceding "There wasn't a God after all" or "God does not really love us then" '.[10] Flew concludes that religious propositions must therefore be rejected as meaningless on purely logical grounds which do not involve one in any prior metaphysical commitment.

It is clear that Flew's falsifiability principle, however, is simply a thinly disguised version of the Logical Positivists' verification principle, for it is only if we understand the principle as signifying that an assertion is meaningful solely if it is known what would count against its truth, *in the way we know what would count against the truth of an empirical or scientific assertion*, that it becomes something more than a logical truism and enables us to exclude non-empirical truths (among them religious propositions) as meaningless.

REDUCTIVIST ACCOUNTS OF RELIGIOUS LANGUAGE

Many linguistic analysts accepted Ayer's and Flew's contention that religious locutions are not verifiable or falsifiable and so do not have a descriptive (true/false) meaning of any kind. Others, however, pointed out that both Ayer and Flew allowed moral utterances to be meaningful even though they were neither verifiable nor falsifiable and they argued that religious propositions might similarly be meaningful even though non-descriptive in function. Of course, many religious locutions *appear* to be making descriptive assertions about non-empirical 'facts' (God, the Persons of the Trinity, Vishnu, etc.), or about historical facts (Jesus Christ rose from the dead, the Buddha achieved enlightenment under the bo tree, etc.). But *in reality* they are making declarations about attitudes to life and the world. It is worthwhile remarking that a number of nineteenth and early-twentieth-century thinkers had already adopted a similar view of religious locutions: thus Matthew Arnold (1822–88) argued that such locutions had a moral purpose but with an emotive form of expression ('morality touched by emotion'); again, as we have seen, the French Catholic thinker Edouard Le

Roy (1870–1954), claimed that the function of religious assertions was a 'practical' one, that is, they prescribe rules of practical conduct, not just ethical conduct but in a much more general sense. Thus, 'Jesus is risen' means 'Always think of Jesus as a contemporary'.[11] These accounts in effect deny that religious locutions have a meaning of their own and reduce them to other terms, moral, poetic, expressive, prescriptive and so on.

R. B. Braithwaite

Among the linguistic analysts the most uncompromising version of this position is that put forward by the Cambridge philosopher R. B. Braithwaite in his essay *An Empiricist's View of the Nature of Religious Belief*.[12] Following Matthew Arnold, Braithwaite argues that religious utterances are similar to moral statements in that they declare an intention to act in a certain way. They are, Braithwaite says, 'primarily declarations of adherence to a policy of action, declarations of commitment to a way of life' – an 'agapeistic 'way of life,[13] as he calls it, that is to say the life of selfless love (*agape*) St Paul proposes in the First Epistle to the Corinthians, chapter 13. But what, then, of the doctrines of Christianity? They are not, Braithwaite answers, to be taken as literally true as descriptive (true/false) locutions, but rather as 'stories' which help us to live the agapeistic life. Thus, 'God is love' is simply a way of declaring that I intend to follow a certain kind of life, and when I recite the Nicene Creed and say that Jesus Christ suffered and died and rose from the dead, I am in effect simply telling myself 'stories' to encourage myself to carry through the agapeistic way of life I have chosen.[14] (Analogous translations would, of course, have to be made for other religious traditions such as Hinduism, Buddhism, Islam.)

In terms of Braithwaite's position, then, it is possible to hold that the proposition 'God exists', taken as a factual statement, is meaningless, but also that the whole corpus of Christian doctrine, together with all the historical statements that go with it, are false if taken literally, and yet claim that one is a Christian believer using religious language in a meaningful way. If it is possible to be accounted a religious believer and a Christian in these conditions, how, one might ask, is it possible to be an atheist? For Braithwaite, presumably, an atheist would be one who did not choose to live agapeistically and who did not find it necessary to tell himself the Christian 'stories'. But whether it would be possible to justify the choice of an agapeistic way of life as the right one, as against the atheist, Braithwaite does not say. In this connection it is worthwhile citing the sardonic reflection of the Australian philosopher John Passmore: 'I heard Braithwaite give his lecture at Oxford. Afterwards I spent half an hour trying to persuade an intelligent, newly arrived, American graduate student that it was not intended as a defence of atheism. His final conclusion: "Well, the English sure are queer!" should perhaps have been met by the reply, "Non Angli, sed Anglicani!" '[15]

R. M. Hare

A more nuanced version of Braithwaite's position has been put forward by another Oxford philosopher, R. M. Hare.[16] Hare begins by admitting that religious statements cannot be factual assertions, for if they were we would have to admit the possibility of evidence counting against their truth, that is to say, we would have to admit that it was, for example, logically possible that God does not exist or does not have the attributes (omnipotence, omniscience, goodness etc.) which he is supposed to have. Nevertheless, if religious utterances do not function as factual assertions, they do function quite meaningfully as 'bliks'. Hare invents the term 'blik' to describe certain basic 'metaphysical' attitudes towards the world and our knowledge of it. So he says:

> As Hume saw, without a blik there can be no explanation; for it is only by our bliks that we decide what is and what is not an explanation. Suppose we believed that everything that happened, happened by pure chance. This would not of course be an assertion, for it is compatible with anything happening or not happening, and so, incidentally, is its contradictory. But if we had this belief, we should not be able to explain or predict or plan anything. Thus, although we should not be asserting anything different from that of a more normal belief, there would be a great difference between us; and this is the sort of difference that there is between those who believe in God and those who really disbelieve in him.[17]

If, then, religious utterances function as 'bliks', this means (i) that they do not assert anything about any facts and as such are neither verifiable nor falsifiable, (ii) that they do nevertheless entail a certain kind of behaviour: that is to say, just as one who has a blik about everything happening by pure chance would tend not to bother to plan and tend not to trust predictions, so one who has a religious and Christian blik would, presumably, tend to behave in a certain way, (iii) that they are justifiable (though this is left unclear in Hare's account) in that it is, apparently, possible to decide which is the right, or most appropriate blik to have.

In a later essay, Hare admits that religious belief involves 'belief in the truth of certain factual statements', but he says that these facts that religious discourse deals with are 'perfectly ordinary empirical facts'. What makes them 'religious' is the fact that 'our whole way of living is organised round them; they have for us value, relevance, importance, which they would not have if we were atheists'.[18] It seems then that it is our attitude to the empirical facts which is expressed in religious utterances. However, Hare goes on to argue that the distinction between facts and attitudes is not a clear-cut one, for even our belief that there are objective facts independent of our dispositions is itself dependent on an attitude. As Hare puts it: 'There is no distinction between fact and illusion for a person who does not take up a certain attitude to the world'.[19]

Hare goes on to make the radical suggestion that, in part at least, Christian belief is a way of expressing these 'metaphysical' attitudes on the basis of which our cognitive relationships with the world are alone possible. Thus, he says:

> Christians believe that God created the world out of chaos, or out of nothing. What I am now going to say I say very tentatively. Is it possible that this is our way of expressing the truth that without belief in a divine order – a belief expressed in other terms by means of worshipping assent to principles for discriminating between fact and illusion – there could be no belief in matters of fact or in real objects? Certainly it is salutary to recognise that even our belief in so-called hard facts rests in the end on a faith, a commitment, which is not in or to facts, but in that without which there would not be any facts. Plato, it will be remembered, said of the Idea of the Good, that it was not itself a being, but the source or cause of being.[20]

Hare does not explain how a similar translation might be made for Christian doctrines other than that of creation, for example the human and divine natures of Christ, nor whether the same kind of translation could be made of both the quasi-metaphysical statements ('God is good', 'God cares for his creation', etc.) and the historical statements ('Jesus Christ died and then rose from the dead', etc.) that are involved in Christian belief.

Norman Malcolm

A view similar in some respects to those put forward by Braithwaite and Hare has been proposed by the American philosopher Norman Malcolm. Although Malcolm's view of religious utterances appears at times to be a reductionist one, at other times he seems to be arguing that those utterances have their own *sui generis* meaning.

In an essay entitled 'Is it a Religious Belief that "God exists"?' Norman Malcolm criticises the assumption that we must first decide whether God exists and then by a separate act, so to speak, take up an attitude of belief to him. (Malcolm as a student at Cambridge became a close associate of Wittgenstein who, as we shall see, also has an ambivalent attitude to the meaning of religious utterances.) In effect Malcolm questions whether there is such a separation between a belief in God's existence and taking up an affective attitude to him. So he says: 'If one conceived of God as the almighty creator of the world and judge of mankind, how could one believe that he exists, but not be touched at all by awe or dismay or fear?... Would a belief that he exists, if it were completely non-affective, really be a belief that he exists?'[21] It is not clear here whether Malcolm wishes to conclude with Braithwaite that believing in God simply is nothing more than the taking up of certain attitudes to life and the world, or whether he is making the common-sense point that our beliefs are usually accompanied by various affective attitudes, for example, of awe or fear, and make a difference to the believer's behaviour. As Malcolm puts it, 'the man who believes that his sins will be forgiven if he is truly repentant, might thereby be saved from despair. What he believes has, for him, no verification nor falsification, nevertheless they are meaningful in so far as they make a difference to the way a person acts and feels, that is to his general behaviour'.[22] From one point of view Malcolm is a reductivist, but from another point of view he is simply claiming that, within the context of the believer's attitudes and behaviour, religious utterances have their own irreducible meaning.

Wittgenstein: 'The Mystical'

As we have seen, Wittgenstein's early work, the *Tractatus Logico Philosophicus*, culminates in some gnomic utterances about a realm of the Mystical (*das Mystische*) which, so it appears, he saw as one of the main points of the whole book. The sense of the Mystical is a sense of the marvellous and inexplicable character of the world – *that*, for example, the world as a whole, seen *sub specie aeternitatis*, exists at all, as against scientific explanations of *how* the world is.[23] (However, this realm cannot be spoken about nor expressed in true/false propositions. But it can be 'shown'.) To view the world *sub specie aeternitatis* is to see it as being 'outside' space and time, although once again this cannot be expressed in propositions but only 'shown'. It is difficult to say whether this experience is 'objective', that is, about some reality. So a commentator says:

'If someone says he does or does not find the existence of something a matter of wonder, something miraculous, mystical, there is no independent criterion by which he can be proved right or wrong'. In that sense the mystical experience as Wittgenstein describes it is not 'an experience of an objective reality as the term is properly understood', though, it might be added, that does not imply that it is purely 'subjective'.[24] Wittgenstein spoke later of other experiences, for example, 'feeling absolutely right' and 'feeling guilty', as belonging to the realm of the 'Mystical',[25] but it is difficult to see what the sense of the Mystical in the *Tractatus* has in common with these latter experiences. Some have seen the remarks on the Mystical as providing a basis for suggesting that while we cannot meaningfully speak of what transcends the world of facts, we can in some way 'show' that there is a realm of the 'divine'. However, in his later work Wittgenstein does not refer to the realm of the Mystical; instead he insists that our only access to the religious realm is through the language that we use, together with the 'practices' that accompany our linguistic behaviour. Thus an English philosopher-theologian observes: 'Again and again Wittgenstein reminds us that we have no alternative to attending to the signs, the repertoire of gestures and so on that interweave our existence. We have no access to our own minds, non linguistically. We have no access to the divine independently of our life and language. It goes against the grain, so captivated are we by the metaphysical tradition'.[26]

At the end of the *Tractatus* Wittgenstein states that 'God does not reveal himself in the world' (*Tractatus*, 6.432), meaning by this that if there is a God he must be transcendent to the world of facts. It is not clear whether Wittgenstein also means that we cannot reason to the existence of God from certain metaphysical facts about the world, for example that it is contingent, exhibits design and order etc., in the manner of the traditional 'natural theology'.

It must be said that Wittgenstein's rather enigmatic and undeveloped notion of the Mystical does not provide a basis for a philosophy of religion and we are not given any indication of how his thought on these matters might be filled out and developed. It is true that he seems to suggest that, as against Logical Positivism, a metaphysical (*sub specie aeternitatis*) perspective is at least possible. But, since this cannot be spoken about or expressed in propositional form, it is difficult to see how it can be exploited in a philosophy of religion. As we shall see, Wittgenstein's innovations in his later book *Philosophical Investigations*,[27] and above all his views on 'language games' and 'forms of life', offer a more promising, but still very slender, basis for a philosophy of religion.

LANGUAGE GAMES AND FORMS OF LIFE

In *Philosophical Investigations* Wittgenstein abandons his assumption in the *Tractatus* that language is, so to speak, a uniform whole and that there could be a single theory of language. Instead, he introduces the idea of a plurality of distinct and irreducible 'language games'. It is best to see language as a set of tools that people can use to do a variety of quite different things. So he enjoins us to 'think of the tools in a tool-box: there is a hammer, pliers, a saw, a screw-driver a ruler, a glue-pot, glue, nails and screws. The functions of words are as diverse as the functions of these objects'.[28] The use of words in a language game is governed by rules very much as any game (for example, chess) is governed by rules and is not entirely arbitrary. Importantly, any language game is embedded in a tissue of actions, practices, expressive gestures etc. Wittgenstein says that language is 'woven' into this tissue and constitutes what he calls a 'form of life'. The term 'language game', he says, 'is meant to bring into prominence the fact that the speaking of language is part of an activity, or a form of life'.[29] Language games, it is important to note, are quite particular and it would make no sense for Wittgenstein to speak holistically of a 'religious language game', as some of his followers have done. Thus the examples he gives of language games include 'Giving orders and obeying them; Describing the appearance of an object or giving its measurements; Constructing an object from a description (or drawing); Reporting an event; Speculating about an event; Making up a story, and reading it; Making a joke; telling it; Translating from one language game into another; Asking, thinking, cursing, greeting, praying'.[30] Cyril Barrett distinguishes usefully between 'syntactical language games', as in the syntactical moves involved in asking a question or giving a command, and 'cultural language games', as in the complex set of activities and expressive gestures and linguistic behaviour involved in speaking of a religious belief such as the Last Judgment. Thus, he says by way of illustration: 'When someone buying a loaf of bread says, "How much?", he is asking a question and in that sense, playing a syntactical language game; but he is also playing a cultural language game, that of negotiating. Whether this activity is common to all cultures (it is certainly not common to all in the same form) it is a form of life and a cultural activity and, as such, gives meaning to the words uttered'.[31] As we shall see, this concept of forms of life has been developed by the British philosopher D. Z. Phillips and others in the Wittgensteinian tradition in an attempt to show how typically religious language functions meaningfully only within a particular form of life or quasi-cultural context. As the English philosopher Roger Trigg remarks, all attempts to transcend 'local meaning and parochial rationality generated within the context of particular practices' are dismissed (by the Wittgensteinians) as 'metaphysics', as though there could be a context-free or context-transcending approach to the way religious discourse is validated.[32]

It must be admitted that Wittgenstein's notions of language games and forms of life are not transparently clear and it is certainly not evident that we can speak of a discrete and autonomous religious form of life in which certain propositions could be seen to be meaningful. Determining the meaning of a religious locution is for Wittgenstein very much an *ad hoc* task in which the personal history and the various 'practices' and behaviours of the speaker are part of the context, and these latter factors cannot be generalised and formalised. In a curious passage in the collection *Culture and Value* Wittgenstein distinguishes between religion and superstition by speaking of higher and lower 'forms of expression'. 'In religion', he says, 'every level of devoutness must have its appropriate form of expression which has no sense at a lower level. The doctrine, which means something at a higher level, is null and void for someone who is still at the lower level; he *can* only understand it *wrongly*, and so these words are not valid for such a person.' Wittgenstein then refers to the doctrine of predestination: 'At my level the Pauline doctrine of Predestination is ugly nonsense, irreligiousness. Hence it is not suitable for me, since the only use I could make of the picture I am offered would be a wrong one. If it is a good and godly picture, then it is so for someone at a quite different level, who must use it in his life in a way completely different from anything that would be possible for me.'[33]

We need to remember here that Wittgenstein's view of the meaning of religious utterances is strictly governed by his overall view of the descriptive or non-explanatory role of philosophy. As he says at the beginning of *Philosophical Investigations*: 'Philosophy may in no way interfere with the actual use of language; it can in the end only describe it. For it cannot give it any foundation either. It leaves everything as it is.'[34] The philosopher of religion then, like the philosopher as such, is forbidden to offer explanations of any kind, scientific or non-scientific. The only thing the philosopher can do is simply to carefully *describe* the language, in the very broad sense that Wittgenstein gives to that term, that religious believers use. Presumably, the philosopher cannot make any kind of inferences from that linguistic usage; he must 'leave everything as it is'.

It is obvious that Wittgenstein is engaged in much more than this kind of pure description in the *Philosophical Investigations*: why otherwise would he write a book making generalisations about language games and forms of life? In some ways Wittgenstein's approach is similar to that of Edmund Husserl's phenomenological description and his ideal of 'going back to things themselves'. The great difference, however, is that Husserl claimed that it was possible to discern or intuit 'essences' in the 'facts' described by the phenomenologist. For example, from a careful phenomenological description of an act of perception it is possible to intuit the essential features of perception in general.[35]

WITTGENSTEIN AND RELIGION

It seems clear that Wittgenstein was not a religious believer in any formal sense; nevertheless he was, so to speak, haunted by religious themes, especially Christian themes of a rather theologically conservative kind. His remark to a friend is, perhaps, the most revealing: 'I am not a religious man but I cannot help seeing every problem from a religious point of view'.[36] Certainly, his later work is full of religious allusions and examples – belief in the Last Judgment, survival after death, historical narratives in Christianity, predestination, miraculous events, the resurrection of Jesus, proofs of God's existence, what it is to be an 'honest religious thinker', the fact that, according to the Gospels, Jesus had a human mother, and so on.[37] But, unfortunately, Wittgenstein nowhere gives us a fully worked out analysis of any of these issues and we are left with a number of provocative, and sometimes eccentric, aperçus and allusions rather than a coherent position or doctrine.

We have seen that for Wittgenstein analyses with reference to language games and forms of life can only be descriptive in mode (in the sense that they describe what goes on in language games) and without any kind of explanatory force. This meant that any kind of natural theology of a traditional kind was excluded *a priori*. In this regard, two of his remarks from different stages in his philosophical career are worth repeating.[38]

> When someone who believes in God looks around him and asks, 'Where did everything that I see come from?' he is *not* asking for a (causal) explanation, and the point of his question is that it is the expression of such a request. Thus, he is expressing an attitude to all explanations. But how is this shown in his life? It is the attitude that takes a particular matter seriously, but then at a particular point doesn't take it seriously after all, and declares that something else is even more serious.

By this Wittgenstein seems to mean that one who is already a religious believer asking 'Where did everything come from?' does not intend his question to be taken seriously or literally. It is rather an exclamation of wonderment at the existence of things. But why, we may ask, must we assume that one who asks 'Where does everything come from?' is not asking for some kind of causal explanation (though not, of course, of the kind used in scientific discourse)?

The second remark is this: 'A proof of God's existence ought really to be something by means of which one could convince oneself that God exists. But I think that what believers, who have furnished such proofs, have wanted to do is to give their "belief" an intellectual analysis and foundation, although they themselves would never have come to believe as a result of such proofs. Perhaps one could convince someone that God exists by means of a certain kind of upbringing, by shaping his life in such and such a way'.[39]

Wittgenstein explains what he means by this: 'Life can educate us to a belief in God. And experiences too are what brings thus about: but I don't mean visions and other forms of sense experience which show us the existence of this being, but, for example, sufferings of various sorts. These neither show us God in the way a sense impression shows us an object, nor do they give rise to conjectures about him. Experiences, thoughts, can force this concept on us.'[40] However, Wittgenstein does not make clear how experiences, thoughts etc., can 'force' the concept of God's existence upon us and how a concept of God 'forced' upon us differs from indoctrination or brainwashing. Why, we may ask, should we prefer Wittgenstein's account as against that which sees assent to the existence of God as the result of an autonomous and free rational commitment? Why should we not give credence to a person who says that she was once an atheist but then became rationally convinced that God existed and later became a Christian believer? (It is worthwhile remarking here that Wittgenstein was deeply impressed by William James's *The Varieties of Religious Experience* with its first-hand, if rather idiosyncratic, accounts of purported direct experiences of God by religious people and mystics.)

The upshot of our discussion of Wittgenstein's view on religion and religious discourse is that there is undoubtedly a great deal of value in his piecemeal remarks especially about the dangers of conflating religious language in its myriad forms with quasi-scientific language, and again in his insistence in his later work that we attend closely and painstakingly to the ways in which religious language is used and the behaviours with which it is interweaved. Again, his insistence on the fact that the task of philosophy of religion, as with philosophy in general, is a descriptive or non-explanatory one is, with some reservations, an important point if he were suggesting that one of the difficulties with traditional philosophy of religion, both pre-Kantian and post-Kantian, is that historically there has been so little contact between the philosophers of religion and the great religious experientialists such as the Christian mystics (Meister Eckhardt, St Teresa of Avila, St John of the Cross and others), the Islamic Sufi mystics (Rabbia, Rumi, al Hallaj and others), and the long line of the Hindu and Buddhist 'enlightened ones'. But, in fact, Wittgenstein makes do with a rather narrow range of religious experience and there is no doubt that his view of the religious form of life could have been much enlarged and enriched by a wider range of the kind just mentioned.

The crucial point, however, is that Wittgenstein's view of the philosophy of religion was severely compromised by his general theoretical view that philosophy (and the philosophy of religion) was essentially a descriptive and non-explanatory enquiry. Like many other post-Kantian attempts, Wittgenstein's claim is that it is possible to engage in the philosophy of religion without the aid of metaphysics. For him, as for Kant, philosophy could have no transcendent function over and above the analysis of particular language games and forms of life. And this means that philosophy could have nothing to say about the transcendent realm of 'the divine'. Equally, despite Wittgenstein's struggle in the *Tractatus* to suggest that that realm can in some way be 'shown', it is clear in the later *Philosophical Investigations* that this is impossible since it involves the assumption that we can determine the meaning of language from a vantage point outside any language game and form of life.

POST-WITTGENSTEIN

Wittgenstein's ideas on religious language have been much commented on by his various followers since the 1960s. His status as a philosophical thinker of enormous depth and originality has compelled many to seriously consider his views on religion (especially with reference to the *Philosophical Investigations*). English philosophy in the twentieth century has been largely unsympathetic to the idea that philosophers ought to concern themselves with the issues that the domain of religion raises and to recognise that the philosophy of religion is a legitimate part of the philosophical corpus.

Wittgenstein's continued fascination with those issues, however, has encouraged many English and American thinkers to take notice of them.

One of the most interesting of those post-Wittgenstein philosophers of religion has been the Welsh thinker D. Z. Phillips who, over some forty years, has sought to use Wittgenstein's key ideas on language games and forms of life to develop a new style of philosophy of religion. Phillips has been described unjustly as a 'Wittgensteinian fideist', meaning that he is claiming that 'to talk of distinctive language games in relation to religion ... is to claim that only religious believers understand religious belief, that religious belief or believers cannot be criticised, that anything called religion determines what is meaningful and that religious belief cannot be overthrown by any personal or cultural event'.[41] These charges are, so Phillips retorts, 'empty', and one cannot but agree with him. In fact, Phillips's general approach is, if anything, anti-fideist. Thus, he has vigorously criticised certain American proponents of what has been called 'Reformed epistemology' – Alvin Plantinga, Nicholas Wolterstorff and others – who attempt to delineate a theory of knowledge and methodology sympathetic to Lutheran and Calvinist theology, and for whom 'the modern Christian philosopher has a perfect right to start with his belief in God, to take it for granted. This right is established by the failure of any philosopher to produce a criterion of basicality which shows that the Christian philosopher cannot do this.'[42] Phillips rightly sees this position as being incompatible with a wholehearted commitment to philosophical enquiry and with 'Wittgenstein's concern about integrity of style in philosophy'.[43]

Phillips is in fact a kind of Wittgensteinian fundamentalist in that he takes Wittgenstein's various dicta as, so to speak, gospel truth and scarcely ever questions or criticises them. Indeed, it could be said that he is more consistent than Wittgenstein himself in that he resists any attempt to go beyond the 'limits of language', or, as he might put it, the contexts of particular language games, and insists that any attempt to seek a context-free or context-transcendent vantage point is strictly impossible. The English philosopher Roger Trigg, in his perceptive critique of Phillips's position, points to the paradox involved in asserting on the one hand that 'we are all bound to certain contexts', and on the other hand assuming that this assertion (about the impossibility of a context-free vantage point) is 'free of contexts'.[44] We shall, however, return to this point later.

Phillips lays great stress on the role of 'practices' in forms of life, meaning the activities and behaviours and expressive gestures which accompany our locutions. So he says: 'We cannot separate concepts from practice, from what we do, because it is only in practice, in what we do, that concepts have their life and meaning'.[45] This becomes very relevant when we wish to distinguish between authentic religious belief and superstition since the superstitious person may in a sense linguistically mimic the true believer, but the difference lies in how the respective lives of the two are affected. As Phillips puts it: 'The strength of a belief is measured, partly, by what a person is prepared to risk for it, by the way it governs his life. For Wittgenstein, these considerations affect what he wants to say about the character of the belief'.[46]

This of course introduces a 'personal' note into the interpretation of what anyone means by their religious locutions since we need to take account not only of what she says, but more importantly how what she says affects her whole personal life (something which, as Phillips admits, she may not be fully aware of). Thus he says: '*Whether* or not a religious belief *is* superstitious is not up to the individual concerned to decide. Someone else may recognise that his belief is superstitious when he does not'.[47] And this in turn makes the understanding of what a person means by her religious utterances an extraordinarily difficult and complex and *ad hoc* business so that we are far from any kind of autonomous and clearly demarcated religious language games governed by clearly evident 'rules' and so easily to be understood. No doubt, Phillips would argue that we ought to expect this when we are dealing with religious matters; all the same, it introduces a high degree of indeterminacy into our understanding of religious realities which is at odds with the absolute certainty of many believers' religious commitment. This complexity of understanding what is going on in any religious language game is further accentuated by the fact that a language game may be related to other language games. So Phillips says: 'Although Wittgenstein emphasises the distinctiveness of language games, he also speaks of the relations between them. He had in mind the bearings that things we say have on each other. *These bearings do not amount to the same things for any individual* [my italics]. Think of the ways in which conversations develop. Without such bearings, there could be nothing like a growth in understanding, or in an understanding of one's life'.[48]

LANGUAGE GAMES AND REALITY

One of Phillips's central concerns is what might be called the 'reality' problem. After all our analyses of particular language games in which the term 'God' plays a meaningful role, could we ever be entitled to say that there is a reality corresponding to this term? In an essay on the ideas of the American linguistic philosopher John Searle, Phillips reports Searle as saying:

> Wittgenstein wants to insist that to understand religious discourse we need to see the role it plays in people's lives. But of course you would not understand the role that it plays in their lives unless you see that religious discourse refers beyond itself. To put it bluntly, when ordinary people pray it is because they think there is a God up there listening. But whether or not there is a God listening to their prayer isn't itself part of the language game. The reason people play the language game of religion is because they think there is something outside the language game that gives it a point.[49]

Phillips's reply to Searle is that the question of the relationship of language games to reality can only be settled by reference to a linguistic and practical context and that we cannot simply assume that religious discourse refers beyond itself. This would have to be shown by descriptive and *ad hoc* analyses of particular cases. So he says that 'the distinction between the real and unreal is not given prior to the use of various language games. There is no Archimedean point outside all language games by which we assess the adequacy of language in relation to reality'.[50]

It is unfortunate that Phillips does not provide a sample analysis (if one could be plausibly given) of the way in which 'real' and 'unreal' function in connection with God. Once we have distinguished between their use with regard to empirical objects and events and states of affairs, and their use with regard to a being who transcends the empirical world (allowing for the moment that this makes sense), what remains to be done? The philosopher of religion is concerned, in the traditional view, with God as he can be known by 'natural reason' as distinct from revelation. For Aquinas and his followers, the 'God' of natural reason is distinct from the 'God' of Jewish, Christian and Islamic revelation and the philosopher cannot (*qua* philosopher) say anything about the latter. But, as we noted before, Wittgenstein's dogma that philosophy can only have a descriptive function and is excluded *a priori* from any kind of explanation, means that any conception of a transcendent God is also rejected *a priori*. We know beforehand that any analysis of any language game and its form of life will never result in the existence of a God transcendent to the empirical world being found to be meaningful. And, as has been said, this is done in a completely *a priori* and 'Archimedean' way without any reference to a language game or form of life or context. Phillips spends a good deal of time complaining about philosophers of religion who refuse to attend to the way that language games function in practice but in this crucial instance he is as much a sinner as they are.

REINSTATING METAPHYSICS

What has been said about Phillips's position leads one to question the Wittgensteinian dogma on which he relies so much, namely that philosophy must be quasi-descriptive of the ways we use language in various contexts or language games, since that dogma leads to paradox in our reasonings. And this in turn leads one to call for the reinstatement of metaphysics in philosophy of religion. As Trigg has put it: 'There is a perpetual tug between those who wish to appeal to metaphysics and to an all-embracing rationality anchored in it and those who concentrate on the local meaning and parochial rationality generated within the context of particular practices. It will then appear to be impossible to transcend all practices and local assumptions to talk of what is "really" the case'.[51] *Prima facie*, as Trigg suggests, 'the traditional pictures of God which are contained in the inherited religious language seem to imply that there is another realm beyond this one and that talk of a spiritual reality is saying something more than attempting to view our present life in a serious, even an ethical, light'.[52]

In the traditional natural theology developed by medieval Islamic and Christian Aristotelians such as Ibn Sina and Aquinas, given that we cannot know directly by unaided human reason that God exists, we must *infer* his existence from the 'facts' (for example, the contingency of things in the world). And this inference must be to a necessary existent which does not require any extrinsic cause of its own existence. Regardless of whether or not one accepts this 'proof' or explanation as it stands, some kind of metaphysical inference must occur and a philosophy of religion which does not allow the possibility of such an inference, such as one based upon Wittgensteinian linguistic analysis, must be judged to be inadequate. No doubt, this kind of analysis can usefully clarify religious discourse and make us more sensitive to the complex problems of meaning that arise in the religious realm, and to the dangers of approaching religious language with a simple-minded verificationism that assumes that scientific meaning is paradigmatic. Again, D. Z. Phillips and the Wittgensteinians emphasise how important it is to enter sympathetically into the religious 'form of life' if we are to understand religious language. However, in the final resort this style of philosophy of religion remains at best a minimalist one.

5

PHILOSOPHY AS POSTMODERNIST CRITIQUE OF THE RELIGIOUS DOMAIN

The death of God will ensure our salvation because the death of God alone can reawaken the divine.

JACQUES DERRIDA, *Writing and Difference*

POSTMODERNISM AND LINGUISTIC ANALYSIS

There are a number of remarkable analogies between the philosophy of Postmodernism and Wittgensteinian analysis. Both reject any kind of 'foundationalism' which assumes that there must be ultimate grounds or bases for human knowledge (as in Descartes) and for reality itself (as in the Platonic and neo-Platonic tradition). Both emphasise the importance of 'interpretive communities' as the final point of reference in any interpretive exercise, as in Wittgenstein's concept of 'language games' in which we are inescapably involved and the 'forms of life' connected with them, and as in the Postmodernist 'local communities of interpretation'. Both question the traditional assumption that philosophy can be context-free and provide ultimate and absolute explanations, and both claim that everything must be understood and interpreted within specific contexts.

A corollary of this is that, so far as traditional metaphysics was defined as the context-transcendent quest for absolute foundations or grounds or 'first principles', both Wittgensteinian analysis and Postmodernism reject any kind of metaphysics. In other words, both deny that there can be a meta-contextual or 'God-like' vantage point from which we can judge, and justify, our epistemological views about human knowledge as well as our meta-physical or ontological views about the structure of reality. And finally, both refuse to endorse Nietzsche's famous claim that 'God is dead' and that the whole religious domain is, as the Logical Positivists of the 1930s and 1940s claimed, vacuous and meaningless. At the same time, however, both find it difficult to give meaning to that domain, or for that matter to any transcendent realm over and above the world of our immediate experience. For both, the crucial problem is whether it is possible to have a philosophy of religion without the aid of metaphysics which would allow a space for a transcendent realm.

Despite these similarities, however, the philosophical structures of Wittgensteinian analysis and of Postmodernism are radically different. The sources of Wittgenstein's philosophy are totally dissimilar from those presupposed by the central forms of Postmodernism, and again, the philosophical ambitions of Postmodernism are much larger and more ambitious than those of Wittgensteinian analysis. Postmodernism proposes a completely new way of social and cultural being and living and indeed one can speak of a Postmodernist 'way of life' and 'world-view', whereas it would be decidedly odd to speak of Wittgensteinian analysis in this way.[1]

POSTMODERNISM AND THE ENLIGHTENMENT

As its name suggests, Postmodernism defines or locates itself in opposition to modernism, or modernity, and modernity in turn is commonly defined in terms of the values of the European Enlightenment of the seventeenth and eighteenth centuries. As Eagleton, an English social philosopher-cum-literary theorist, has put it: 'Postmodernity is a style of thought which is suspicious of classical notions of truth, reason, identity and objectivity, of the idea of universal progress or emancipation, of single frameworks, grand narratives or ultimate grounds of explanation. Against these Enlightenment norms, it sees the world as contingent, ungrounded, diverse, unstable, indeterminate, a set of disunified cultures or interpretations which breed a degree of scepticism about the objectivity of truth, history and norms, the givenness of natures and the coherence of identities'.[2]

The difficulty with this definition, however, is that the concept of the Enlightenment is itself ill-defined and controversial and as such it has become a quarry for a number of highly contestable and conflicting Postmodernist interpretations. As Eagleton says very pertinently: 'Postmodernism is such a portmanteau phenomenon that anything you assert of one piece of it is almost bound to be untrue of another.'[3]

A further difficulty is that the sources of Postmodernism as a philosophical tendency are extremely eclectic. Among those sources are Nietzsche, Heidegger, semiology and the structuralism of de Saussure and Levi-Strauss, Gadamer and the interpretation of texts (hermeneutics), forms of neo-Kantian sociology ('the social construction of knowledge'), the work of Michel Foucault bearing on the socio-cultural shaping of the conscious subject or self, versions of neo-Marxism and neo-Freudianism, and contemporary feminist thinking on the formation of gender differences. These influences have all contributed over the last forty years to the making of what we now call Postmodernism and this is, no doubt, why so many distinct disciplines – philosophy, sociology, anthropology, literary theory, semiology – have become engaged in Postmodernist discourse.[4] Again, it is also why there are such large differences between the various styles of Postmodernist philosophy, Heidegger and Derrida on the one hand, and on the other hand the Americans Richard Rorty and Stanley Fish, as well as what might be called 'vulgar' Postmodernism where any radical questioning of the *status quo* is called 'Postmodernism'. There is, no doubt, a 'family resemblance' between these various forms or styles, but all the same one might well speak of 'Postmodernisms' in the plural rather than 'Postmodernism' in the singular as though the term designated a coherent movement of thought.

As we shall see, this caveat is especially important when we address the relationship between Postmodernism as a philosophical position and the religious sphere since some Postmodernist thinkers simply assume that Postmodernism is wedded to some form of atheism or secularism, while others, such as Heidegger and Derrida, strongly suggest that there is a space for God and religion, and that even if 'metaphysics' is exorcised we can still have some kind of 'understanding' of the religious domain. For these latter thinkers Nietzsche's claim that God is dead refers to a metaphysical (foundationalist and meta-contextual) God, and if it is possible to speak of God (and the religious domain in general) in a non-metaphysical way then we are not committed to atheism or agnosticism.[5]

To sum up: Postmodernism begins from a recognition of the failings of modernity and its concept of rationality: the scientific and technological

(reductive and 'value free') 'disenchantment of the world' and the manipu-
lation and exploitation of nature; the emergence of extreme individualism
and the consequent collapse of a sense of community; the divorce between
technology and moral values; the denial of the validity of 'local knowledge'
or tradition, with its pluralism and variety, in favour of universal, abstract
systems and 'meta-narratives' or grandiose theoretical frameworks. Eagleton
has expressed this sense of crisis in modernity and its values, and the need to
go beyond it, in the following dramatic way:

> Postmodernism signals the death of ... meta-narratives whose secretly
> terrorist function was to ground and legitimate the illusion of a
> 'universal' human history. We are now in the process of waking from a
> nightmare of modernity, and its manipulative 'reason' and fetish of
> totality, into the laid-back pluralism of the postmodern – that heteroge-
> neous rage of lifestyles and language-games which has renounced the
> nostalgic urge to totalise and legitimate itself... Science and philosophy
> must jettison their metaphysical claims and view themselves more
> modestly as just another set of narratives.[6]

THE ATTACK ON FOUNDATIONALISM

The great seventeenth-century thinker René Descartes (1596–1650) is
usually seen as the founder of philosophical 'modernism' and as the first
'modern' philosopher. Descartes was centrally concerned with discovering
the 'foundations' of our knowledge and with providing a clear and certain
basis for knowledge. So long as we rely upon the evidence of our sensory
knowledge of the external world, we cannot have certain or indubitable
knowledge since it is possible that our senses may have deceived us. The
foundation of our knowledge must then be something that is absolutely
certain and that cannot be doubted. This Descartes finds in his famous *cogito,*
the indubitable experience that one is actually thinking or is engaged in
conscious acts. This experience pre-exists any knowledge we have of the
external world or of other conscious subjects; indeed, I can know that there
are other subjects only by roundabout inference from their external
behaviour. The conscious self may be located in a human body (which
operates according to mechanical principles) at particular points in space and
time, but it can transcend the body and provides a vantage point (above and
beyond space and time) from which the conscious self can judge the world
and achieve universal knowledge. For Descartes, philosophy thus starts from

a privileged vantage point and provides a comprehensive, or total, or transcendent, view of reality and of human experience.

Almost all the central ideas behind the Cartesian project have been rejected by Postmodernist thinkers for whom the whole epistemological enterprise begun by Descartes, and continued by Kant and various successors in the nineteenth and twentieth centuries, was a momentous mistake. In particular these thinkers reject 'foundationalism', that is, an approach to philosophy which sees its primary task as a quasi-Cartesian quest for ultimate and absolute grounds or principles. Indeed, Postmodernism can be seen as a movement which teases out the radical consequences of this anti-foundationalism which the American literary theorist and legal scholar Stanley Fish describes as follows: 'Anti-foundationalism teaches that questions of fact, truth, correctness, validity and clarity, can neither be posed nor answered in reference to some extra-contextual, ahistorical, non-situational reality or rule or value; rather, anti-foundationalism asserts, all these matters are intelligible and debatable only within the precincts of the contexts, or situations, or paradigms, or communities that give them their local and changeable shape'. Fish notes that 'the resistance ... of foundationalism usually takes the form of a counterattack in which the supposedly disastrous consequences of anti-foundationalism are paraded as a reason for rejecting it. These consequences are usually said to extend to the loss of everything necessary to rational enquiry and successful communication.'[7] As we shall see, the charge of pernicious relativism is a constant accusation made by the opponents of Postmodernism.

In parenthesis, another point on which the Cartesian project has been subject to criticism by Postmodernist thinkers is its view of the conscious subject or self as an autonomous entity independent of both the external world and other selves. For Descartes I could still function as a conscious subject or *cogito* even if I were the only being in existence. Michel Foucault and other Postmodernist thinkers reject this idea and argue that the self itself is a 'construct' and not some kind of 'inner citadel' or impregnable preserve that is simply 'given'. The idea that our views about the world and human beings are powerfully influenced by social and cultural factors, including the structure of the language in which we think, is of course a common one. But Foucault and other Postmodernist thinkers have given a radical philosophical twist to this sociological commonplace by arguing that the conscious subject is not merely influenced by external social and cultural factors, but rather that it is 'constructed' by them. Thus the Cartesian *cogito* is a cultural fabrication reflecting certain historical forces in the seventeenth century and it is now losing whatever validity it appeared to have in the past and new concepts of the self are emerging. We can even contemplate the end, or 'death', of Cartesian subjectivity.[8]

ANTI-FOUNDATIONALISM AND THE RELIGIOUS DOMAIN

As we have noted, the Postmodernist critique of foundationalism is allied with the idea that we cannot know anything that is outside a context or pretends to transcend all contexts and to provide a God-like vantage point. In other words, all authentic knowledge is contextual or situational and it is because classical metaphysics attempts to flout this 'principle' that metaphysics is rejected by the Postmodernists. This view of contextualism is most fully elaborated in the work of the French-Algerian philosopher Jacques Derrida, whose key idea is the hermeneutical principle that 'there is nothing outside the text'.[9] This is, of course, a commonplace of hermeneutics or the theory of interpretation, but it is given a philosophical (dare one say, metaphysical?) twist by Derrida who uses it not only of written or literary texts but, following the structuralists, of human behaviour in general and even socio-cultural complexes like the Enlightenment. As Paul Ricoeur puts it, 'text' is used of 'any set of signs as a text to decipher, hence a dream or neurotic symptom, as well as a ritual, myth, work of art, or a belief'.[10] 'There is nothing outside the text' becomes then a universal and, it would seem, an *a priori* principle. For Derrida, since there is no outside reference point by which the meaning of a text can be determined, there can be no 'correct' interpretation of a text since any text allows a multiplicity of interpretations and no one of these discloses a core, or central, or basic, or privileged meaning. In other words it is impossible to 'fix' or determine, once and for all, the meaning of a text. In fact, every text implicitly allows a (limited) multiplicity of meanings and there is always the possibility of 'free play' between the various meanings a text may have – a possibility exploited by poetry. In his work *Writing and Difference*, Derrida says that 'the interpretive imperative is interpreted differently by the rabbi and the poet. The rabbi interprets a text to discover "literal meaning"; the poet interprets to explore the free play of interpretation.'[11] Derrida has often been accused of promoting a permissive (anything goes) view of interpretation, but he has declared quite firmly, 'I am not a pluralist and would never say that every interpretation is equal'.[12] Culler reports a remark by Derrida on a sentence quoted by Nietzsche, 'I have forgotten my umbrella': of this Derrida says that 'a thousand possibilities remain open'. On this, in turn, Culler remarks: 'They [these possibilities] remain open not because the reader can make the sentence mean anything whatever, but because other specifications of context or interpretations of the "general text", are always possible.'[13]

Prima facie, the critique of foundationalism and the Postmodernist theory of the interpretation of texts have devastating implications for the religious domain, at least as it presented in the great monotheistic religions, Judaism, Christianity and Islam, for whom God is often represented as the ultimate ground of the being of all things, and of our knowledge of that ultimate ground. The various forms of philosophy of religion, however, conceptualise their foundationalism in very different ways, so that not all philosophical Gods, so to speak, are foundationalist Gods. Plato's Form of the Good, for example, is clearly a foundationalist principle both epistemologically and ontologically; since without it we would not really know anything, nor would there be any 'real' things. Again, Plotinus's 'One' is obviously a foundationalist divinity since everything 'emanates' from it and returns to it and, as with Plato, the One is the ground or basis of our knowledge. The kind of God, however, that emerges from the natural theology of Aquinas and the medieval Aristotelians, Jewish, Christian and Islamic, is much more difficult to characterise. Ibn Sina's and Aquinas's God is certainly the supreme and ultimate cause of the contingent beings in the world, but we do not know, by philosophical reason, God as he is in his essence. By reason we know merely *that* a supreme cause must be inferred to exist but we do not know, in any sense, *what* God is. The other 'names' or attributes of God can only be known, for the most part, by the 'way of negation'. In other words, we 'know' what God is like by knowing what he is *not* like, that is, by denying or negating the attributes that belong to the things within our immediate experience – temporal attributes, spatial attributes, material attributes, mutable attributes, and so on. For the medieval Aristotelians, then, the God known by philosophical reason is a very minimal one and it is not at all clear whether or not this God can be said to be a foundationalist God.

In parenthesis, it is worth remarking that the 'negative way' presupposes that we know positively that God exists in some way and is transcendent to the world of created beings. It is only then possible to negate of God any attributes – spatial, temporal, mutable, etc. – that can only properly be applied to created and contingent things. If our *total* knowledge of God were negative then of course we would not know that there was a God at all.

Kant's position, of course, is ambivalent: within the realm of pure reason there is no way of providing a foundation for the religious domain though it can be shown that there is a space for that domain; but within the realm of practical reason God is invoked as the foundation of the sphere of morality.

The Postmodern theory of contextual interpretation also has, at least *prima facie*, damaging implications for the religious sphere since, as we have seen, it involves a rejection of any kind of 'metaphysical' understanding that goes beyond any 'local' contexts and enables us to gain access to some kind of domain transcendent to the world of our immediate experience. The classical monotheistic religions implicitly presuppose some kind of metaphysics of this kind and the crucial question is whether it is possible to have access to a realm of the 'divine' without metaphysics. This will be considered later in this chapter.

Apart from this, Postmodernist contextualism raises further questions for the monotheistic religions in that they are all 'religions of the Book' and so are subject to the same exigencies of textual interpretation as apply to other secular texts. Islam attempts to avoid the need for interpretation by claiming that the text of the Qur'an has been directly dictated by God to the Prophet. Some Christian Churches claim that they have divinely sanctioned institutional structures entrusted with the definitive interpretation of their sacred texts and also with ensuring the continuity of religious truths across profound historical and cultural changes. For the Postmodernists, with their emphasis on the historical and socio-cultural shaping of all the truths available to us, and of the interpreting agents themselves, the very notion of 'revelation' – a-historical, once-and-for-all, unaffected by socio-cultural factors – and of its transmission through a non-contextual 'Church' or analogous institutions, becomes extremely problematic.

POSTMODERNISM AND CHRISTIAN THEOLOGY

In a recent essay, the American theologian Thomas Guarino has given a perceptive account of a number of crucial aspects of the Postmodernist challenge to traditional Christian theology of the kind we have been discussing.[14] First, the theologian can no longer pretend that he is some kind of 'transcendental subject', like Descartes's *cogito*, surveying the world and human affairs from a God-like vantage point. In fact the theologian is inevitably and always embedded in a particular historical and cultural context or situation and the way she or he does theology, so to speak, must reflect the fact that any interpretation involves not just the text but also what the reader brings to the text. This means that contemporary theology must come to terms with a new view of theological truth since Postmodernism has shown us that 'truth is entirely mediated by historical flux, societal norms and cultural warrants'.[15] Citing Jurgen Habermas's recognition of 'the historicist, saturated and embedded character of reason', Guarino calls on Christian theologians to do theology in a way that takes this into account in both content and style. Again, Postmodernist theologians insist that the role of hermeneutics in Christian theology has to undergo radical change. For example, the naive idea that we can distinguish between the unvarying content of revelation and doctrine and the various cultural and historical forms in which it is expressed, has to be subjected to critical analysis. The same remark applies to biblical interpretation. Thus an English Postmodern theologian says that the future of biblical interpretation 'will be a paradise of different readings with none privileged and all equally valid... The Enlightenment rupture between medievalism and postmodernity will be healed by a return to a future of uncompetitive diverse readings. Readers of the Bible will also be able to cross from community to community as and when they please choosing the reading community which suits their needs best. A veritable reading utopia will have dawned and the old hierarchies and hegemonies will have gone forever'.[16] This is, no doubt, an exaggerated picture with its emphasis on the pluralistic and relativistic aspects of the Postmodernist view of interpretation, but it gives some idea of the analogous changes that may take place in any Postmodernist theology.

It is worthwhile here to look briefly at the work of a contemporary Christian theologian, Jean-Luc Marion, who is attempting to engage in theology in a self-consciously Postmodernist way. In his book *God Without Being* (*Dieu sans l'être*)[17] Marion goes counter to the Thomistic philosophical tradition with its emphasis on 'being' (*esse*) and he attempts to show that the language of 'being' distorts the notion of God. Above all, it obscures the 'otherness' of God and makes it appear that God is in some way subject to our control. Marion distinguishes between *idol* and *icon* and he argues that the Thomistic description of God as 'subsistent being' (*ipsum esse subsistens*) is 'idolic' in that it does not leave any place for God's otherness and makes God a 'prisoner of being'.[18] Instead, God's primary attribute is 'the Good'. As Marion says: 'Dionysius, following Christ, says that the Good is God's primary name.'[19] Marion uses the pseudo-term 'GXd' to signify the otherness of the divine order and he emphasises that the GXd of revelation should be seen as a 'free gift' which we cannot control or imprison. Here Marion, following Heidegger and Derrida, calls upon the mystical writers in the 'apophatic' or 'way of negation' tradition – Pseudo-Dionysius, Meister Eckhart and others – to illustrate his 'iconic 'approach to God. It is for the same reason that theology cannot be, as Aquinas pretended, a 'science' or organised body of knowledge based on principles. Theology, Marion says, has nothing like an *object*, nor does it have any of 'the characteristics of scientificity, especially not its objectivity'.[20] For traditional theologians Marion's attempt to reconstruct Christian theology may seem to be based not on arguments but more on imaginative suggestions which seek to persuade the reader, and the believer, to look at theology in a completely new way. Rorty remarks that Derrida, like Nietzsche and Heidegger, is engaged in 'forging new ways of speaking, not making surprising discoveries about old ones', and one might apply that remark to Marion also.[21]

For believers in the classical monotheistic religions the questions we have just been discussing about Postmodernism's repercussions on theology are subordinate to the question of the existence of a transcendent God, since if such a God does not exist in some non-reductionist, and meta-contextual, way, issues about the role of the theologian, the notion of truth in theology, biblical intepretation, etc., do not have much point. That latter question has been addressed most directly by Heidegger and Derrida and we must now look more specifically at their positions and their attempts to formulate an understanding of what Heidegger calls the 'divine God', as distinct from the traditional metaphysical God.

HEIDEGGER AND DERRIDA

Martin Heidegger and Jacques Derrida are both heirs of Kant in that they develop an anti-metaphysical philosophical position – anti-foundationalist and denying that there can be any meta-contextual knowledge of a realm that transcends our immediate experience. This implies that any philosophy of religion which depends upon 'metaphysics', in the pejorative sense Heidegger gives to that term, must be rejected out of hand. Many sympathisers with this form of Postmodernism have assumed without more ado that Postmodernism is therefore essentially atheistic, or at best secularist, apropos the religious sphere. For them Postmodernism provides the philosophical means to realise the Nietzschean poetic prophecy of the death of God and the dissolution of the domain of religion.

However, both Heidegger and Derrida reject this conclusion. They both distinguish between the philosophical God of the main Christian tradition and what Heidegger calls the 'divine God'. So Heidegger refers to 'the godless thinking which must abandon the god of philosophy, god as *causa sui*, as perhaps closer to the divine God'.[22] And Derrida claims that both the 'negative theology' of Pseudo-Dionysius and the 'mysticism' of Meister Eckhart, Angelus Silesius and others, lead to an 'understanding' of God which does not involve metaphysics. So he says: 'The divine has been ruined by God, that is God as the agent of totalisation', and again, 'The death of God will ensure our salvation because the death of God alone can reawaken the divine.'[23] As the American Postmodernist thinker Mark C. Taylor, has said: 'Followers of Derrida have preferred to overlook the theological and religious aspects of his thought, no doubt suspecting that they represent a vestige of the nostalgia which he criticises so relentlessly'.[24] It is quite clear, however, that Derrida's interest in the religious domain is far from being some kind of metaphysical nostalgia.

In parenthesis, one might mention that although Derrida was born in Algeria, he has a Jewish background and in many of his writings he refers to themes and liturgical practices both Kabbalistic and Rabbinic. He has also written a meditative study of the seventeenth-century Christian mystic Angelus Silesius and his work *The Cherubinic Wanderer*.[25]

DECONSTRUCTION AND THEOLOGY

Both Heidegger and Derrida suggest that what the Postmodernists call 'deconstruction' has an important part to play in revealing 'the primordial experiences' which underlie belief and practice. Unfortunately, the term has been interpreted by some as having a negative and sceptical connotation, but both Heidegger and Derrida insist very strongly that it has a positive and revelatory sense. So Heidegger, at the beginning of his great work *Being and Time*, writes that his task 'is one in which by taking the question of Being as our clue, we are to destroy the traditional content of ancient ontology until we arrive at those primordial experiences in which we achieved our first ways of determining the nature of Being – the ways which have guided us for ever since'. Heidegger goes on to say that deconstruction (*Destruktion* in the German) in this sense has nothing to do with a 'vicious relativising' of standpoints.[26]

In the same way Derrida has stressed that:

> Deconstruction is not negative. It is not destructive, not having the purpose of dissolving, distracting or subtracting elements in order to reveal an internal essence. It's a matter of gaining access to the mode in which a system or structure, or ensemble, is constructed or constituted, historically speaking. Not to destroy it, or demolish it, nor to purify it, but in order to accede to its possibilities and its meaning, to its construction and history.[27]

Derrida suggests that it is through a form of deconstruction that we are able to speak of 'moving beyond being'. Thus he says 'What there is in Plotinus of the movement beyond being … is something that interests me greatly. I think that deconstruction is also a means of carrying out this going beyond being, beyond being as presence, at least.'[28]

Unfortunately, Derrida does not tell us how this kind of deconstruction might lead us 'beyond being', although both he and Heidegger indicate that it is in mysticism and 'negative theology' that we may find a clue. In the negative theology of Pseudo-Dionysius and his later medieval followers we understand what God is by knowing what he is *not*. That is, by a process of 'unknowing', we divert or attention 'from concepts of God to the true God who cannot be conceptualised'.[29]

Similarly, the great medieval mystics, such as Meister Eckhart, emphasise the impossibility of conceptualising God while proposing 'unknowing', silence and 'detachment' (involving the spiritual annihilation of the self) as being the only legitimate ways of approaching the realm of divinity. Heidegger has devoted long and serious attention to Eckhart and he speaks of 'the extreme precision and depths of thought to be found in great and authentic mystics'.[30] Similarly, it has been suggested that for Eckhart, 'God lives without a "why", without a ground; and we can only be one with God when we have overcome all desire to ground our belief in God.'[31] As we have seen, for Heidegger and Derrida 'the divine God' (as distinct from the meta-physical 'God') cannot be known by conceptual knowledge but can be 'understood'. Thus Derrida writes that 'the mystics' avowal of God does not essentially belong to the order of cognitive determination. It has nothing to do with knowing as such. As an act of charity, love and friendship in Christ it is meant for God and his creatures'.[32] It may be thought that Derrida is suggesting here that when the mystics (and perhaps the ordinary believer) speak of God they are not describing (and making true or false statements about) any transcendent entity. They are rather making an avowal of 'love and friendship in Christ', as though 'I believe in God' could be translated as 'I avow or declare my love and friendship for Christ'. This would be rather like the reductionist position of the English philosopher R. B. Braithwaite for whom 'I believe in God' may be translated as 'I intend to follow an agapeistic way of life as exemplified in the life of Jesus Christ'. But it would seem that Derrida means more than this, though it is not easy to see what that is.

At the end of his detailed examination of Heidegger's 'divine God', Hart concludes: 'Heidegger offers the possibility of a divine God being revealed to us, though one that is far removed from the God of biblical revelation, and about whom we cannot say anything at all. The burden is on Heidegger to describe what sort of revelation would count as a revelation of God, rather than Being, and nowhere does he offer such a description.'[33] Much the same could be said of Derrida's God of the mystics and negative theologians. Despite his very interesting remarks about the non-metaphysical God that emerges from the process of deconstruction we are little the wiser as to what a basic religious utterance such as 'I believe in God' really means.

As we have noted, Postmodernism, at least of the kind aligned with Heidegger and Derrida, does not endorse Nietzsche's doctrine of 'the death of God'. What it does is to reject a particular philosophical view of God, which has had an enormously large and influential currency since the beginnings of Greek philosophy, and which defines God as an ultimate metaphysical foundation or ground. But the Postmodernist argument against this view of God works in exactly the same way against the classical forms of atheism in so far as they rely upon a metaphysical ground as in, for example, materialism, empiricism and positivism. In other words, we cannot adopt a transcendent, context-free, or God-like vantage point to show that God does not exist. As Hart puts the matter: 'Deconstruction is neither theistic nor atheistic in any normal sense of the words.' And he goes on to say: 'Deconstruction offers a critique of theism to be sure, but it is directed to the "ism" rather than the "theos", that is it offers a critique of the use to which "God" is put. In fact, to the extent to which deconstruction is a critique of theism, it is also a critique of any discourse which denies that there is a God'.[34] This suggests that theism is beyond the reach of philosophy so that philosophical reason by itself can say nothing either for or against theism, and equally for or against atheism.

As we have already remarked, Hart argues that it is possible to develop from Derrida's work a 'non-metaphysical theology' in which God can be understood, in a very weak sense of that word, but not known or conceptualised, and that this is 'the only possible way in which theology can resist the illusions of metaphysics'.[35] But, as we have seen, philosophy can have almost no real contact, either for or against, with the sphere of religion and it would seem therefore that for the Postmodernists there cannot be a philosophy of religion in any meaningful sense.

RORTY'S POSTMODERNISM AND SECULARISM

Quite apart from Derrida's position, there is the form of Postmodernism proposed by the American philosopher Richard Rorty by which Postmodernist ideas are linked with James's and Dewey's pragmatism according to which truth and falsity are judged (and 'justified') in terms of the consequences of holding certain beliefs. Rorty has not been explicitly concerned with God or the religious domain but some idea of his attitude towards that domain can be gathered from his book *Philosophy and the Mirror of Nature*.[36] In common with all the Postmodernists Rorty rejects the quest for an absolute foundation for any discourse by reference to which our beliefs can be justified or validated and our interpretations adjudicated. He then considers the conflict in the seventeenth century between Cardinal Bellarmine, typically seen as the representative of obscurantist religion, and Galileo, the champion of scientific rationalism. 'Much of the seventeenth century's notion of what it was to be a "philosopher", and much of the Enlightenment's notion of what it was to be "rational" ', so Rorty says, 'turns on Galileo's being absolutely right and the Church absolutely wrong.' But Rorty claims that there is no way of showing that Galileo was absolutely right and the Church absolutely wrong and, more generally, that scientific reason is 'objective' and that religion is not. This distinction is 'justified' only in terms of the socio-cultural consequences of maintaining these distinctions. 'We are', Rorty says, 'the heirs of 300 years of rhetoric about the importance of distinguishing sharply between science and religion, science and politics, science and art, science and philosophy and so on. But to proclaim our loyalty to these distinctions is not to say that there "objective" and "rational" arguments for adopting them. Galileo, so to speak, won the argument and we all stand on the grid of relevance and irrelevance which modern philosophy developed as a consequence of this victory.'[37]

It is notorious that James's and Dewey's pragmatism faces very large difficulties in that it is not clear how the 'consequences' of holding specific beliefs are to be measured and weighed and evaluated, and it is certainly not clear that the socio-cultural consequences of holding Bellarmine-type religious beliefs on the one hand and Galileo-type scientific beliefs on the other hand can be meaningfully compared and weighed. Rorty's calm assumption that the Galileo-type consequences outweigh the Bellarmine-type consequences is in fact nothing more than an assumption and it is difficult to resist the judgement that his position is a form of irrationalism in that it implicitly uses canons of objectivity and rationality in order to deny them.[38] In a more recent, and quite extraordinary, essay,[39] Rorty has attempted to show that secularism is, so to speak, the preferred 'religious' stance for the interpretive community constituted by American believers in democratic ideals. Rorty sees democracy in Postmodern terms as an anti-authoritarian polity dedicated to pluralism and to 'the creation of a greater diversity of individuals, larger, fuller, more imaginative and daring individuals'.[40] And he argues that there are obvious affinities or correspondences between this anti-authoritarian pluralism and the secularism which is the civic religion, so to speak, of democratic societies. Rorty cites the poet Walt Whitman, '*And I call to mankind, Be not curious about God,/ For I who am curious about each am not curious about God*', and he goes on to comment: 'Whitman thought that there was no need to be curious about God because there is no standard, not even a divine one, against which the decisions of a free people, can be measured.'[41]

According to Rorty, for Whitman and Dewey America was the first nation to identify wholeheartedly with the democratic ideal: 'Other nations thought of themselves as hymns to the glory of God. We redefine God as our future selves'.[42] Rorty concludes: 'America will, Dewey hoped, be the first nation to have the courage to renounce hope of justification from on high – from a source which is immovable and eternal'.[43] In other words, the American polity has renounced any kind of political and religious authoritarianism and foundationalism. From this point of view it would appear that for Rorty democracy (American style) and its attendant secularism constitute the Postmodern 'religious' stance *par excellence*.

No doubt Rorty would claim that this endorsement of secularism does not amount to a foundationalist justification since it is 'justified' only by its pragmatic consequences, but it is not clear what kind of an argument this is. It is certainly not a persuasive political-historical argument since the claim that democratic societies have had an affinity with secularist societies neglects the fact that, in most democratic polities, there is a distinction between church and state which entails that the state opts out of the religious sphere and vice versa. But that the American state, for example, is committed in this way to a civic secularism does not mean that the whole civic community will be committed to secularist or anti-religious values. Again, it is difficult to see how a pragmatic or consequentialist argument for secularism might be mounted of the same kind that Rorty uses to show that Galileo-type scientific values are to be deemed more 'objective' and 'rational' than Bellarmine-type religious values.

CONCLUSION

As we have seen, Postmodernism, at least of the kind asssociated with Heidegger and Derrida, does not necessarily involve the 'death of God', although it does involve the rejection of a particular view of God, defined as a metaphysical ground or foundation, which can be known only in some kind of meta-contextual way. The Postmodernist argument against this God works equally against the classical forms of atheism in so far as they rely upon some form of metaphysical foundationalism. The Postmodernist cannot, therefore, say either that God exists or that God does not exist and to that extent there cannot be a Postmodernist philosophy of religion. Of course, both Heidegger and Derrida suggest that negative theology and mysticism can provide (in a non-metaphysical way) some kind of non-conceptual understanding of God but, as we have seen, it is not clear what this involves. The realm of the 'Mystical', as Wittgenstein famously remarked in the *Tractatus*, is that whereof one cannot speak and about which one must be silent.

Of course, a Postmodernist philosopher will be able to use decon-struction in a critical or therapeutic way to purify religious and theological discourse from improper metaphysical contamination. This is especially important in Western theology because of its dependency on Greek meta-physical modes of thought from Platonism, Plotinian neo-Platonism (through the immensely influential Pseudo-Dionysius), and medieval (Islamic and Christian) Aristotelianism. As has been said, however, it is difficult to see that in any positive sense there can be a Postmodernist philosophy of religion akin to the classical varieties considered in preceding chapters.

Quite apart from these considerations, one might also raise the crucial question of whether the Postmodernist critique of metaphysics in general, and of metaphysically based religion and theology in particular, is not itself caught in a fatal paradox of much the same kind as Wittgenstein faced in the *Tractatus*. As we saw in the previous chapter, the *Tractatus* declares that all philosophical propositions are 'nonsense' and cannot be 'said'. But then Wittgenstein's own propositions in the *Tractatus* must themselves be 'nonsense' and without meaning. Similarly, one might ask whether Postmodernism (if it can be taken as a whole) escapes the objection that, in expressing itself as a philosophical position, it turns inevitably into an absolute or 'metaphysical' position and lays itself open to a deconstructive critique. For example, as we have already seen, the American Postmodernist thinker Stanley Fish claims that 'questions of fact, truth, correctness, validity, and clarity can neither be posed nor answered in reference to some extra-contextual, ahistorical, non-situational reality or rule, or law or value: rather … all these matters are intelligible and debatable only within the precincts of the contexts or situations or paradigms or communities that give them local shape'.[44] But what of Fish's own anti-foundationalist position here? Does it not involve reference to some 'extra-contextual, ahistorical, non-situational reality or rule'? After all, an *a priori* interpretive rule that applies to and binds *all* interpretive communities can hardly itself be a locally and historically shaped rule within a particular interpretive community.

One might note here also that the terms 'context', 'situation', 'interpretation', 'justification', are often used by Postmodernist thinkers in a univocal way as though they mean exactly the same when they are used of philosophical contexts, scientific contexts, mathematical contexts, moral contexts, literary contexts, legal contexts, linguistic contexts and so on. But it is obvious that interpretation in a philosophical context is radically different from interpretation in a mathematical or scientific context, which in turn is essentially different from interpretation in a literary context. When we talk of a religious context within which certain locutions about God have meaning, we are clearly talking about a very special and rarified but, so the believer would claim, real situation. Medieval Aristotelians like Aquinas were very well aware that 'exists', 'cause', etc., cannot be predicated univocally of God and of his dependent creatures, but only in a very different or 'analogous' way. Aquinas's theory of the 'analogy of proportion' is a philosophically sophisticated way of coping with this issue and the Postmodernist philosophers need something similar to remind them of the differences in kind of contexts or situations and of the interpretations they make possible.[45] In parenthesis, we might remember that a surreptitiously univocal use of the term 'verification', where *scientific* verification was assumed to be the paradigm for all forms of verification, enabled the English analyst A. J. Ayer to construct a universal 'verification principle' which was used to dismiss all metaphysical propositions, and religious propositions, as meaningless. In the case of Derrida's Postmodernism it appears as though the principle 'No text without a context' applies paradigmatically to linguistic and literary texts, but one may question the way in which it is used of religious texts or texts in a natural theology situation.

Critics of Postmodernism have also pointed to other, more particular, contradictions within its general position. Eagleton, for example, has remarked on the difficulties that Postmodernists face in providing a basis for moral and social values: 'In seeking to cut the ground from under its opponents' feet, Postmodernism finds itself unavoidably pulling the rug out from under itself, leaving itself with no more reason why we should resist fascism than the feebly pragmatic plea that fascism is not the way we do things in Sussex or Sacramento'. Again, he notes that while Postmodernism rejects 'universalism' as an attempt to homogenise differences, it at the same time exploits all kinds of universals of its own: 'It is brimful of universal moral prescriptions – hybridity is preferable to purity, plurality to singularity, difference to self-identity – and denounces such universalism as an oppressive hangover of Enlightenment'.[46] These contradictions are especially evident in some Postmodernists' approaches (for example, that of Rorty) to the religious and theological domain.

We return then to much the same conclusion we reached apropos the relevance of Wittgensteinian analysis to the religious domain and the possibility of a Wittgensteinian philosophy of religion. Like linguistic analysis, Postmodernism can have a valuable therapeutic and quasi-deconstructive function *vis-à-vis* the religious and theological domain, but it is difficult to see how it can lead to a philosophy of religion of the classical, or indeed any, kind.

6

CONCLUSION

People have always thought that reflection would destroy Christianity and is its
natural enemy. I hope I have shown, with God's help, that religious reflection can
retie the knot which a superficial reflection has unravelled for so many years.

SOREN KIERKEGAARD, *The Works of Love*

We have been concerned to isolate five main conceptions of the philosophy
of religion that have appeared in the history of Western thought, and to
analyse their respective logical anatomies. Each type represents an original
and thoroughgoing attempt to reconcile the demands of philosophical reason
with the demands of that which is in some way 'beyond' reason – the
'divine', the 'numinous', the 'supernatural'. Each type exhibits its own
peculiar understanding of what philosophy is, on the one hand, and what
religion is on the other. Each has its own philosophical and religious benefits
and attractions and its own equal and opposite difficulties and drawbacks: in
the philosophy of religion, as in life, you pay a price for every advantage
gained.

For the most part, the religions that Western philosophy has had to
confront and to come to terms with have been Judaeo-Christianity and Islam.
There are of course large differences between the various sectarian interpretations of Judaeo-Christianity, but their family resemblance becomes
manifest when they are contrasted, for example, with Hinduism or
Buddhism or Taoism. Fundamentally, the religious phenomena that religious

philosophers as diverse as Augustine, Pseudo-Dionysius, Aquinas, Pascal, Kant, Kierkegaard and Tillich have to confront and 'save', are broadly the same. Consequently, to the extent that by the 'philosophy of religion' we have understood here 'the philosophy of the Judaeo-Christian and Islamic religions', our findings and conclusions are correspondingly limited in scope. If we had, for example, focused our attention on Hinduism or Buddhism instead, it might be that other quite different issues would have arisen for consideration and that the whole question of philosophy's relations with the religious order would have appeared in a rather different light.

However, as we remarked at the beginning of this work, what we know as the philosophy of religion is, as a matter of historical fact, a child of the conjunction between Greek philosophy and the great monotheistic religions of the Middle East, so that our concentration upon the phenomena provided by this latter tradition is not as serious a limitation as it might appear. Certainly there has been a vast amount of quasi-philosophical speculation within both Hinduism and Buddhism, and it is salutary to be made aware of these other radically variant approaches to religion and the different range of religious phenomena with which they confront us.

None the less it remains true that it was with the Greeks that philosophy was first distinguished from mythical and religious speculation and achieved an autonomy and independence that it did not ever reach in Eastern cultures; and it is also true that Judaism, Christianity and Islam lent themselves to (indeed, invited) being philosophised about, so to speak, in a way in which other religions have not. Whether it be due to providence or historical luck, it is a fact that Greek philosophy and the three monotheisms have been amazingly complementary to each other. And it is from this happy conjunction, as we have said, that the philosophy of religion was born. It was within this particular context that the attempt to reconcile reason with that which is beyond reason seemed to be an urgent and possible enterprise in a way in which it has not seemed either pressing or possible in other religious contexts. No doubt, as Postmodernist philosophers have reminded us, there have been pluses and minuses in the conjunction between Greek philosophy and Christian faith, and many contemporary Christians would question whether it has really been a 'happy' conjunction. Nevertheless, it has at least been the source of an extraordinarily impressive intellectual creation which one cannot but admire.

Despite the various particular criticisms made of the five views of the philosophy of religion, we have not attempted to adjudicate between them.

Any such comparative judgement could only be made by reference to two distinct, though related, sets of criteria. There are, first, purely philosophical considerations arising from the specific conception of philosophy's nature and role presupposed to each type of the philosophy of religion. Thus the Platonic/neo-Platonic version of the philosophy of religion is only viable if some kind of 'transcendental' metaphysics is possible. Aquinas's philosophy of religion likewise presupposes the possibility of philosophy having a meta-physical and transcendental role. In the same way the Kantian and neo-Kantian view of the philosophy of religion depends for its validity upon the philosophical adequacy of Kant's 'critical' philosophy; and the Wittgensteinian view of religious language also assumes the truth of Wittgenstein's 'analytical' or 'therapeutic' (anti-metaphysical) view of philosophy's role. The same is true of Postmodernism's view of the religious domain. Heidegger's and Derrida's views of religious discourse depend upon their Postmodernist philosophical positions which deny, in effect, that philosophy has any 'metaphysical' or 'foundationalist' role. Which view of the nature and role of philosophy is the correct or more adequate one would have to be argued on purely philosophical grounds, and consequently any judgement between the five types of philosophy of religion would have to be argued in the same way.

There are, however, other considerations to be taken into account in making such a judgement in that any philosophical account of religion that leads to systematic theological 'reductionism' is clearly inadequate. It is extremely difficult to define exactly what constitutes 'reductionism' and what its limits are, but Hegel, Arnold and Santayana (to take what are, one hopes, non-contentious examples) may perhaps be considered to offer clearly reductionist accounts of religion. Thus for Hegel a philosophical account is given of religion which results in it being interpreted or re-described as a species of metaphysics; for Arnold the meaningfulness of reli-gious language is 'saved' by construing the latter as a type of moral language; while for Santayana religious attitudes are identified with quasi-aesthetic attitudes. In such accounts as these religion is clearly reduced to something else that is not religion; they are philosophies of religion that effectively deny that there is such a thing as religion to be philosophised about and they are on that account defective.

However, it is not easy to distinguish sharply between the legitimate 'interpretation' of religious phenomena that any philosophy of religion necessarily involves, and reductionism of the kind just described. If, for example, one judges Arnold to be an ethical reductionist, is it as clear that Kant's philosophy of religion may be described in the same way? Or if Hegel is said to be a metaphysical reductionist, in that for him religion becomes a species of metaphysics, is the same true of Plato and Plotinus? Or again, how are we to judge Spinoza? Is Spinoza guilty of reducing religion to philosophy, or is he attempting to give philosophy a religious dimension; is he an atheist or a 'God-intoxicated' man? There is a further difficulty when we consider accounts of specific religious traditions such as Christianity. Is it obvious, for example, that Tillich's philosophy of religion results in a reductionist denaturing of the Christian religion? It has been charged that Tillich's position violates 'essential Christian belief' and that 'the proper place for Tillich and many of his followers today is in the Hindu religion'. Certainly we may admit that Tillich's view of the Christian religion is at odds with traditional theology, but then Tillich is obviously concerned to proffer a reinterpretation of Christianity which will reveal its true essence, hitherto obscured by traditional theology. Once again, as we have said, it is not easy to distinguish nicely between legitimate reinterpretation of the data of Christianity and reductionism. Nevertheless, despite the difficulties of applying this criterion it remains true that a philosophy of religion that effectively evacuates religion of any specific meaning of its own by reducing it to that which is not religion, is deficient as a philosophy of religion.

These are the kinds of criteria that would have to be invoked if we were to try to adjudicate between the various types of philosophy of religion we have discussed. Fortunately, it is not our business to carry out that work of adjudication here. Our task has been the more modest one of describing and critically analysing the main ways in which philosophy and religion have wrestled with each other in the past two thousand years of Western thought.

As was stated at the beginning of this book, that two-thousand-year-old tradition has represented an extraordinary intellectual achievement in Western culture which has not been fully recognised.

NOTES

INTRODUCTION

1. *Philosophy of Religion: the Historic Approaches* (New York, Herder and Herder, 1972).
2. See the brilliant works of the French historian of ideas Pierre Hadot, for example the collection *Philosophy as a Way of Life*, ed. Arnold I. Davidson (Oxford, Blackwell, 1988). See also Max Charlesworth, 'The Diversity of Revelations' in Charlesworth, *Religious Inventions, Four Essays* (Cambridge, Cambridge University Press, 1997). On Gnosticism old and new, see Harold Bloom, *Omens of Millennium: the Gnosis of Angels, Dreams and Resurrection* (New York, Riverhead Books, 1990).
3. On the Muggletonians and other seventeenth-century antinomian sects see Charlesworth, *Religious Inventions*, pp. 144–6.
4. See Steven Runciman's classic work, *The Medieval Manichee: A Study of the Christian Heresy* (Cambridge, Cambridge University Press, 1947); and on the Cathars the marvellous study by E. Le Roy Ladurie, *Montaillou: Cathars and Catholics in a French Village: 1294–1320* (Harmondsworth, Penguin, 1980).
5. See Raimundo Pannikar, 'Religious Pluralism: The Metaphysical Challenge', in Leroy S. Rouncer ed., *Religious Pluralism* (Boston, 1984).
6. Jacques Dupuis, *Jesus Christ at the Encounter of World Religions* (New York, Orbis Books, 1991), p. 4.
7. See, for example, Clifford Geertz, *Local Knowledge: Further Essays in Interpretive Anthropology* (New York, Basic Books, 1983).

8. The early work of the English anthropologist E. Evans-Pritchard has been important in this respect: see his classic study, *Theories of Primitive Religion* (Oxford, Clarendon Press, 1965).

9. See the excellent study by Kevin Hart, *The Trespass of the Sign: Deconstruction, Theology and Philosophy* (Cambridge, Cambridge University Press, 1989).

10. See Charlesworth, *Religious Inventions*, pp. 42–3.

11. Luce Irigaray, *This Sex Is Not One* (Ithaca, Cornell University Press, 1985); Sara Coakley, 'Gender and Knowledge in Western Philosophy: The "Man of Reason" and the Feminine "Other" in Enlightenment and Romantic Thought', in Ann Carr and Elisabeth Schussler Fiorenza, eds., 'The Special Nature of Women', *Concilium*, 1991/6; Ursula King, ed., *Religion and Gender* (Oxford, Blackwell, 1995). See also Alison M. Jaggar and Iris Marion Young eds., *A Companion to Feminist Philosophy* (Oxford, Blackwell, 2000), Part V, 'Religion'.

12. Evelyn Fox Keller, 'Feminism and Science', *Signs*, 3 (1982), p. 593. See also the same author's *Reflections on Gender in Science* (New Haven, Yale University Press, 1985).

13. See Deirdre Carbine, *The Unknown God: Negative Theology in the Platonic Tradition: Plato to Eriugena* (Louvain, Peeters, 1995).

CHAPTER ONE

1. G. Kaufman, 'Philosophy of Religion and Christian Theology', *Journal of Religion* (1957), p. 236.

2. Rudolf Bultmann, 'The Question of Natural Revelation', in Bultmann, *Essays: Philosophical and Theological* (London, 1957), p. 90.

3. 'Qu'est ce qu'un dogme?', *La Quinzaine* (16 Apr 1905), p. 517: 'Primarily a dogma (i.e. a theological statement) has a *practical* meaning. Primarily, it states a presumption of a practical kind.' p. 518: 'Christianity is not a system of speculative philosophy, but a source and rule of life, a discipline or moral and religious action, in short, a set of practical means for obtaining salvation.'

4. Cf. W. F. R. Hardie, *Aristotle's Ethical Theory* (Oxford, 1968), p. 340: 'Aristotle was not a democractic liberal, and did not shrink from the idea that happiness, at least in its best form, is for the fortunate few not the meritorious many.'

5. Le Roy, p. 523.

6. See A. D. Nock, *Conversion: The Old and the New in Religious from Alexander the Great to Augustine of Hippo* (Oxford, 1933), esp. chap. xi, 'Conversion to Philosophy'.

7. On the medieval 'dialecticians' and 'anti-dialecticians' and St Anselm's intellectualism, see M. J. Charlesworth, *St Anselm's 'Proslogion'* (Oxford, 1965), pp. 25–6.

8. See Étienne Gilson, *Reason and Revelation in the Middle Ages*, pp. 55–65.

9. Alain De Libera, *Penser au Moyen Age* (Paris, 1991), pp. 321–333.

10. *Republic*, 364–7.

11. Ibid., 379a–380d.

12. A. Diès, *Autour de Platon*; ii. (Paris, 1927), 591. This old but still valuable study has two excellent chapters, 'Le Dieu de Platon' (chap. iii), and 'La Religion de Platon' (chap. iv). See also Michael C. Morgan, 'Plato and Greek Religion' in *The Cambridge Companion to Plato*, ed. Richard Kraut (Cambridge, MA, Harvard University Press, 1985), esp. chap. vii, 'Philosophical Religion'.

13. *Philebus*, 28d; *Laws*, 889e–890a; *Gorgias*, 482c–484c.

14. Cited in Diès, *Autour de Platon*, ii, p. 533; Cf. p. 536: 'The main proofs of the existence of God are, with Plato, echoes not only of Socrates' teachings but also of an entire literature that existed before him.'

15. W. Jaeger, *The Theology of the Early Greek Philosophers* (Oxford, 1967), p. 36.

16. Ibid., p. 54: 'He was profoundly impressed by the way in which philosophy was disturbing the old religion, and it was this that made him insist upon a new and purer conception of the divine nature.'

17. Ibid., p. 72.

18. *Phaedo*, p. 80a–b.

19. *Sophist*, p. 249a.

20. *Republic*, p. 509b.

21. See, for example, Plato's *Seventh Letter*, 341c–402, regarding the divine: 'There is no writing of mine on this subject, nor will there ever be; for it cannot be put into words like other objects of knowledge.'

22. Cf. A. J. Festugière, *Personal Religion among the Greeks* (Berkeley and Los Angeles, 1934), p. 133: 'If *nous* is taken in its twofold meaning as both intellectual faculty and mystical faculty, there will result a philosophical contemplation leading, in its final stage, to mystical contact; here we have the true Platonic tradition, that adopted, for example, by Plotinus.' See also the same author's *Contemplation et vie contemplative selon Platon*, 2nd ed. (Paris, 1950).

23. Cf. R. Hackforth, 'Plato's Theism', in *Studies in Plato's Metaphysics*, ed. R. E. Allen (London, 1965), p. 440: 'For Plato the Demiurge is a *theos*, so is the created universe, so are the stars and planets and the gods of popular theology, and the (possible) plurality of good souls in *Laws*, x; the adjective *theios* is commonly applied to the Forms.'

24. Hackforth, ibid. Cf. Diès, *Autour de Platon*, ii, 592–3: 'The dialectical ascent and the mystical or religious ascent are fundamentally the same movement – the movement of the entire soul towards being, towards the intelligible, towards God.'

25. 966c–d.

26. 90a.

27. F. Solmsen, *Plato's Theology* (New York, 1942), p. 126, claims that Plato's religious intellectualism was balanced by the influence upon him of the mystery religions and their 'general feeling of man's dependence on the gods and the atmosphere of religious awe'. Cf. also W. K. C. Guthrie, *Orpheus and Greek Religion* (London, 1935), pp. 158–69. But it remains true, as Solmsen admits, that the ecstasy typical of the mystery cults has no place in Plato's religion. J. B. McMinn, 'Plato as a Philosophical Theologian', in *Phronesis* (1960), 30, argues that Plato resorts to 'mythological constructs' in his philosophical theology because he recognises 'the inadequacy of rational explanation' in this sphere. McMinn concludes that Plato's acceptance of a 'noncognitive factor' in religion is akin to the views of the those contemporary philosophical theologians who claim that religious knowledge is 'non-cognitive' or 'non-rational'. But it is clear that for Plato any such conception of 'non-cognitive knowledge' would be sheer nonsense, and that mythological thinking is an inferior mode of thinking incapable of really disclosing the divine.

28. Diès, *Autour de Platon*, ii, p. 603.

29. W. D. Ross, *Aristotle's Metaphysics* (Oxford, 1924), p. clii.

30. Ibid., p. cliv.

31. Gerald F. Else, *Aristotle's Poetics: The Argument* (Cambridge, Mass., 1957), p. 475.

32. W. Jaeger, *Aristotle: Fundamentals of the History of his Development*, 2nd ed. (Oxford, 1948); cf. J. H. Randall, *Aristotle* (New York, 1960), p. 7: 'This theology of the Unmoved Mover, the expression of Aristotle's early Platonistic faith, was gradually pushed into the background.' There is an enormous literature on Jaeger's thesis. For critical views see A. Mansion, 'La genèse de l'oeuvre d'Aristote d'après les travaux récents', *Revue Néoscolastique de Philosophie* (1927), pp. 307–31, 423–66; F. Nuyens, *L'Evolution de la psychologie d'Aristote* (Louvain, 1948). Cf. W. K. C. Guthrie, 'The Development of Aristotle's Theology', *Classical Quarterly* (1934), p. 98: 'Aristotle's system, instead of showing a development altogether away from Platonism, might rather be described as in some respects the furnishing of logical grounds for preserving what he regarded as the essential parts of Platonism intact... To put this in a more general form, it was his progress in the exact sciences itself which was helping him, not to cast off Platonism, but to substantiate more and more of the Platonic position.'

33. It is not quite exact to say, as W. D. Ross does, that the object of Book viii of the *Physics* is merely to account for 'the presence of movement in the world and for its having the characteristics it has': *Aristotle's Physics* (Oxford, 1936), p. 85. Its object is rather to account for the mixture of potentiality and actuality that the material world exemplifies.

34. Sextus Empiricus, *Phys.*, 1. pp. 20–3: 'Aristotle used to say that men's thoughts of gods spring from two sources – the experiences of the soul, and the phenomena of the heavens… Seeing by day the sun running his circular course, and by night the well-ordered movement of the other stars, they came to think that there is a God who is the cause of such movement and order.' Cited in *The Works of Aristotle*, ed. Sir David Ross (Oxford, 1952), xii (*Select Fragments*), p. 84.

35. Ibid., 1074b 1–14; cf. W. K. C. Guthrie, 'Development of Aristotle's Theology', p. 92. 'Astronomy had a strange but undeniable fascination for Aristotle… It was one of the few outlets left to him to show his sympathy with religion. In acknowledging the supremacy of the stars he was paying homage to an age-old belief… It was the one religious tenet which he felt the rationalist could retain.' I cannot agree, however, with Guthrie's implication here that Aristotle's rationalism was at odds with his sympathy for religion.

36. *Metaphysics*, x 10, 1075a 14.

37. W. I. Verdenius, 'Traditional and Personal Elements in Aristotle's Religion', *Phronesis*, v (1960), p. 61: 'In his strictest form the Aristotelian god is the final cause of the world, residing in his own sphere and acting on the world as a model of perfection. But the final cause sometimes develops an efficient aspect. Consequently, the Aristotelian god, who is the ultimate source of the good, brings about the order of the world, primarily as the object of the world's desire, but secondarily as a regulative force.'

38. P. Merlan, *The Cambridge History of Later Greek and Early Medieval Philosophy*, ed. A. H. Armstrong (Cambridge, 1967), p. 52. In Aristotle's actual practice in the *Metaphysics*, however, it is clear that 'theology' is a *part* of a more general inquiry.

39. 430a 20–5.

40. Merlan, *Cambridge History*, p. 118. Alexander's interpretation of the *De Anima* has been hotly contested by later commentators, but his reading is nevertheless a plausible one.

41. x 7, 1177a 12–18.

42. x 8, 1178b 7.

43. 1178b 18–23.

44. Cf. E. R. Dodds, *The Greeks and the Irrational* (Berkeley, 1951), pp. 117–21.

45. 1177a 13–16; cf. W. F. R. Hardie, *Aristotle's Ethical Theory* (Oxford, 1969), p. 345.

46. 1177a 25–32.

47. vii 15, 1249b 17–20: 'That choice, then, or possession of the natural goods – whether bodily goods, wealth, friends, or other things – which will most produce the contemplation of God, that choice or possession is best, this is the noblest standard. But any that through defect or excess hinders one from the contemplation and service of God is bad.'

48. *De Anima*, ii 5, 430a 23.

49. Cf. Nuyens, *L'Évolution de la psychologie d'Aristote*, p. 309.

50. 1074b 32.

51. 1238b 18.

52. Cf. R. Norman, 'Aristotle's Philosopher-God', in *Phronesis*, xiv (1969), p. 67: 'When Aristotle describes the Prime Mover as "thinking itself", he is not referring to any activity that could be called "self-contemplation", he is simply describing the same activity that human minds perform when they engage in abstract thought ... its thinking is entirely of the "theoretic" kind and not at all of the "receptive" kind. Since "self-thinking" is the same as ordinary human abstract thought, it is not this that characterises the Prime Mover, but rather the fact that it thinks of perfection, and does so eternally'.

53. *Metaphysics*, p. cliv.

54. Ibid. Cf. also E. Gilson, *God and Philosophy* (New Haven, 1941), p. 34: 'With Aristotle, the Greeks had gained an indisputably rational theology, but they had lost their religion.'

55. Cf. Jaeger, *The Theology of the Early Greek Philosophers*, p. 32. Speaking of Anaximander, Jaeger says: 'His first principle is immortal and without beginning. It is not infinite but also truly eternal. It would be a mistake to blind ourselves to the religious significance implicit in this exalted conception of the Divine because of any preconceived notions of what genuine religion ought to be and what kind of knowledge it should seek. We have no right, for instance, to complain that Anaximander's god is not a god one can pray to, or that physical speculation is not true religion. Surely no one will deny that we simply cannot conceive of any advanced form of religion as lacking the idea of endlessness and eternity which Anaximander links with his new concept of the Divine.'

56. Solmsen, *Plato's Theology*, p. 177.

57. A. H. Armstrong, ed., *Cambridge History*, p. 239.

58. 'Enn.' vi 7.21.

59. On Plotinus see *Cambridge History*, part iii, by A. H. Armstrong; and on Porphyry, Proclus and the later neo-Platonists, see part iv of the same work by A. C. Lloyd. See also J. M. Rist, *Plotinus: The Road to Reality* (Cambridge, 1967), and Paul Henry, 'The Place of Plotinus in the History of Thought', in J. Dillon ed., *Plotinus: The Enneads* (London, Penguin, 1991); and Pierre Hadot's introduction to his translation of the *Treatise 38, V, 7 of the Enneads* (Paris, Les Editions du Cerf, 1987), pp. 11–69.

60. Nock, *Conversion*, p. 175. On Plotinus, see Porphyry's *Vita Plotini*, in *Enneads*, trans. S. MacKenna (London, 1917), pp. 1–20. Cf. p. 17: 'Pure of soul, ever striving towards the divine which he loved with all his being, he laboured strenuously to free himself and rise above the bitter waves of this blood-drenched life, and this is why to Plotinus – God-like and lifting

himself often, by the ways of meditation and by the methods Plato teaches in the *Banquet* to the first and all-transcendent God – that God appeared, the God who has neither shape nor form but sits enthroned above the Intellectual-Principle and all the Intellectual-Sphere... To this God, I also declare, I Porphyry, that in my sixty-eighth year I too was once admitted and entered into Union.' On the similarities between Plotinus and Eastern religious thought see E. Bréhier, *La Philosophie de Plotin* (Paris, 1928) chap. vii, 'L'Orientalisme de Plotin'.

61. R. A. Markus, in *Cambridge History*, p. 343.

62. Markus, ibid., p. 344. Regarding Origen see R. A. Norris, *God and World in Early Christian Theology* (New York, 1965), p. 133. 'However much Origen may differ from the Platonism of the Pagan schools – and his teaching in fact diverges from it widely at certain crucial points – there can be no doubt that his conception of the point and purpose of Christian teaching is shaped by the Platonist idea of the soul's intellectual quest for union with intelligible reality.' On St Gregory of Nyssa see W. Jaeger, *Early Christianity and Greek Paideia* (Cambrige, Mass., 1961), p. 90: 'As the Greek philosopher's whole life was a process of *paideia* through philosophical ascesis, so for Gregory Christianity was not a mere set of dogmas but the perfect life based on the *theoria* or contemplation of God and on even more perfect union with him.'

63. *Confessions*, iii 4.

64. See E. R. Dodds ed., *Proclus: The Elements of Theology*, 2nd ed. (Oxford, 1963), pp. xxvi–xxviii.

65. Cf. I. P. Sheldon-Williams, in *Cambridge History*, p. 573, n. 3: 'Contemporary opinion differs as to whether the author was a pagan who prudently disguised his thorough-going neo-Platonism under a thin Christian veneer, or a sincere Christian, and even a Christian mystic, who found the neo-Platonic formularies a suitable mode of expression for his thought.'

66. See Arnaldo Momigliano, 'Cassiodorus and Italian Culture of His Time', *Proceedings of the British Academy* (1955), p. 213: 'Many people have turned to Christianity for consolation. Boëthius turned to paganism. His Christianity collapsed – it collapsed so thoroughly that perhaps he did not even notice its disappearance. The God of the Greek philosophers gave peace to his mind.' For a more balanced assessment of Boëthius and the *De Consolatione* see H. Liebeschutz, *Cambridge History*, pp. 550 ff.

67. See L. Gardet and M. M. Anawati, *Introduction à la théologie musulmane* (Paris, 1948); R. Walzer, *Greek into Arabic* (Oxford, 1962); R. Walzer, 'Early Islamic Philosophy', in *Cambridge History*, part viii; M. M. Sharif, *A History of Muslim Philosophy* (Wiesbaden, 1963), i, part 3.

68. 'Rhazes on the Philosophic Life', trans. A. J. Arberry, *Asiatic Review*, xlv (1949), pp. 703–13.

69. Cited in Sharif, *A History of Muslim Philosophy*, p. 439.
70. Cited in *Cambridge History*, p. 655.
71. Cited in ibid., p. 656.
72. See, for example, George Santayana, *The Life of Reason*, vol. iii; *Reason in Religion* (New York, 1905); J. H. Randall, *The Role of Knowledge in Western Religions* (Boston, 1956).
73. *Al Farabi's Philosophy of Plato and Aristotle*, ed., M. Mahdi (New York, 1962), pp. 44–5.
74. R. Walzer, in *Cambridge History*, p. 668. See also Sharif, *A History of Muslim Philosophy* (Wiesbaden, 1963–66), pp. 49 ff., on Ibn Sina's theory of prophecy, and A. J. Arberry, *Avicenna on Theology* (London, 1951).
75. L. Gauthier, *Ibn Rochd* (Paris, 1948); *Ibn Rochd: Traité Décisif* (Algiers, 1948).
76. Ibid., p. 267.
77. Cf. Jaeger, *Early Christianity and Greek Paideia*, p. 53: 'The distinction between the "simpler" Christian minds of mere "believers" and the theologian who "knows" the true meaning of the holy books is common to both Clement and Origen. *Gnosis* is the fashionable word for this trend to transcend the sphere of *pistis*, which in Greek philosophical language always had the connotation of the subjective'.
78. *Lectures on the Philosophy of Religion*, iii, ed. E. B. Spiers and J. B. Sanderson (London, 1962), p. 148. On the general interest in philosophical religion or the 'religion of reason' during the Enlightenment era, and on the ideas of the various deistic thinkers such as Lord Herbert of Cherbury (1583–1648) and Lessing (1729–81), see Peter Gay, *The Enlightenment: An Interpretation* (London, 1967), and *Deism: An Anthology* (Princeton, 1968). See also Ernst Cassirer, *The Philosophy of the Enlightenment* (Boston, 1951), esp. chap. 4, 'Religion'. Lessing's statement is a typical one: 'All revealed religion is nothing but a reconfirmation of the religion of reason.' See also, on the 'rational theology' of the seventeenth century 'Cambridge Platonists' (Smith, Cudworth, More), Basil Willey, *The Seventeenth Century Background* (London, 1953), chap. viii, and the splendid anthology of texts, *The Cambridge Platonists*, ed. C. A. Patrides (London, 1969).
79. J. Steinmann, ed., *Pensées* (Monaco, 1961), p. 455.
80. H. Meynell, *Sense, Nonsense and Christianity* (London, 1964), chap. iv, assumes that the orthodox or traditional interpretation of the Christian religion is in some way normative, so that any attempt to give Christianity a sense at variance with that interpretation *ipso facto* involves 'reductionism' and the denaturing of Christian doctrine.
81. J. N. Findlay, *Hegel: A Re-examination* (London, 1958), p. 354. See also G. R. G. Mure, 'Hegel, Luther and the Owl of Minerva', *Philosophy* (1966), p. 127: 'Too little attention is now paid to the peculiar influence of his personal religion on Hegel's mature philosophical speculation.'

82. *G. W. Leibniz: Theodicy*, ed. A. Farrer (London, 1951), Introduction, pp. 9–10. Leibniz's philosophy of religion is, however, in some respects more akin to that of Aquinas than to that of Spinoza and Hegel.

83. iii 150–1.

84. *Ethics*, part iv, prop. 28, ed. J. Gutman (New York, 1949), p. 207.

85. Ibid., part v, prop. 32, corollary, p. 273.

86. Ibid., corollary, p. 273.

87. *A Theologico-Political Treatise* (New York, 1951) p. 185.

88. Ibid., p. 194.

89. Ibid., p. 186.

90. Ibid., p. 190.

91. Cf. S. Hampshire, *Spinoza* (London, 1951), p. 151. For Spinosa 'the various religious myths of the world are essentially the presentation in imaginative and picturesque terms of more or less elementary moral truths. The great majority of mankind, who are capable only of the lowest grade of knowledge, will only understand, and be emotionally impressed by, myths which appeal directly to their imagination... They cannot understand what is meant by the perfection and omnipotence of God, as a metaphysician understands these ideas.'

92. Schopenhauer, *Essays and Aphorisms*, trans. R. J. Hollingdale (Harmondsworth, 1970), p. 96.

93. *Phenomenology of Mind*, trans. J. B. Baillie, 2nd ed. (London, 1949), pp. 780–2. Cf. Findlay, *Hegel: A Re-examination*, p. 342. For Hegel 'a religious term like "God" will, when stripped of pictorial associations, reveal itself as meaning no more than the "I" of self-consciousness, which is for Hegel also the element of universality and unity present in all thinking, which is inseparable from the finite particular self to which it may *seem* transcendent, but which uses the latter as the vehicle through which it achieves its self-consciousness.'

94. Cf. W. T. Stace, *The Philosophy of Hegel* (London, 1924), pp. 486–7, for a useful discussion of *Vorstellung*.

95. *Ethics*, p. 19.

96. Ibid.

97. *Lectures on the Philosophy of Religion*, iii 148.

98. Ibid., pp. 87–8.

99. Letter lxxiii, *The Correspondence of Spinoza*, ed. A. Wolf (London, 1925), p. 344. Cf. Hampshire, *Spinoza*, pp. 145–6, on 'the radical lack of the idea of history' in Spinoza's thought. For Spinoza, 'We ordinarily think of the world as a mere succession of events, in the manner of the historian, only because we have not yet arrived at the eternal truths which present the true order of Nature as an unchanging system'. For a contrary view see R. Mason, *The God of Spinoza* (Cambridge, 1997).

100. *Lectures on the Philosophy of Religion*, pp. 78 ff. Lessing – in his religious ideas, a link between Spinoza and Hegel – has a very acute awareness of the problem that arises over the relation between the historical and necessary elements in religion. If religion is to be rational it must deal in necessary and universal truths; on the other hand religious belief is as a matter of fact always rooted in particular historical claims. How then move from the one to the other? 'Contingent historical truths can never serve as proof for necessary truths of reason... To jump from historical truth to an entirely different class of truths, and to ask me to alter all my metaphysical and moral concepts accordingly ... if that is not a "transformation to another kind" then I do not know what else Aristotle meant by this term... This is the ugly, wide ditch over which I cannot leap, however often and earnestly I try. If anyone can help me over, I pray, I conjure him to do so. God will recompense him'. *Schriften*, ed. Lachmann, Munckner (1886–1924) xiii 5. See also H. Chadwick, *Lessing's Theological Writings* (Palo Alto, Calif., 1956).

101. Hegel's philosophy, however, is all things to all men, and it can also be interpreted in an 'historicist' sense. Thus A. MacIntyre, 'Herbert Marcuse: From Marxism to Pessimism', in *Survey*, lxii (1967): 39, claims that there is a 'spectrum' of interpretations of Hegel. 'At one end of this spectrum lies a Hegel for whom the world of historical experience is merely the phenomenal clothing of the timeless logical categories which constitute the successive phases of the self-development of the Absolute... This interpretation of Hegel is fundamentally a theological interpretation and although in this Hegelian scheme the metaphysical reality behind finite experience does not enjoy the independence of its this-worldly manifestations which it does in Christian theology, nonetheless it is this element in Hegel which enabled Right Hegelianism and Lutheranism to cement a relationship. At the other end of the spectrum lies the interpretation of Hegel according to which the categories of the logic are thought of as having no more reality than that bestowed upon them by their embodiment in historical form... This history of philosophy, of categories and concepts, and the history of social transactions are but two sides of the same coin. This interpretation emphasises the empirical aspect of Hegel's thought, and especially the fact that the logical progress in both societies and conceptual schemes is something that can be discerned only after the event. We cannot discover the patterns of development without a close study of which actually happened. The owl of Minerva flies only at dusk.'

102. *The Principles of Logic* (London, 1922), 'Terminal Essays', viii, pp. 688–9. Cf. pp. 689–70: 'I will venture once more to speak through the mouth of my supposed Christian. Imagine him asked whether, thinking as he does, he cares nothing for "the historical truth" of Christianity, any more than for the detail of Christian creeds and symbols – and possibly his answer might surprise us. "I understood you to be speaking", he might reply, "about mere

temporal events and happenings, just as you might speak again about mere material things such as this crucifix or that flag. These by themselves are all abstractions, mistaken for realities by what too often is called Common Sense; and these most assuredly are not the genuine facts and beliefs of religion. Religious events and symbols, though on one side things and happenings in your "real world", are something on the other side whose essence and life is elsewhere. Identified with what is beyond, they are no mere occurrences in time or things in space. They represent, and they are the actual incarnation of eternal reality, and for the least of them a man might feel called on do die.' Bradley himself does not identify his Absolute with God nor does he argue for any kind of religious view.

103. Letter xxi, in A. Wolf, ed., *Correspondence of Spinoza*, p. 173.

104. F. Copleston, *A History of Philosophy* (London, 1958), iv, 245.

105. *Dialogues concerning Natural Religion*, ed. N. Kemp Smith (Oxford, 1945), p. 281. Cf. A. Seth Pringle-Pattison, *The Idea of God* (New York, 1920), p. 22: 'How can a proposition possess any religious significance if, as Philo truly describes it here, "it affords no inference that affects human life".' It might be remarked that this kind of objection presupposes a sharp disjunction between the speculative and practial orders (*à la* Kant), and that it loses a good deal of its force in an Aristotelian context, for example, where the end of the moral life is primarily a contemplative one and where the 'practical reason' is dependent upon 'pure reason',

106. Though some contemporary Christian theologians seem to deny that the notion of revelation is tied to a 'supernaturalist' undersanding of it according to which revelation is a 'miraculous supernatural intervention in the natural order of existent beings'. See on this Paul Tillich, 'Revelations in the Philosophy of Religion', in *Twentieth Century Theology in the Making*, ed. J. Pelikan (London, 1970), ii, p. 51.

107. See S. Runciman, *The Medieval Manichee* (Cambridge, 1947).

108. See Aelred Graham, *Conversations between Christians and Buddhists* (London, 1969), p. 44: 'Muso says that if one is going to be a Zen disciple at all he has to be of the first class.'

109. J. M. E. McTaggart, *Some Dogmas of Religion* (London, 1906), pp. 292, 297, 298.

110. 1 Cor. 15.

111. H. Price, 'Is Theism Important?', in *The Socratic* (Oxford, 1952), p. 41.

112. McTaggart, *Some Dogmas of Religion*, p. 74.

113. A. N. Whitehead, *Process and Reality* (Cambridge, 1929), p. 484. On Whitehead's concept of God see W. A. Christian, 'The Concept of God as a Derivative Notion', in *Process and Divinity*, ed. W. L. Reese and E. Freeman (La Salle, Ill., 1964), pp. 181–203. See also James Collins, *God in Modern Philosophy* (Chicago, 1959), pp. 315 ff. Cf. also the work of Whitehead's fellow traveller, Charles Hartshorne, *Man's Vision of God and the Logic of Theism* (Chicago and New York, 1941).

114. See C. F. Mooney, *Teilhard de Chardin and the Mystery of Christ* (London, 1966). It is very interesting in the case of Teilhard to see how he finds himself up against the same difficulties as the philosophers of religion we have examined above – for example, how to preserve the notion of the supernatural and of revelation, and how to escape 'necessitarianism' and to allow for the dimension of historical contingency. In other words, the demands of traditional Christianity appear to conflict with the demands of his philosophy of religion.

CHAPTER TWO

1. See W. Jaeger, *Early Christianity and Greek Paideia* (Cambridge, Mass., 1961); A. H. Armstrong and R. A. Markus, *Christian Faith and Greek Philosophy* (London, 1960), esp. chap. 10, 'Faith and Philosophy'.
2. On Philo the definitive work is *Philo: Fundations of Religious Philosophy in Judaism, Christianity and Islam*, by H. A. Wolfson (Cambridge, Mass., 1948), 2 vols. See also the old but still valuable work, *The Christian Platonists* by Charles Bigg (Oxford, 1886), Lecture 1.
3. Wolfson, *Philo*, i, 141.
4. For the history of the 'handmaid' analogy see ibid., i, 145.
5. Ibid., i, 115.
6. Ibid., i, 116.
7. Ibid., i, 125.
8. H. Chadwick, *Early Christian Thought and the Classical Tradition* (Oxford, 1966), p. 5.
9. See R. M. Grant, *Gnosticism and Early Christianity* (New York, 1966), esp. chap. 5, 'From Myth to Philosophy'.
10. Origen, *Contra Celsum*, trans. H. Chadwick (Cambridge, 1965), i, 9; p. 12.
11. Cf. Clement of Alexandria's judgement on the simple faithful: 'The so-called orthodox believers are like beasts working out of fear; they do good works without understanding what they do.' *Stromateis*, i, 45.6.
12. See Chadwick, *Early Christian Thought*, p. 3.
13. On Justin see R. A. Norris, *God and World in Early Christian Theology* (New York, 1965), chap. 11.
14. *Apologia*, i 46: trans. *The Library of Christian Classics* (Philadelphia, 1953), vol. i.
15. R. A. Norris, *God and World in Early Christian Theology* (New York, 1965), p. 53.
16. *Strom*, i, 30.
17. Ibid., i, 94.
18. On Clement's 'Christian gnosticism' see Bigg, *Christian Platonists*, pp. 86 ff.
19. Origen, *Contra Celsum*, trans. Chadwick, vii, 42; p. 430.

20. Ibid.
21. Ibid., p. 430.
22. Ibid.; J. Daniélou, *Origen* (London, 1955), chap. v, sees Origen's rejection of Celsus's religious esotericism as a central feature of his thought. See p. 108: 'In his view, the vision of God is beyond the reach of all men without exception when they are left to their natural resources, while on the other hand it is given by God as a favour to all who ask and turn to him for it, whether they are philosophers or not.'
23. *De Principiis*, i.3.1.
24. *Comm. Matt.*, 12.5.
25. See Daniélou, *Origen*, part ii.
26. On this see J. J. O'Meara, *The Young Augustine* (London, 1954), chaps. ix, x. The following paragraphs are taken from my book *St Anselm's 'Proslogion'* (Oxford, 1965), pp. 26–7.
27. *Epist*, 120; P. L. 38, 453.
28. *Sermo*, 126; P. L. 38, 699: 'God made you a rational animal ... and formed you in His own image... Therefore lift up your mind ... look at the things you see, and look for Him whom you do not see'.
29. *Sermo* 43; P. L. 38, 257.
30. See E. TeSelle, 'Nature and Grace in Augustine's Exposition of Genesis 1: 1–5', *Recherches augustiniennes*, v (1968), 114. For Augustine, 'what is required for the vision of God is not a supernatural perfection of the intellect by which it might be enabled to attain to a knowledge beyond its capabilities, but a fervour and steadfastness of the will by which the mind can be borne towards God. Augustine assumes that God is not only present to the mind but fully knowable to the pure in heart.'
31. Ibid., p. 112.
32. *De Lib. Arbit.*, II, ii 5, trans. M. Pontifex, *The Problem of Free Choice* (London, 1955), pp. 77–8.
33. Ibid., II xv; Pontifex, p. 120.
34. Ibid.
35. Cf. *De Trinitate*, vi, Boëthius: *The Theological Tractates*, trans. H. F. Stewart and E. K. Rand (London, 1919), p. 31. 'If, God helping me, I have furnished some support in argument to an article which stands by itself on the firm foundation of Faith, I shall render joyous praise for the finished work to him from whom the invitation comes.'
36. See Jean Cottiaux, 'La conception de la théologie chez Abélard', *Revue d'histoire ecclésiastique*, xxvii (1932), pp. 248–95, 533–51, 788–828.
37. *Tractatus*, pp. 19–29.
38. Cottiaux, 'La conception de la théologie,' p. 799.
39. J. R. McCallum, *Abelard's Christian Theology* (Oxford, 1948).
40. See A. V. Murray, *Abelard and St Bernard* (Manchester, 1967).

41. McCallum, *Abelard's Christian Theology*, p. 68. Abelard goes on to cite the text from Plato's *Timaeus* to which Origen also refers: 'Plato, greatest of philosophers, saw this point when he said in the *Timaeus*: "The craftsman of the universe, and its begetter, is hard to find, and even when found, difficult to define".'

42. *Introductio ad theologiam*, P. L. 178, 1050. For a balanced view on Abelard's position on faith and reason see M. de Gandillac, *Oeuvres choisies d'Abélard* (Paris, 1945), pp. 33 ff.

43. *Theologia*, P. L. 178, 1226A.

44. *Introductio*, 1085.

45. See the analysis of Anselm's central work *Cur Deus Homo?* in M. J. Charlesworth, *St Anselm's 'Proslogion'* (Oxford, 1965), pp. 30–7.

46. In I Sent.II. Cited in T. Tshibangu, *Théologie positive et théologie speculative* (Louvain, 1965), p. 51.

47. Ibid.

48. *Summa Theologica*, ed. Quarrachi (1924), cap. i. On the application of the Aristotelian idea of 'science' to theology see M. D. Chenu, *La Théologie comme science au XIIIème siècle* (Paris, 1957) and Tshibangu, *Théologie positive*.

49. See Maimonides's *The Guide of the Perplexed*, trans. S. Pines (Chicago, 1963).

50. Ibid., ii, 16; pp. 293–4.

51. Ibid., ii, 22; p. 320.

52. Ibid.

53. Ibid., ii, 25; p. 328.

54. Ibid., 25; pp. 329–30.

55. Ibid., p. 329.

56. Étienne Gilson, *Reason and Revelation in the Middle Ages* (New York, 1938), p. 83.

57. Cited in Gilson, *Reason and Revelation*, p. 64. It was ironic that some of Aquinas's own propositions were also condemned at the same time by Bishop Tempier. For general background see Gillian Evans, *The Medieval Theologians: An Introduction to Theology in the Medieval Period* (Oxford, Blackwell, 2001).

58. *Summa Theologiae*, I, i.

59. Ibid. See also II, ii 2.3.

60. II, ii, 2.4.

61. See II, ii, 2.4. 'Whether it is necessary to believe those things which can be proved by natural reason?'

62. Ibid., ad 2.

63. I, i, 3.

64. I, i, 6.

65. I, i, 2. See Tshibangu, *Théologie positive*, pp. 68–96, on Aquinas's views of theology as an Aristotelian 'science'.

66. II, ii, 2.2.

67. II, ii, 6.1.
68. See Y. Congar, *La Foi et la théologie* (Paris, 1959), pp. 83 ff., on the various post-Thomistic theories of the act of faith. See also R. Aubert, *Le problème de l'acte de foi*, 3rd ed. (Louvain, 1945).
69. Heb. 11:1. In the *Summa Contra Gentiles*, iii 40, Aquinas says that *as knowledge* faith is the most imperfect act of the intellect (*operatio intellectus imperfectissima*), though with respect to its *object* it is the most perfect.
70. I 12.13. Cf. G. Van Riet, 'Y a-t-il chez saint Thomas une philosophie de la religion?', in *Revue Philosophique de Louvain*, lxi (1963), p. 54.
71. II, ii, 2.3. 'Wherever one nature is subordinate to another, we find that two things concur towards the perfection of the lower nature, one of which is in respect of that nature's proper movement, while the other is in respect of the movement of the higher nature.' Aquinas applies this principle to reason (the lower and subordinate) and faith (the higher).
72. *The Letter on Apologetics* (1896); English trans., Maurice Blondel, *The Letter on Apologetics and History and Dogma*, trans. Alexandra Dru and Illtyd Trethowan (London, 1964), pp. 147–8.
73. For a highly interesting attempt to develop a coherent theory of the relationship between the natural and the supernatural on the bais of St Thomas's ideas see *The Mystery of the Supernatural* by H. de Lubac, English trans. (London, 1967).
74. I 6 and 2. See also II, ii, 2.10, where Aquinas says that the adducing of reasons in support of what we believe by faith is 'consequent to the will of the believer'. 'For when a man's will is ready to believe, he loves the truth he believes, he thinks out and takes to heart whatever reasons he can find in support thereof, and in this way, human reason does not exclude the merit of faith, but is a sign of greater merit.'
75. II, ii, 2.10: 'When a man either has not the will, or not a prompt will, to believe, unless he be moved by human reasons ... in this way human reason diminishes the merit of faith'.
76. I 2.2.
77. Aquinas often seems to confuse the two senses of dependence in that he seems to think that, because a person happens to believe by faith a truth (e.g. one of the preambles of faith) that can *of itself* be known by reason, the former is not logically dependent upon the latter.
78. I, i, 8. See also *In Boëtium de Trinitate*, IX, ii, 4: 'Sacred doctrine makes a threefold use of philosophy. The first is is to demonstrate those truths that are preambles of faith and that have a necessary place in the science of faith... The second is to give a clearer notion, by certain similitudes, of the truths of faith... The third is to resist those who speak against the truth, either by showing that these statements are false, or by showing that they are not necessarily true.'
79. See I 12.7.

80. Timothy Potts, 'Theology and Philosophy', *Tablet* (18 Sept 1965), p. 1026.

81. See P. T. Geach, 'Nominalism', *Sophia*, iii, 2 (1964), pp. 3–14.

82. 'Anselm's Ontological Arguments', *Philosophical Review*, lxix (1960), p. 60. Cf. Geach, 'Nominalism', p. 6. 'If all the arguments against a mystery of faith can be cleared up, then surely, people may object, the mystery ceases to be a mystery. This objection is confused. What I am maintaining is that for each single argument against faith there is a refutation, in terms of ordinary logic; not that there is some one general technique for refuting all arguments against faith, or even all arguments against a particular dogma of faith. I do not claim that we can prove, or even clearly see, that the propositions expressing mysteries of faith are consistent... And as regards the doctrine of the Trinity in particular we can see that a demand for a consistency proof could never be satisfied. For the propositions expressing this dogma, relating as they do to the inner life of God without bringing in any actual or possible creatures, cannot be only possibly true; if they are possibly true they are necessarily true. So a proof that the doctrine is consistent would be a proof of its truth, which is certainly impossible.'

83. S. T., I 2.3. On the 'Five Ways' see E. L. Mascall, *He Who Is – A Study in Traditional Theism* (London, 1943) and A. Kenny, *The Five Ways* (Oxford, 1969).

84. Exodus iii 3:14.

85. See I 13.11: 'Whether this name, "He Who Is", is the most proper name of God?'

86. John L. McKenzie, 'God and Nature in the Old Testament', in his *Myths and Realities* (London, 1963), p. 94. Cf. p. 131: '[The Hebrews] saw nature as integrated into the moral and religious order; it was the expression of the blessing or of the wrath of Yahweh, which came as a response to human behaviour.'

87. See also K. Rahner, 'Dieu dans le Nouveau Testament', *Ecrits Théologiques*, i (Paris, 1959), p. 33: 'Old Testament monotheism does not rest upon an investigation of human reason seeking the ultimate unity of the world and looking for it finally in an all-embracing principle that is transcendent to the world. It is based on the experience of the men of the Old Testament of the saving action accomplished by Jahweh at the heart of the world and in the history of their people.'

88. See J. L. McKenzie, 'The Hebrew Attitude toward Polytheism', in *Myths and Realities*, pp. 142–3: 'Even the words for "god" in Hebrew are not susceptible of refinement and precision of expression. Hebrew had no words for god except "el", "elohim"; to express its own peculiar concept of deity which was applicable to Yahweh alone, it had no word except the name Yahweh itself. The words for god had, in Hebrew as in other Semitic idioms, a broader use than the Hebrew concept of deity, strictly speaking, would permit.

89. B. Vawter, 'The God of the Bible', in *God, Jesus and Spirit*, ed. D. Callahan (London, 1969), p. 4.

90. 'Dieu dans le Nouveau Testament', p. 64.

91. See R. Garrigou-Lagrange, *God – His Existence and Nature* (St Louis, 1934); Gilson, *Reason and Revelation* and *Christianisme et Philosophie* (Paris, 1936); J. Maritain, *Approaches to God* (London, 1955).

92. See E. L. Mascall, *He Who Is: A Study in Traditional Theism* (London, 1943); A. Farrer, Finite and Infinite (London, 1943); see also *Anglicanism: The Thought and Practice of the Church of England, Illustrated from the Religious Literature of the 17th Century*, ed. P. E. More and F. L. Cross (London, 1935), sec. vi, 'Natural Theology'.

93. On background to Newman see Ian Ker, *Newman: A Biography* (Oxford, Oxford University Press, 1985) esp. chap. 16, 'The Justification of Religious Belief'.

94. The best edition of Newman's *Essay...* is that of Ian Ker (Oxford, Clarendon Press, 1985). It is cited here as *Grammar.*

95. Cited by Ker, introduction to *Grammar*, p. xx.

96. See Ian Ker and Alan G. Hill, eds., *Newman After a Hundred Years* (Oxford, 1990).

97. Cited by Ker, introduction to *Grammar*, p. xxvii.

98. Owen Chadwick, *Newman* (Oxford, Oxford University Press, 1985), p. 28.

99. *Grammar*, p. 25.

100. An English translation of the essay can be found in M. J. Charlesworth, ed., *The Problem of Religious Language* (New Jersey, Prentice Hall, 1974).

101. Ibid., p. 178.

102. Ibid., p. 188.

103. Ibid., p. 189.

104. Ibid.

105. Ibid., p. 22.

106. ibid., p. 194.

107. See V. White, *The Unknown God and Other Essays* (London, 1948) on the importance of the 'negative way' in Aquinas's conception of God.

108. On Aquinas's theory of analogy see E. L. Mascall, *Existence and Analogy* (London, 1949).

109. It is difficult to accept the interpretation of Aquinas's philosophical theology advanced by Victor Preller in his book *Divine Science and the Science of God: A Reformulation of Thomas Aquinas* (Princeton, 1967). Preller claims that the Five Ways are not really meant by Aquinas to be strict proofs of the existence of God but rather 'external and probable evidence of the truths of the theological claim that the mind of man is ordered to an Unknown God and can reflect on that order' (p. 25).

110. *Summa Contra Gentiles*, bk iii, chap. 25, 'That understanding God is the end of every intellectual substance'; chap. 37, 'That ultimate happiness consists in the contemplation of God'.

111. See Tshibangu, *Théologie positive*, part ii, for an account of the movement in late-nineteenth- and early-twentieth-century Catholic theology against this a-historical tendency. See also the great work of Maurice Blondel, *History and Dogma* (1903), English trans. A. Dru and I. Trethowan (London, 1964). Criticising the a-historical approach of the Thomist school, Blondel says: 'All they ask of the facts is that they should serve as signs to the senses and as commonsense proofs. Once the signs have been supplied, an elementary argument deduces from them the divine character of the whole to which these signifying facts belong. Then, with the help of rational theses, they deduce the required universal conclusion from the premisses, and take up an embattled position in the place to which history, it would seem, has yielded up the key, thanking her for her provisional services. From then on the place belongs to others, and she has only to take her leave' (p. 226). Again, for the Thomists, 'The Bible is guaranteed *en bloc*, not by its content, but by the external seal of the divine: why bother to verify the details? It is full of absolute knowledge, ensconced in its eternal truth; why search for its human conditions or its relative meaning ... the ageless facts are without local colour ... and disappear beneath the weight of an absolute by which they are crushed' (p. 229).

112. *The Last Years: Journals 1853–1885*, ed. R. Gregor Smith (London, 1965), pp. 99–100.

CHAPTER THREE

1. Pascal, *Pensées*, 273.
2. *Memorial*, 'God of Abraham, God of Isaac, God of Jacob, not of the philosophers and scientists'.
3. Col. 2:8.
4. Rom. 1:19.
5. Matt. 11:25; Luke 10:21.
6. *Some Dogmas of Religion*, p. 298. He goes on: 'This criticism applies, naturally, not to the teacher who made the exclamation, but to the teachers who turned it into a principle. It may be remarked that the principle is applied rather capriciously. Many men would be prepared to use it as a ground for distrusting Hegel, and for trusting the peasantry of Ireland or Wales (as the case may be). But they would not admit it as a ground for accepting the peasantry of Morocco as a safer guide in religion than Thomas Aquinas. And yet Thomas Aquinas was a wise man, and the religion of a peasant in Morocco would be eminently childish. But, of course, it is only ignorant

orthodoxy that is childlike simplicity. Ignorant heterodoxy is childish superstition.'

7. Gilson, *Reason and Revelation in the Middle Ages*, p. 8.

8. 'On Prescription against Heretics', vii, in *The Ante-Nicene Fathers* (Buffalo, 1887), iii, p. 246.

9. *De Carne Christi* c. 5: 'The Son of God died – this is believable because it is absurd: and he was buried and rose again – this is certain because it is impossible.'

10. *Pensées*, 267.

11. On Peter Damian, see Jean Leclercq, *Saint Pierre Damien et la culture profane* (Louvain, 1956).

12. 'Contra quaedam capitula errorum Abaelardi,' *S. Bernardi Opera* (Paris, 1939), p. i.

13. See P. Boehner (ed.), *William of Ockham: Selected Philosophical Writings* (London, 1957), pp. xix–xx.

14. See 'The Second Letter of Nicholas of Autrecourt to Bernard of Arezzo', trans. E. A. Moody, in *Medieval Philosophy: Selected Readings*, ed. H. Shapiro (New York, 1964), pp. 524–5. On Nicholas see J. Weinberg, *Nicholaus of Autrecourt* (Princeton, 1948) and the interesting paper by H. Rashdall, 'Nicholas of Ultricuria: A Medieval Hume', *Proceedings of the Aristotelian Society* viii (1907), pp. 1–27.

15. See R. Guelluy, *Philosophie et théologie chez Guillaume d'Ockham* (Paris, 1947), p. 364: 'Ockham refuses to separate the domain of theology from that of metaphysics and ... does not seem to have as his aim the opposing of faith to reason.' On Biel, see H. A. Oberman, *The Harvest of Medieval Theology: Gabriel Biel and Late Medieval Theology* (Harvard, 1963), p. 81: 'Biel is interested in safeguarding the peculiar character of faith and is keen not to have it subsumed under some form of higher reason. He thus makes every effort to distinguish between philosophy and theology by marking as clearly as possible where the one ends and the other begins. But there is no indication that this distinction is carried so far as to become a divorce between faith and reason.' On the Catholic orthodoxy of Ockham's and Biel's position on faith and reason, see Oberman, pp. 423–8.

16. Cited in P. Althaus, *The Theology of Martin Luther* (Philadelphia, 1966), p. 66.

17. Ibid., pp. 69–70. 'Reason despises faith'; 'It is up to God alone to give faith contrary to nature, and ability to believe contrary to reason'. Reason is 'the greatest whore that the Devil has'; 'Philosophy is a practical wisdom of the flesh which is hostile to God'.

18. Luther admits, however, that reason has a place within theology: 'Reason enlightened by the Spirit helps us to understand the Holy Scripture'; 'Reason in godly men is something different, since it does not fight with faith but rather aids it'. Cited ibid., p. 71.

19. Calvin, *Institutes of the Christian Religion*, i 3, in *Library of Christian Classics*, ed. J. T. McNeill and F. L. Battles (London, 1961), p. 43.
20. Ibid., i 3; p. 44
21. Ibid., i 4; p. 47.
22. Ibid., i 4; p. 49.
23. Ibid., i 5; p. 58.
24. Heb. 2:3
25. Rom. 1:19.
26. *Institutes*, i 5; p. 68.
27. Ibid., i 6; p. 71.
28. W. Niesel, *The Theology of Calvin* (London, 1956), p. 50; see chap. 2, sec. 3, 'The Question of Natural Theology'. See also E. A. Dowey, *The Knowledge of God in Calvin's Theology* (New York, 1952).
29. Owen Chadwick, *The Reformation* (London, 1964), p. 94.
30. A. Boyce Gibson, *Theism and Empiricism* (London, 1970), p. 115.
31. *Pensées*, 267.
32. On Al Ghazzali see W. Montgomery Watt, *Muslim Intellectual – A Study of Al Ghazzali* (Edinburgh, 1963); D. B. Macdonald, art. 'Al Ghazzali', in *Encyclopedia of Islam* (London, 1927), ii 146–9; 'Al Ghazzali', by M. Saeed Sheikh in *A History of Muslim Philosophy*, ed. M. M. Sharif (Wiesbaden, 1963), chaps xxx, xxxi, See also Alain de Libera, *La philosophie médiévale* (Paris, 1995), pp. 95–7.
33. English trans. W. Montgomery Watt, *The Faith and Practice of Al Ghazzali* (London, 1963).
34. Ibid., pp. 37–8.
35. Ibid., p. 34.
36. Macdonald, art. 'Al Ghazzali', p. 146.
37. English trans. by Sabih Ahmad Kamali (Lahore, 1958). See the analyses of this work in Montgomery Watt, *Muslim Intellectual*, pp. 57–65, and Sharif, *A History of Muslim Philosophy*, pp. 588–616.
38. *The Inconsistency*, p. 181.
39. *The Inconsistency*, p. 186. See the discussion of Al Ghazzali's theory of causality in *A History of Muslim Philosophy*, pp. 614–15.
40. Ibid., p. 189.
41. *The Deliverance*, p. 61.
42. Ibid., p. 54.
43. *Pensées*, 469.
44. Ibid., 347.
45. Ibid., 273.
46. Ibid., 72.
47. Ibid.
48. Ibid., 470.
49. Ibid., 233.

50. Ibid.
51. Ibid., 241. On the 'wager' see J. Chevalier, *Pascal* (London, 1970), pp. 242–53 and appendix iv, 'Historical and Critical Note on Pascal's "wager".'
52. *Pensées*, 83.
53. Ibid., 229.
54. Ibid., 230.
55. Ibid., 555.
56. Ibid., 278.
57. Ibid., 277.
58. Ibid., 282.
59. See the 'Memorial', cited in Chevalier, *Pascal*, pp. 94–5.
60. *Pensées*, 587.
61. Ibid., 267, 268, 269, 270, 271, 272.
62. For a brief analysis of these early works of Kant see A. E. Taylor, 'Theism', in *Encyclopedia of Religion and Ethics*, ed. Hastings (1921), xii 275–6. See also Kant, *Selected Pre-Critical Writings*, translated and introduced by G. R. Kerferd, and D. E. Walford (Manchester, 1965), for Kant's *Enquiry Concerning the Clarity of the Principles of Natural Theology and Ethics* (1763).
63. Taylor, 'Theism', p. 276.
64. See N. Kemp-Smith, *Hume's Dialogues Concerning Natural Religion* (Oxford, 1935), pp. 38–9.
65. See *Dialogues*, p. 234. On this see A. Flew, *Hume's Philosophy of Belief* (London, 1961), pp. 230–1.
66. *Dialogues*, p. 230.
67. Ibid., pp. 232–3.
68. Ibid., p. 282.
69. J. Collins, *The Emergence of Philosophy of Religion* (New Haven, 1967), p. 76. The same author goes on to say: 'To Holbach and other atheistic friends of Hume, the reasonable expectation was that, upon exposure of the frailties and fallacies involved in natural theology and upon presentation of an areligious moral humanism as the social ideal, religious belief would shrivel up and disappear. It was freely predicted that this result would follow at least for those honest minds who gave sufficient time, study, and reflection to the problem of the intellectual standing of theism. But Hume's own experience ran counter to this prediction, even though he did not care to give any comfort to the proponents of traditional theism and the institutional forms of religion. One's assent to God's reality may be deprived of many customary supports in argument, without thereby being annihilated or reduced merely to an uncommonly stubborn social custom, destined for eventual disappearance.'
70. On Hume's attitude to religion see Kemp-Smith, *Hume's Dialogues*. Kemp-Smith cites Boswell's interview with Hume in 1777: 'He [Hume] said he

never had entertained any belief in Religion since he began to read Locke and Clarke.' However, while rightly stressing Hume's philosophical and personal antagonism to religion, Kemp-Smith perhaps underestimates the strength of Hume's lifelong fascination with the phenomenon of religion. This is brought out very well by Collins, *The Emergence of Philosophy of Religion*, pp. 3–4, 76–7.

71. *Dialogues*, p. 282. Cf. p. 162: 'You propose then, Philo, said Cleanthes, to erect religious faith on philosophical scepticism; and you think, that if certainty or evidence be expelled from every other subject of enquiry, it will all retire to these theological doctrines, and there acquire a superior force and authority.'

72. T. H. Green and T. H. Grose, eds, *Essays: Moral, Political and Literary* (London, 1875), II 107.

73. Ibid., II 399.

74. Ed. L. A. Selby-Bigge (Oxford, 1894), p. 131.

75. *Dialogues*, p. 166.

76. Ibid.

77. Ibid., p. 230.

78. Ibid., p. 158.

79. Ibid., pp. 172–3.

80. A Leroy, *David Hume* (Paris, 1953), pp. 308–9, argues that Hume's position differs from that of the Christian fideists such as Pascal, Hamann and Kierkegaard, in that his scepticism is not directed to arousing an act of supernatural faith, nor does it abase human reason to make room for revelation. This is true enough as far as Hume's own personal intentions go. But the intrinsic logic of Hume's position – philosophical agnosticism making room for faith – is nevertheless very similar to that of the fideists mentioned.

81. 'To Christian Garve, 21 Sept 1798', in *Kant: Philosophical Correspondence, 1759–99*, ed. A. Zweig (Chicago, 1967), p. 252: 'It was not the investigation of the existence of God, immortality, and so on, but rather the antinomy of pure reason – "the world has a beginning; it has no beginning, and so on", right up to the 4th (*sic*): "There is freedom in man, versus there is no freedom, only the necessity of nature" – that is what first aroused me from my dogmatic slumber and drove me to the critique of reason itself ...' On Kant in general see D. P. Dryer, *Kant's Solution for Verification in Metaphysics* (Toronto, University of Toronto Press, 1966); James Van Cleeve, *Problems from Kant* (New York, 1999). See also Gordon Michalson, *Kant and the Problem of God* (Oxford, Blackwell, 1999), p. 144.

82. P. F. Strawson, *The Bounds of Sense: An Essay on Kant's Critique of Pure Reason* (London, 1966), p. 16; cf. *Critique of Pure Reason*, trans. N. Kemp-Smith (London, 1929), B 195: 'All concepts, and with them all principles, even such as are possible *a priori*, relate to empirical intuitions, that is, to the data for a possible experience. Apart from this relation they have no objective validity.'

83. Ibid., B 76; A 52.

84. Ibid., A 619; B 647: 'The ideal of the supreme being is nothing but a regulative principle of reason, which directs us to look upon a connection in the world *as if* it originated from an all-sufficient necessary cause. We can base upon the ideal the rule of a systematic and, in accordance with universal laws, necessary unity in the explanation of that connexion; but the ideal is not an assertion of an existence necessary in itself.'

85. Ibid., A 483; B 511.

86. Ibid., A 636; B 664.

87. Cf. Hume, *Letters*, i, 157: 'All our inference [from design in nature to God] is founded on the similitude of the works of nature to the usual effects of the mind. Otherwise they must appear a mere chaos. The only difficulty is, why the other dissimilitudes do not weaken the argument. And indeed it would seem from experience and feeling, that they do not weaken it so much as we might naturally expect. A theory to solve this would be very acceptable.'

88. *Critique of Pure Reason*, A 638; B 666.

89. Ibid., A 639; B 667.

90. D. P. Dryer, *Kant's Solution for Verification in Metaphysics* (London, 1966), p. 526. Despite its formidable style this is one of the most perceptive commentaries on the *Critique of Pure Reason*.

91. *Critique of Pure Reason*, A 641; B 669.

92. Ibid., B xxx.

93. On Kant's notion of 'faith' see L. W. Beck, *Studies in the Philosophy of Kant* (New York, 1965), p. 51. Rational faith is 'a faith which demands the same degree of assent required for theoretical knowledge and yet avoids the speculative claims of those who believe metaphysics to be a theoretical science'.

94. Cf. Strawson, *Bounds of Sense*, p. 15: 'Wherever he [Kant] found limiting or necessary features of experience, he declared their source to lie in our own cognitive constitution; and this doctrine he considered indispensable as an explanation of knowledge of the necessary structure of experience. Yet there is no doubt that this doctrine is incoherent in itself'.

95. *Émile*, trans. B. Foxley (London, 1911), p. 228.

96. Ibid., p. 272.

97. Ibid., p. 254

98. Ibid., p. 277. On Rousseau's view of religion see R. Grimsley, *Rousseau and the Religious Quest* (Oxford, 1968); P. M. Masson, *La Religion de J.-J. Rousseau*, 3 vols (Paris, 1916); K. Barth, *From Rousseau to Ritschl* (London, 1959), chap. ii. See also the valuable annotations in the Pléiade edition, *Jean-Jacques Rousseau: Œuvres Complètes*, Vol. iv (Paris, 1969). Judith Shklar, *Men and Citizens: A Study of Rousseau's Social Theory* (Cambridge, 1969), pp. 113–120, has some acute observations on Rousseau's religious ideas. On Rousseau's influence on Kant see E. Cassirer, *Rousseau, Kant, Goethe* (Princeton, 1945) and Beck, *Studies in the Philosophy of Kant*, pp. 5–10.

99. Cited by H. J. de Vleeschauwer, *The Development of Kantian Thought* (London, 1969), pp. 39–40. Vleeschauwer argues (p. 42) that Rousseau's influence was crucial in Kant's change from his Wolffian beginnings: 'I believe that Rousseau must be held responsible for this change of tone, for he revealed to Kant the superiority of morality to knowledge.'

100. *Émile*, p. 245.

101. To J. C. Lavater, 1775; Zweig, *Philosophical Correspondence*, pp. 79–82.

102. Ibid.

103. Kemp-Smith, trans., *Critique of Pure Reason*, B xxiv–vi.

104. Ibid., B xxvi.

105. L. W. Beck, trans., *Critique of Practical Reason, and Other Writings in Moral Philosophy* (Chicago, 1950).

106. Ibid., bk ii, chap. ii, sec. v, p. 227.

107. Ibid., p. 229.

108. Ibid., p. 232: 'Morals is not really the doctrine of how to make ourselves happy, but of how we are to be *worthy* of happiness. Only if religion is added to it can the hope arise of some day participating in happiness in proportion as we endeavoured not to be unworthy of it.'

109. Ibid., A 811; B 839.

110. Cf. W. H. Walsh, 'Kant's Moral Theology', *Proceedings of the British Academy*, xlix (1963) 266: 'This is simply a causal argument which attempts to infer God's existence from the particular way in which things are constituted; in form it is identical with Descartes's argument from the fact that we possess the idea of God, or again with the teleological argument itself. And it shares all the weaknesses of these purported demonstrations, as Kant himself would have been the first to point out.'

111. Beck, trans., *Critique of Practical Reason*, p. 229.

112. Ibid., pp. 229–30.

113. Ibid., p. 231.

114. Ibid., p. 232. Cf. Walsh, *Kant's Moral Theology*, p. 285: 'Interpreted on these lines, the theology of Kant becomes identical in essentials with the theology of Professor Braithwaite as expressed in his well-known lecture "An Empiricist's View of the Nature of Religious Belief"... Though Braithwaite and Kant follow somewhat different lines in working this alternative out, they end up with what is fundamentally the same view, namely that the whole force of a declaration of belief in God's existence is to be found in the adoption of a practical attitude. Braithwaite virtually identifies belief in God with acceptance of the command that we love one another; Kant equates it more generally with manifest confidence that the moral struggle will not be in vain.'

115. Ibid, p. 245.

116. Cf. Beck, *Studies in the Philosophy of Kant*, p. 52: 'Since it is practical and not speculative reason which finally warrants Kant's use of the concept of God, theology for him can have no theoretical content, and religion is only the

attitude of performing all duties as divine commands. The judgement, "There is a God" is not a theoretical judgement; it is not a hypothesis in a theoretical context. It is a practical postulate, a point of orientation. In the ordinary sense of the word "know" we do not know that it is true, yet there is an *a priori* guaranty for it.'

117. In the manner of J. H. Newman's argument in *A Grammar of Assent* (London, 1901), pp. 109–10; see also A. J. Boekraad and H. Tristram, *The Argument from Conscience to the Existence of God According to J. H. Newman* (Louvain, 1961), and A. E. Taylor's thesis in *The Faith of a Moralist* (London, 1930). See also H. P. Owen, *The Moral Argument for Christian Theism* (London, 1965).

118. H. L. Mansel, *The Limits of Religious Thought*, 3rd ed. (London, 1859), p. 70.

119. Kant's oscillations on this point are vividly exemplified in *Critique of Practical Reason*, bk ii, chap. ii, sec. vii, pp. 236–43: 'How is it possible to conceive of extending pure reason in a practical respect without thereby extending its knowledge as speculative?'

120. A. R. C. Duncan, *Practical Reason and Morality* (London, 1957), pp. 134–5.

121. For a full discussion of this work see C. C. J. Webb, *Kant's Philosophy of Religion* (Oxford, 1926), chap. v.

122. Ibid., p. 151.

123. Cited ibid., p. 169. An English translation of part of this work is included in *Kant's Political Writings*, ed. H. Reiss (Cambridge, 1970).

124. Cited in Webb, *Kant's Philosophy of Religion*, p. 171.

125. Ed. E. Adickes (Berlin, 1920), p. 819.

126. Ibid., p. 820; cf. p. 824: 'There is a Being in me, distinguished from myself as the cause of an effect wrought upon me, which freely – that is without being dependent on laws of nature in space and time – judges me within, justifying or condemning me; and I as man am myself this being, and it is no substance external to me, and – what is most surprising of all – its causality is no natural necessity but a determination of me to a free act.'

127. Erich Adickes, p. 781. See the discussion of these passages in F. E. England, *Kant's Conception of God* (London, 1929), pp. 198–200.

128. *Kant: Philosophical Correspondence 1759–99*, ed. A. Zweig, pp. 217–20. In this letter, however, it is clear that Kant sees the essence of Christianity to consist in its moral content, the theoretical articulation of Christian doctrine being accidental and dispensable. 'It was, I maintain, my duty to make clear the status of rational religion. It should have been incumbent on my accusers to point out a single case in which I depreciated Christianity either by arguing against its acceptance as a revelation or by showing it to be unnecessary. For I do not regard it as a depreciation of a revealed doctrine to say that, in relation to its practical use (which constitutes the essential part of all religion), it must be interpreted in accordance with the principles of pure rational faith and must be urged on us openly. I take this

rather as a recognition of its morally fruitful content, which would be deformed by the supposedly superior importance of merely theoretical propositions that are to be taken on faith... I have insisted on the holy, practical content of the Bible, which, with all the changes in theoretical articles of faith that will take place in regard to merely revealed doctrines, because of their coincidental nature, will always remain as the inner and essential part of religion.'

129. Cited in Barth, *From Rousseau to Ritschl,* p. 195. While recognising that Kant wished to limit theology to the study of the accidental and dispensable historical expression of religion, Barth sees a genuine insight in Kant's sharp distinction between theology and philosophy. Cf. p. 196: 'It is only necessary to take quite seriously what Kant said half in mockery, in order to hear something very significant, even though we reserve in every respect our right to object to his formulations. Or is it not the case that the philosopher of pure reason has said something very significant to the theologian in telling him in all succinctness that "The biblical theologian proves that God exists by means of the fact that He has spoken in the Bible"?' Barth's view of the Bible as the self-authenticating word of God, however, is profoundly different from Kant's.

130. Cf. Mansel's criticism of Kant in *Limits of Religious Thought,* p. 14. 'Throughout every page of Holy Scripture God reveals Himself not as a Law but as a Person... By what right do we venture to rob the Deity of half his revealed attributes, in order to set up the other half, which rest on precisely the same evidence, as a more absolute revelation of the truth? By what right do we enthrone, in the place of the God to whom we pray, an inexorable Fate or immutable Law?'

131. Though Kierkegaard, despite his continual sarcasms at Hegel's expense, always retained a reluctant admiration for him. In a footnote written for the *Postscript,* Kierkegaard wrote: 'I cherish a respect for Hegel which is sometimes an enigma to me; I have learnt much from him, and I know that on returning again to him I could still learn much more... His philosophical knowledge, his astonishing learning, the sharpsightedness of his genius, and whatever else can be alleged to the advantage of a philosopher, I am as ready as any disciple to concede – but no, not to concede, that is too proud an expression; I would say rather, willing to admire, willing to let myself be taught. But for all that, one who is thoroughly tried in life's vicissitudes and has recourse in his need to the aid of thoughts, will find him comic – in spite of the great qualities which are no less certain.' Cited by W. Lowrie, *Kierkegaard's Concluding Unscientific Postscript,* trans. D. F. Swenson and W. Lowrie (Princeton, 1944), p. 558. For a balanced assessment of Kierkegaard's attitude to Hegel see J. Collins, *The Mind of Kierkegaard* (London, 1954), chap. 4.

132. *Søren Kierkegaard – The Last Years: Journals 1853–55*, ed. and trans. by R. Gregor Smith (London, 1965), p. 30.

133. p. 54.

134. Ibid., p. 504.

135. *Philosophical Fragments*, trans. D. F. Swenson (Princeton, 1936), p. 35. Cf. *Concluding Unscientific Postscript*, p. 495: Every man can distinguish 'between what he understands and what he does not understand ... and he can discover that there is something which is, in spite of the fact that it is against his understanding and way of thinking'.

136. *Philosophical Fragments*, p. 35.

137. *The Last Years*, p. 246.

138. *Philosophical Fragments*, p. 37.

139. *The Last Years*, p. 100.

140. *Concluding Unscientific Postscript*, p. 55: 'The subject is in passion infinitely interested in his eternal happiness... But in order to philosophise he must proceed in precisely the opposite direction, giving himself up and losing himself in objectivity, thus vanishing from himself... Christianity does not lend itself to objective observation, precisely because it proposes to intensify subjectivity to the utmost'.

141. Ibid., p. 23.

142. Ibid., p. 124.

143. *Philosophical Fragments*, pp. 31–2. Cf. *Concluding Unscientific Postscript*, p. 107: 'An existential system is impossible... System and existence are incapable of being thought together; because in order to think existence at all, systematic thought must think it as abrogated, and hence as not existing. Existence separates, and holds the various moments of existence discretely apart, the systematic thought consists of the finality which brings them together.'

144. *Papirer*, X2 a 354, cited by J. Heywood Thomas, *Subjectivity and Paradox* (Oxford, 1957), p. 121.

145. Kierkegaard suggests that even speculative thought presupposes 'a resolution of the will' in order to get it going. Cf. *Concluding Unscientific Postscript*, p. 103: 'Only when reflection comes to a halt can a beginning be made, and reflection can be halted by something else, and this something else is something quite different from the logical, being a resolution of the will'.

146. Cf. ibid., p. 53: 'The comical inheres precisely in the incommensurability between his [the speculative philosopher's] interest and the speculative objectivity... If, therefore, he says that he bases his eternal happiness on his speculation, he contradicts himself and becomes comical, because philosophy in its objectivity is wholly indifferent to his and my and your eternal happiness.'

147. *Philosophical Fragments*, p. 52.

148. *Concluding Unscientific Postscript*, p. 497.
149. Ibid.
150. *The Last Years*, p. 354. On Kierkegaard's ideas on grace see L. Dupré, *Kierkegaard as Theologian* (London, 1964), chap. iii.
151. Trans. D. F. and L. Swenson (Princeton, 1946), p. 248.
152. Heywood Thomas, *Subjectivity and Paradox*, p. 16.
153. *Concluding Unscientific Postscript*, p. 196.
154. Ibid., p. 339.
155. *The Last Years*, pp. 354–5.
156. *Concluding Unscientific Postscript*, p. 514.
157. Cf. on this Dupré, *Kierkegaard as Theologian*, p. 146: 'Since faith is para-doxical, reason is assigned the negative but indispensable task of pointing up the incomprehensibility of faith. Consequently, reason must know precisely what is and what is not outside its competence, and such knowledge is a prerequisite for defining with accuracy the sphere of faith. Instead of dispelling the mysteriousness of faith, reason must set itself the task of bringing it into relief. This requires that it be able to distinguish between the contradictory and the incomprehensible.'
158. Cf. S. Kierkegaard, *Fear and Trembling & Dialectical Lyric* (Princeton, 1941), p. 85: Abraham, the man of faith *par excellence*, 'cannot be mediated; in other words, he cannot speak. As soon as I speak, I express the universal, and when I remain silent, no one can understand me.'
159. *Concluding Unscientific Postscript*, p. 181.
160. Ibid., pp. 179–80.
161. Boyce Gibson, *Theism and Empiricism*, p. 117.
162. Cf. Collins, *The Mind of Kierkegaard*, p. 155: 'Existential thoughts ... always retain this orientation to a free plan about one's personal existence and moral condition. But if this accounts sufficiently for existential thinking, then the latter does not differ *in the cognitive order* from other sorts of thinking. Only the use and personal reference of the thinking are different. The conclusion is inescapable that only a non-cognitive shift of attitude is needed to convert abstract thinking ... into existential thinking.'
163. Mansel, *Limits of Religious Thought*, p. xliv.
164. Ibid., p. 48.
165. Ibid., p. 153. On Mansel's undeservedly neglected work, see Kenneth D. Freeman, *The Role of Reason in Religion – A Study of Henry Mansel* (The Hague, 1969). J. S. Mill has a rather external critique of Mansel's book in *An Examination of Sir William Hamilton's Philosophy*, 2nd ed. (London, 1865), chap 7. Mill alleges (p. 89) that Mansel's position involves that 'no argument grounded on the incredibility of the [religious] doctrine, as involving an intellectual absurdity, or on its moral badness as unworthy of a good or wise being, ought to have any weight, since of these things we are incompetent to judge'. And Mill goes on to say (p. 90): 'My opinion of this

doctrine, in whatever way presented, is, that it is simply the most morally pernicious doctrine now current.'

166. Richard R. Niebuhr, *Schleiermacher on Christ and Religion* (New York, 1964), p. 195: 'A silent assumption of the attack on natural theology by recent Protestant theology is that knowledge is a form of power. This assumption no doubt reflects the extent to which technological science has become the norm of all our conceptions of knowing. In any case, a natural knowledge of God seems to represent some form of human power over, or claim upon, God, according to this way of thinking, and this in part accounts for the vehemence with which crisis theology rejects the notion of a seed of religion present in all men, an innate idea of God, obscured and vitiated, but still abiding in human nature.'

167. Rudolph Otto, *The Idea of the Holy* (Harmondsworth, 1959), p. 129.

168. Ibid., p. 33.

169. *Die Kategorie das "Heiligen" bei Rudolf Otto*, cited in J. L. Adams, *Paul Tillich's Philosophy of Culture, Science and Religion* (New York, 1965), p. 220.

170. See Barth, *From Rousseau to Ritschl*, pp. 195–6.

171. See H. Zahrnt, *The Question of God* (London, 1969), pp. 27–8, for a discussion of Kierkegaard's influence on Barth.

172. Cf. the attack on Barth's supposed 'irrationalism' by Brand Blandshard, *Critical Reflections on Karl Barth*, in *Faith and the Philosophers*, ed. J. Hick (London, 1964), pp. 159 ff.

173. See K. Barth, *Fides Quaerens Intellectum*, English trans. (London, 1960).

174. R. Bultmann in *The Theology of Rudolf Bultmann*, ed. C. W. Kegley (London, 1966), p. 276.

175. Ibid., p. 274. The essay 'Philosophy and Theology in Bultmann's Thought', by John Macquarrie, in *The Theology of Rudolf Bultmann*, is the clearest account in English of Bultmann's implicit philosophy of religion.

176. Cf. 'The Historicity of Man and Faith', in *Existence and Faith*, trans. S. M. Ogden (London, 1961), p. 95: 'A philosophy would be unusable if it undertook to ascertain the "meaning" of human existence in the sense of trying to show that the latter is "meaningful" (or, on the contrary, as in Nietzsche, that it is "meaningless"). It would then try to take from the concrete man the question as to his "meaning", a question that is posed uniquely to him and can only be answered by him as an individual person; it would try to give a universal answer to man's question, "What is truth?" which as his question is a question of the moment. On the other hand, a legitimate philosophical analysis of human existence shows precisely that it is the concrete man himself who must alone pose the question about his "meaning", the question, "What is truth?" and give an answer to it. And just this is what it means for such an analysis to exhibit the "meaning" of human existence, i.e. to show what man means, what *meaning* "being" has when one speaks of man. If philosophy by no means

deceives itself into thinking that its work as inquiry leads to absolute knowledge, then naturally theology also ought not to suppose that philosophy provides it with a normative ontology with which it is then able to work as it pleases.'

177. 'Symbol and Knowledge', *Journal of Liberal Religion*, ii (1941), p. 203.

178. On Tillich's position, see Adams, *Paul Tillich's Philosophy of Culture, Science and Religion*, p. 215: 'All in all the epistemological method presented is a way of faith whereby one through decision puts his trust in that effulgent and powerful mystery which vibrates through every part of creation, supporting and threatening, form-creating, form-bursting, form-transforming. One cannot prove or disprove its reality. One can only recognise that in it and through it we live and move and have our being. This is rather an affirmation about the ultimate, a decision for that without which being and meaning and truth lose their life-blood. It is, in short, a method that presupposes the reality it is supposed to lead to. Tillich himself calls it an "original decision" in response to grace.' Adams's study, at once sympathetic and discerningly critical, is the best account in English of Tillich's philosophy of religion. See also Stuart C. Brown, *Do Religious Claims Make Sense?* (London, 1909), pp. 154 ff., on 'Tillich's A-Theism'.

179. *The Limits of Religious Thought*, p. xxxii.

180. Gordon Kaufman, *God: The Problem* (Cambridge, Mass., 1972), p. 7. See also Gordon Michalson, *Kant and the Problem of God* (Oxford, 1999).

181. Ibid, p. 85.

182. Ibid.

183. (Philadelphia, 1981).

184. Ibid.

185. See Don Cupitt, *Taking Leave of God* (London, 1980), and *Reforming Christianity* (London, 2000). See also Teresa Wallace, ed., *Time and Tide; The Sea of Faith Beyond the Millennium* (London, 2000). On Cupitt see Scott Cowdell, *Atheist Priest? Don Cupitt and Christianity*, and also A. C. Thistleton, *Interpreting God and the Post-modern* (Edinburgh, 1995), esp. chaps. 14–17.

CHAPTER FOUR

1. See the collection of mainly reductivist essays, A. Flew and A. MacIntyre, eds, *New Essays in Philosophical Theology* (London, 1955). See also M. J. Charlesworth, *The Problem of Religious Language* (Englewood Cliffs, Prentice Hall, 1974).

2. *Tractatus*, 6.45. On Wittgenstein's thought in general see Hans-Johann Glock, *A Wittgenstein Dictionary* (Oxford, Blackwell, 1996). See entries, 'religion', 'language-game', 'form of life', 'mysticism'.

3. See Cyril Barrett, *Wittgenstein on Ethics and Religious Belief* (Oxford, Blackwell, 1991), chap. 2.

4. Ibid., p, viii.
5. Ibid., pp. x–xi.
6. D. Z. Phillips, 'Searle on Language Games and Religion", in Phillips, *Wittgenstein and Religion* (Baskingstoke, 1993), p. 31, fn. 2.
7. A. J. Ayer, *Language, Truth and Logic* (London, 1936), p. 107.
8. Ibid.
9. Ibid., p. 117.
10. A. Flew, 'Theology and Falsification', in *New Essays in Philosophical Theology*, eds, Flew and MacIntyre, p. 98.
11. See the collection of reductivist accounts in Charlesworth, ed., *The Problem of Religious Language.*
12. Cambridge, 1955.
13. Ibid., p. 14.
14. Ibid., p. 27.
15. J. A. Passmore, 'Christianity and Positivism', *Australian Journal of Philosophy*, xxxiv (1956), p. 133.
16. See his essay, 'Theology and Falsification', in *New Essays in Philosophical Theology*.
17. Ibid., p. 102.
18. Ibid.
19. Ibid., p. 190.
20. In John Hick, ed., *Faith and the Philosophers* (London, 1964), p. 37.
21. Ibid., pp. 103–110.
22. Ibid.
23. I rely here on Barrett's careful exegesis of the *Tractatus* in his *Wittgenstein on Ethics and Religious Belief.*
24. Ibid., p. 78.
25. See 'Wittgenstein's Lecture on Ethics', *Philosophical Review* (Jan. 1961), pp. 3–12.
26. Fergus Kerr, *Theology after Wittgenstein* (Oxford, Blackwell, 1986), p. 117.
27. (Oxford, 1953).
28. Wittgenstein, *Philosophical Investigations*, pp. 11–12; 6–7.
29. Ibid.
30. *Philosophical Investigations*, pp. 11–12.
31. Barrett, *Wittgenstein on Ethics and Religious Belief*, p. 117.
32. Roger Trigg, *Rationality and Religious Belief* (Oxford, Blackwell, 1998), p. 134. Trigg offers a stringent critique of the Wittgensteinian position on religious discourse.
33. *Ludwig Wittgenstein: Culture and Value*, trans. P. Winch (Oxford, Blackwell, 1980), p. 32. These views are discussed by D. Z. Phillips in his essay 'Religion in Wittgenstein's Mirror' (1991) in Phillips, *Wittgenstein and Religion* (London, Macmillan, 1993).
34. PI, 1, para. 24.

35. See, for example, M. Merleau-Ponty, *The Phenomenology of Perception* (London, Routledge and Kegan Paul, 1962).
36. See Rush Rhees ed., *Recollections of Wittgenstein* (London, Oxford University Press, 1984).
37. See Barrett, *Wittgenstein on Ethics*, chap. 9, pp. 178–208.
38. These remarks are taken from Kerr, *Theology after Wittgenstein*, pp. 154–5.
39. *Culture and Value*, p. 85.
40. Ibid., p. 86.
41. D. Z. Phillips, *Wittgenstein and Belief* (London, Macmillan, 1993), Introduction, p. xii. This is a collection of 15 essays written between 1968 and 1991. See also his book *Belief, Change and Forms of Life* (London, 1986).
42. Phillips, 'Advice to Philosophers who are Christians' in Phillips, *Wittgenstein and Religion*, p. 232. See also Nicholas Wolterstorff, 'Can Belief in God be Rational', in Alvin Plantinga and N. Wolterstorff, eds., *Faith and Rationality* (Notre Dame, USA, 1983), p. 1.
43. Ibid., p. xx.
44. Roger Trigg, *Rationality and Religious Belief* (Oxford, Blackwell, 1998), p. 135.
45. Ibid., p. xiii.
46. Ibid., pp. 249–50.
47. Ibid., p. 247.
48. Ibid., pp. xii–xiii.
49. Cited in Phillips, 'Searle on Language-games and Religion', in Phillips, *Wittgenstein and Religion*, p. 23.
50. In ibid., p. xi.
51. Trigg, *Rationality and Religious Belief*, p. 134.
52. Ibid., p. 149.

CHAPTER FIVE

1. See David Lyon, *Concepts of Social Thought: Postmodernity* (Minneapolis, University of Minnesota Press, 1994).
2. Terry Eagleton, *The Illusions of Postmodernism* (Oxford, Blackwell, 1996), p. vii.
3. Ibid., p. viii. On the concept of the Enlightenment see the recent revisionist work by Jonathan Israel, *Radical Enlightenment: Philosophy and the Making of Modernity, 1650–1750* (Oxford, Oxford University Press, 2001). Israel locates the sources of the new movement in Holland and makes the 'God intoxicated' philosopher, Baruch de Spinoza, and sympathisers in Germany and Scandinavia (rather than French thinkers) its central figures.
4. Perhaps the most perceptive book on this background is that by Jonathan Culler, *On Deconstruction: Theory and Criticism after Structuralism* (New York, Cornell University Press, 1982).

5. See Kevin Hart's remarkable study, *The Trespass of the Sign* (Cambridge, Cambridge University Press, 1989). Here I rely heavily on Hart's work even though I disagree with him on several crucial issues.

6. Eagleton, 'Awakening from Modernity', *Times Literary Supplement*, 20 February, 1987, p. 5.

7. Stanley Fish, *Doing what Comes Naturally: change, rhetoric and the practice of theory in literary and legal studies* (Durham, USA, Duke University Press, 1989), p. 8.

8. See Michel Foucault, *Madness and Civilisation* (1975); *The Birth of the Clinic* (1973); *Discipline and Punish* (1977); and *History of Sexuality* (1978–86). See also Foucault's essay 'The subject and power' in H. Dreyfus and P. Rabinow, eds, *Michel Foucault: beyond structuralism and hermeneutics* (Chicago, University of Chicago Press, 1983).

9. Jacques Derrida in Raoul Mortley, ed., *French Philosophers in Conversation* (London, Routledge, 1991), pp. 96–7. Derrida's main works (in English translation) are *Of Grammatology* (Baltimore, Johns Hopkins University Press, 1997); *Writing and Difference* (Chicago, University of Chicago Press, 1987); *Speech and Phenomena* (Evanston, Northwestern University Press, 1973); *Glas* (Lincoln, University of Nebraska Press, 1986).

10. Paul Ricoeur, *Freud and Philosophy, an essay in interpretation* (New Haven, Yale University Press, 1970), p. 29.

11. Derrida, *Writing and Difference*, p. 87.

12. Cited in Hart, *Trespass of the Sign*, p. 144.

13. Culler, *Deconstruction*, p. 131. Culler notes (p. 157) that the 'general text' refers to the 'discursive structures and systems of signification' presupposed by any text.

14. Thomas Guarino, 'Postmodernism and Five Fundamental Theological Issues', *Theological Studies*, 57 (1996), pp. 654–89.

15. Ibid., p. 661.

16. Robert P. Carroll, 'Poststructuralist Approaches: Historicism and Postmodernism', in John Barton, ed., *The Cambridge Companion to Biblical Interpretation* (Cambridge, Cambridge University Press, 1998), p. 62.

17. Jean-Luc Marion, *God Without Being* (Chicago, 1991).

18. Ibid., pp. 104–6, 37.

19. Ibid., p. 37.

20. Ibid., p. 163.

21. R. Rorty, *Consequences of Pragmatism* (Brighton, Harvester Press, 1982), p. 98.

22. M. Heidegger, *Identity and Difference*, p. 72.

23. Derrida, *Writing and Difference*, pp. 243, 184.

24. Mark C. Taylor, *Deconstructing Theology* (New York, Crossroads, 1982), p. xx.

25. Derrrida, *Sauf le nom* (Paris, Editions Galilee, 1993).

26. Heidegger, *Being and Time* (Oxford, Blackwell, 1973), p. 44.

27. Derrida in Raoul Mortley, ed., *French Philosophers in Conversation*, pp. 96–7.
28. Ibid.
29. Hart, *Trespass of the Sign*, p. 27. On negative theology in general see the excellent study by Deirdre Carbine, *The Unknown God: Negative Theology in the Platonic Tradition: Plato to Eriugena* (Louvain, Peeters, 1995).
30. Heidegger, *Le principe de raison* (Paris, Gallimard, 1962), p. 10. On Eckhart see Alain de Libera, *Eckhart, Tauler et Suso* (Paris, Editions Bayard, 1997).
31. Hart, *Trespass of the Sign*, p. 256, commenting on Eckhart's sermon 'Quasi stella matutina' in E. College and B. McGinn, eds., *Meister Eckhart* (New York, Paulist Press, 1981), p. 60.
32. Derrida, *Sauf le nom*, p. 23.
33. Hart, *Trespass of the Sign*, p. 94.
34. Ibid., p. 27.
35. Ibid., p. 39.
36. (Princeton, Princeton University Press, 1979).
37. Ibid., pp. 330–1.
38. See Georgia Warnke, 'Rorty's Irrationalism', in her *Gadamer: Hermeneutics, Tradition and Reason* (Stanford, Stanford University Press, 1987), pp. 151–6. See also Susan Haack, *Evidence and Enquiry: towards reconstruction in epistemology* (Oxford, Blackwell, 1993), chap. 9, on Rorty's *Philosophy and the Mirror of Nature*.
39. Richard Rorty, *Achieving our Country* (Cambridge MA., Harvard University Press, 1999).
40. Ibid., p. 30.
41. Ibid., p. 16.
42. Ibid., p. 22.
43. Ibid.
44. Stanley Fish, *Doing what Comes Naturally*, p. 354.
45. On Aquinas's very nuanced discussion of analogous predication see David Burrell, 'Aquinas and Jewish and Islamic Thinkers' in N. Kretzmann and E. Stump, eds., *The Cambridge Companion to Aquinas* (Cambridge, Cambridge University Press, 1993).
46. Eagleton, *Illusions of Postmodernism*, p. 28.

INDEX

211